FREEDOM OF RELIGION

In most European societies today, religion and questions about religion are increasing in relevance and importance. This development can be explained in several ways, for example by continuous demographic changes and new societal standards and values.

As a consequence, the debate on the interpretation and scope of the right to freedom of religion has intensified in politics, media and, of course, law. The right to freedom of religion is complex and varies within different legal contexts at the international, European and national levels. This has resulted in a right that is ambiguous and sometimes difficult for individuals to claim and for states to assert.

This book presents a variety of perspectives on the concept of freedom of religion in different European countries against the background of the European Convention on Human Rights, the EU Charter of Fundamental Rights and other international treaties. It contains contributions from leading legal scholars working in these fields in Sweden, the Nordic countries and wider Europe.

Freedom of Religion

An Ambiguous Right in the Contemporary European Legal Order

Swedish Studies in European Law
Volume 14

Edited by
Hedvig Bernitz
and
Victoria Enkvist

•HART•
OXFORD • LONDON • NEW YORK • NEW DELHI • SYDNEY

HART PUBLISHING

Bloomsbury Publishing Plc

Kemp House, Chawley Park, Cumnor Hill, Oxford, OX2 9PH, UK

1385 Broadway, New York, NY 10018, USA

HART PUBLISHING, the Hart/Stag logo, BLOOMSBURY and the Diana logo are trademarks of Bloomsbury Publishing Plc

First published in Great Britain 2020

A catalogue record for this book is available from the British Library.

Library of Congress Cataloging-in-Publication data

Names: Bernitz, Hedvig, 1970- editor. | Enkvist, Victoria, editor.

Title: Freedom of religion : an ambiguous right in the contemporary European legal order / [edited by] Hedvig Bernitz, Victoria Enkvist.

Description: Chicago : Hart Publishing, an imprint of Bloomsbury Publishing, 2020. | Series: Swedish studies in european law; 14 | Includes bibliographical references and index.

Identifiers: LCCN 2019048480 | ISBN 9781509935864 (hardback) | ISBN 9781509935871 (Epub)

Subjects: LCSH: Freedom of religion—Sweden. | Human rights—Sweden. | Freedom of religion—European Union countries.

Classification: LCC KKV2693 .F74 2020 | DDC 342.2408/52—dc23

LC record available at https://lccn.loc.gov/2019048480

ISBN: HB: 978-1-50993-586-4
ePDF: 978-1-50993-588-8
ePub: 978-1-50993-587-1

Typeset by Compuscript Ltd, Shannon

Preface

THIS VOLUME, *FREEDOM of Religion: An Ambiguous Right in the Contemporary European Legal Order*, deals with an area of law that has proved to be increasingly important in modern society. The interest in religious legal issues and the relationship between religion and law has increased over the past few years. One reason, among others, is immigration into Europe from other parts of the world that leads to a new approach to the role of religion in society.

In many ways, religion has shaped European traditions and European policy, and has gone from being a cause of war and controversy to today's agreements on common protection in European and international law. Religion has a major impact on societies and civil matters including, for example, family concerns, workplace issues, clothing and food.

Each European state has its own national laws concerning religion and religious freedom. Freedom of religion is a fundamental right for individuals and groups, protecting both the majority and minorities. The European Convention on Human Rights and the case law of the European Court of Human Rights give freedom of religion a wider European perspective. In addition to this, EU law provides an important EU dimension from both fundamental rights perspective within the Union and as part of other legal areas such as, for example, EU labour law. This system of national and international laws is distinct from the laws and traditions of religious communities and organisations.

Clashes between different religious groups and between religious and non-religious public interests arise frequently in Europe. Over the past few years there have been a number of important legal disputes concerning the freedom of religion at a European level, as well as at a national level in several European countries. Both individual and collective rights have come to the fore. The disputes raise questions about the role of religion in democratic states, both secular and non-secular.

On behalf of the Swedish Network for European Legal Studies, we are proud to present the fourteenth volume in the series Swedish Studies in European Law. This edited volume is based on a well-attended conference on the topic held in Stockholm on 9–10 April 2018. The conference was sponsored by the Swedish Network of European Legal Studies and Impact of Religion. The speakers were well-known experts and a selection of scholars from Sweden, the other Nordic countries as well as from other parts of Europe, representing different academic fields but with a common interest in the relationship between religion and law.

In Part I of the volume Professor Pamela Slotte, Professor Joakim Nergelius and Professor Reinhold Fahlbeck analyse how national and European law deal with religion and religious freedom from a conceptual as well as a historical perspective. In Part II Professor Ronan McCrea, Senior lecturer Patrik Bremdal, Senior Lecturer Karin Åström, doctoral student Emma Ahlm, and human rights and political science graduate Willem Vancutsem focus on religious issues in European legislation as well as in the case law of the European Court of Justice and the European Court of Human Rights. In Part III Professor Lotta Lerwall, Senior Lecturer Hedvig Bernitz and Senior Lecturer Kavot Zillén deal with freedom of religion in specific legal areas, that is, the education system and healthcare. Finally, Senior Lecturer Victoria Enkvist concludes the trends discussed in the book.

Pamela Slotte from Åbo Akademi University focuses on the subjects of 'codified freedom' and freedom of religion, and discusses how international law grapples with the ambivalence and ambiguities of religious freedom and tentatively explores why this is the case at this exact point in time, and why this situation has arisen in the first place.

Joakim Nergelius presents a historical exposé on religious freedom in Sweden from the early sixteenth century until the present day, illustrating the political importance of religion in Sweden and how freedom of religion has developed over the centuries.

Reinhold Fahlbeck analyses how religion, despite the return of religion as a factor of importance in social life, continues to be a factor without any significance in the Swedish legislative process.

Ronan McCrea highlights the challenges that EU law is likely to face in the future when the EU (probably) has to allow religions a degree of indirect influence over law by allowing them to form national cultural preferences that the Union then accommodates.

Patrik Bremdal discusses how the European Court of Human Rights has attributed certain characteristics to the Islamic headscarf and how this characterisation has affected the conclusions drawn by the Court and its subsequent case law.

Karin Åström investigates the relationship between freedom of religion and other human rights such as freedom of expression, freedom of assembly and the right to demonstrate, both from a Swedish Constitutional perspective as well as from the perspective of the European Convention on Human Rights.

Emma Ahlm addresses the communal aspects of religious freedom from a European perspective. In particular she analyses religious organisations acting as employers, and how they allegedly establish a 'special legal system' for churches and organisation with a religious ethos, but only so far as the EU Member States allow for it in the national legal order.

Willem Vancutsem underlines the fact that in many of the supposedly secular societies of Western Europe, religion has once again become a topic of discussion. Particularly Islam, a religion that is relatively new to some European countries, is widely debated, especially in the wake of the rise of the Islamic State and the terrorist attacks carried out by its members. As a result, several countries in Europe have implemented restrictions on freedom of religion. Vancutsem investigates this development, and asks whether the direction taken by European institutions is the right one.

Lotta Lerwall from Uppsala University analyses whether it is possible to restrict religious schools according to the European Convention on Human Rights.

Hedvig Bernitz discusses the thin line between the indoctrination of pupils and society's desire to educate children to become active citizens in a democratic society.

Kavot Zillén deals with the interesting topic of religious refusals in the health care sector as a matter of freedom of religion.

Victoria Enkvist concludes on the trends discussed in the volume and analyses how questions relating to religious freedom are dealt with in Europe today. The concept 'religion' is shown to be interpreted differently depending on tradition, culture and past experience. Other aspects that affect the interpretation depend on the views of the majority society concerning religious minorities, the actual context and the present political situation both in European states and in the world of today.

This collection of essays is being published at a time when religious issues are highly topical in Europe. The book is of interest to any reader who is curious about religion and law.

We would like to thank the Swedish Network of European Legal Studies for giving us the possibility to edit this volume. Finally, we would like to thank our coordinator, Marie Kagrell at Stockholm University, for her fantastic help and support in organising the conference and preparing this volume.

Hedvig Bernitz and Victoria Enkvist
May 2019

Contents

PART III

List of Contributors

Emma Ahlm is PhD Candidate in European law at the Department of Law, Uppsala University.

Hedvig Bernitz is Senior Lecturer in Constitutional Law at the Faculty of Law, Stockholm University.

Patrik Bremdal is Senior Lecturer in Public Law and Human Rights at the Department of Law, Uppsala University.

Victoria Enkvist is Senior Lecturer in Public Law at the Faculty of Law, Uppsala University.

Reinhold Fahlbeck is Professor Emeritus in Labour Law at the Department of Law, Lund University.

Lotta Lerwall is Professor in Administrative Law at the Department of Law, Uppsala University.

Ronan McCrea is Professor in Constitutional and European Law at the Faculty of Laws, University College London.

Joakim Nergelius is Professor in Constitutional Law at the School of Law, Psychology and Social Work, Örebro University.

Pamela Slotte is Associate Professor at the Faculty of Arts, Psychology and Theology, Åbo Akademi University and Vice-director of the Centre of Excellence in Law, Identity and the European Narratives, University of Helsinki.

Willem Vancutsem is parliamentary assistant for the Belgian Green Party at the Belgian Federal Parliament.

Kavot Zillén is Associate Professor in Public Law and Senior Lecturer in legal science at the Faculty of Law, Stockholm University.

Karin Åström is Senior Lecturer at the Department of Law, Umeå University.

Table of Cases

European Court of Human Rights

European Union

Germany

Sweden

Table of Legislation

International

Council of Europe

European Union

International Labour Organisation

National

Belgium

Germany

Sweden

Part I

1

Religion and Human Rights

Ambiguities and Ambivalences of Freedom

PAMELA SLOTTE

I. INTRODUCTION

As Ludwig Wittgenstein remarked: 'How words are understood is not told by words alone'.[1] Indeed, it would be possible to spend plenty of time deconstructing religion and human rights, which are 'capacious categories'[2] in their own right that do not make up 'self-evident unit[s] of meaning'.[3] However, this chapter takes for granted to a certain extent the ongoing scientifically insightful explorations into 'religion' and 'human rights', and the meanings they are attributed in their diverse roles within social practices.[4]

[1] L Wittgenstein, *Zettel*, edited by GEM Anscombe and GH von Wright, translated by GEM Anscombe, 2nd edn (Oxford, Blackwell Publishers, 1981) §144. The present chapter develops the main points of a keynote address, 'Religion and human rights: ambiguities and ambivalences of freedom', delivered at the IMPACT conference in Uppsala, Sweden in April 2018. The chapter has been written as part of the author's academy research fellow project 'Management of the Sacred: A Critical Inquiry', funded by the Academy of Finland 2013–18 (grant number: 265887) and work as vice-director of the Centre of Excellence in Law, Identity and the European Narratives, Academy of Finland 2018–25 (grant number: 312430).

[2] Terminology borrowed from A Pagden, B Straumann and N Bhuta, 'Series Editors' Preface' in M Koskenniemi, M García-Salmones and P Amorosa (eds), *International Law and Religion: Historical and Contemporary Perspectives*. The History and Theory of International Law (Oxford, Oxford University Press, 2017) v.

[3] M Koskenniemi, 'International Law and Religion: No Stable Ground' in M Koskenniemi, M García-Salmones and P Amorosa (eds), *International Law and Religion: Historical and Contemporary Perspectives*, The History and Theory of International Law (Oxford, Oxford University Press, 2017) 3. '[A]ny study of "religion" or "international law" must confront the fact that both terms are complex wholes of ideas and practices whose scope and meaning is contested by people most intimately connected to them'. Koskenniemi, ibid, 17.

[4] These explorations have generated a rich literature. The following provide just a sample of contributions to the discussion: T Asad, *Genealogies of Religion: Discipline and Reasons of Power*

Instead, it is the subtitle of the present chapter that is of particular interest here. It focuses on ambiguity and ambivalence in relation to what is below termed 'codified freedom' in religious matters. Thus it provides an overview and discussion of certain tendencies in contemporary discussions of religious freedom.

The Merriam-Webster Dictionary defines the word 'ambiguity' as 'the quality or state of being ambiguous especially in meaning'. Something that is ambiguous 'can be understood in two or more possible ways'. 'Ambiguity' is defined secondly as 'uncertainty'. A synonym for 'ambiguous' is 'dubious'.[5] Ambivalence, in turn, is defined as 'simultaneous and contradictory attitudes or feelings (such as attraction and repulsion) toward an object, person, or action'. Ambivalence can also mean 'continual fluctuation (as between one thing and its opposite)', as well as 'uncertainty as to which approach to follow', an ambivalence about goals.[6]

Freedom, on the other hand, is usually evaluated positively in the abstract. It is seen as an ideal. Can an ideal trigger an ambivalent response and, if so, in what sense? In what sense is freedom both affirmed and questioned? What kinds of tensions does the subtitle of the present chapter point at? The subtitle could be read as asserting that the concept of freedom contains internal logical contradictions. It is also clear that certain (theoretical) understandings of freedom are championed by some and rejected by others, and may logically cancel each other out.[7] However, the subtitle could also refer to the material configurations of freedom: to how freedom takes actual political expression, the concrete

in Christianity and Islam (Baltimore, John Hopkins University Press, 1993); C Douzinas, *The End of Human Rights* (Oxford, Hart Publishing, 2000); C Douzinas, *Human Rights and Empire: The Political Philosophy of Cosmopolitanism* (Abingdon, Routledge-Cavendish, 2007); T Fitzgerald (ed), *Religion and the Secular: Historical and Colonial Formations* (London, Equinox Publishing, 2007); B Nongbri, *Before Religion: A History of a Modern Concept* (New Haven, Yale University Press, 2013); T Stack, N Goldenberg and T Fitzgerald (eds), *Religion as a Category of Governance and Sovereignty*, Supplements to Method & Theory in the Study of Religion 3 (Boston, Brill Academic Publishing, 2015). See also D Decosimo, 'The New Genealogy of Religious Freedom' (2018) 33 *Journal of Law and Religion* 3, 38.

[5] www.merriam-webster.com/dictionary/ambiguity.

[6] www.merriam-webster.com/dictionary/ambivalence.

[7] See, eg J Modée, 'Frihet till och frihet från religion' in J Modée and H Strandberg (eds), *Frihet och gränser: Filosofiska perspektiv på religionsfrihet och tolerans* (Stockholm, Brutus Östlings Bokförlag Symposium, 2006) 21–38, for an overview of different conceptualisations of freedom. For example, it includes a discussion of negative freedom and positive freedom (Isaiah Berlin), and freedom as an 'opportunity concept' or alternatively as an 'exercise concept' (Charles Taylor). Modée himself talks of this respectively as deregulated negative freedom and regulated positive freedom (that includes societal supportive operations), and he speaks of 'absence of limitation' and 'possibility for self-realisation' which both are important in relation to religious liberty. Modée, ibid, 23–28, 31; I Berlin, 'Two Concepts of Liberty' in *Four Essays On Liberty* (Oxford, Oxford University Press, 1969) 118–72; C Taylor, 'What's Wrong with Negative Liberty?' in D Miller (ed), *Liberty* (New York, Oxford University Press, 1991) 141–62. Catharina Stenqvist, in turn, considers it 'important to distinguish between external and inner freedom, freedom from and freedom to something, absolute freedom, codified freedom and freedom as an existential category'. C Stenqvist, 'Situerad frihet och gränsens problem' in J Modée and H Strandberg (eds), *Frihet och gränser: Filosofiska perspektiv på religionsfrihet och tolerans* (Stockholm, Brutus Östlings Bokförlag Symposium, 2006) 81.

state of things. Thus the subtitle can be taken to imply that talk of freedom and action in its name, the striving to realise something like freedom, has ambiguous, dubious consequences, consequences we feel ambivalent about. If this is the case, then we can raise the further question of whether this results from freedom in and of itself, or if, on the contrary, the reasons for it can be located in the context in which freedom is being realised, in conditions external to freedom, or indeed in a combination of these two.

The fact that freedom as 'situated freedom' is not limitless, but only 'possible in one bounded form or the other',[8] does not need to be regarded as a sign of ambiguity per se. As the late Swedish philosopher of religion Catharina Stenquist has observed: 'The question of what are the limits of freedom is in fact the question of what is freedom'.[9] Ambiguity and resultant ambivalent attitudes refers to something else, even if it is clear that a connection may exist with how freedom is effectively circumscribed.

This chapter will say no more than the preceding about freedom as a philosophical concept and the ways in which freedom, a complex notion if ever there was one, has been conceptualised through the ages and today, and how different understandings are at variance with each other.[10] Instead, in what follows we will concentrate on freedom in relation to religion, and upon ambiguity and ambivalence in relation hereto, and on 'freedom as stipulated in law'.[11] In addition, we will concentrate on how this law – primarily, albeit not exclusively, international human rights law – simultaneously constrains and enables religious life. Hence, this chapter will say something about 'codified freedom',[12] and about freedom of religion rather than, for example, about freedom in a religious sense: that is, freedom as an existential category.

II. NAVIGATING SPACES OF ANXIETY

In his book *Questioning Secularism*, Hussein Ali Agrama observes that as ever more domains of life become the subject of law, a process we can call 'juridification', they are subjected to regulation that enables state intervention and as a rule has afforded interpretative prerogative precisely to the state. Moreover, this regulation time and again generates what Agrama calls 'spaces of anxiety', owing to the fact that law cannot, without exception, regulate human life in a

[8] Stenqvist (n 7) 81.

[9] ibid 89. My translation. See also Decosimo (n 4) 31, 36.

[10] Stenqvist calls freedom a 'porous concept' (*poröst begrepp*). Stenqvist (n 7) 81. She draws on the thought of the philosopher Friedrich Waismann, who according to Stenqvist, in his concept of porosity alludes to 'a vagueness that cannot be expressed and which characterises all empirical concepts'. Stenqvist (n 7) 81 (fn 2) my translation.

[11] Terms taken from Stenqvist (n 7) 82.

[12] Terms taken from ibid, 81.

total and fully foreseeable manner. We cannot elude the questions 'what is legal' and 'what is illegal'.[13] This produces uncertainty.

As far as international law and religion are concerned, Martti Koskenniemi notes in an edited volume on international law and religion, which investigates how religion and theology has contributed to the development of modern international law and continues to interrelate and be in an alliance with it, that anxiety about speaking of matters related to religion has taken root in the international legal context and community at the expense of 'self-confident secularism'.[14]

Of course, religious matters and freedom in relation to these have never been totally uncontroversial. Still, Koskenniemi directs our attention to something important, to a change that he situates in the wider context of what he calls 'the deformalization of international law', and which focuses attention on precisely the kind of spaces that Agrama speaks of explicitly as spaces of anxiety. According to Koskenniemi, law, despite far-reaching detailed regulation, houses an inescapable space for discretion – a void of sorts. Outcomes are not determined in advance, as applying the law inevitably means that choices, decisions, must be made. Power is exercised. This usually will involve, at least as far as other than completely technical decisions are concerned, value-based considerations that could be perceived of as arbitrary, ambiguous and unpredictable, and also be contested. According to Koskenniemi:

> The deformalization of international law by recourse to broad standards of equity, reasonableness, and 'balancing' between conflicting values that characterizes practical work across the field is … [among other things] the result of a certain running-out of rules and the reason that seeks to deduce judgments from them. Practitioners are called upon to exercise contextual sensitivity, to be responsive to the call of the moment, and to adjust conflicting principles reasonably. The turn to the hermeneutics of judging is all about how to reach that moment of when, in an indeterminate environment everything will fall into place.[15]

Koskenniemi claims – and I assume that at this point he has in mind in particular a 'western context' and history of international law – that there used to exist a vocabulary (for example, the talk of virtues) for capturing what it could mean to exercise power in a legal as well as morally and theologically responsible manner. However, 'the modern political and legal culture' is not very good at equipping people for what the task requires, 'even if it relentlessly points beyond its internal principles and rationales'.[16] Law is porous. And so, those 'trying to

[13] HA Agrama, *Questioning Secularism: Islam, Sovereignty, And The Rule Of Law In Modern Egypt* (Chicago, University of Chicago Press, 2012) 35. For a general discussion of juridification as it pertains to religion in particular, see H Årsheim and P Slotte, 'The Juridification of Religion?' (2017) 1(2) *Brill Research Perspectives in Law and Religion* 1–89.

[14] Koskenniemi (n 3) 4.

[15] ibid 7.

[16] ibid 7: 'Moral theology and Kantian moralists discussed this predicament in terms of the virtues needed to operate power in a way that is legally – and thus both morally and theologically – responsible'.

operate the institutional vocabularies of modern law and governance … grapple between the formal demands of the law and the knowledge that the legal vocabularies fall short of fully dictating what is a "right" or "good" or "just" thing to do'.[17]

Thus there exists this space, this void, which cannot be filled on purely legally internal grounds, a place in which you will necessarily be drawing on things from 'outside' strict law. This matter has not been necessarily fully theorised, even if recent years have seen attempts to theorise the 'void' at the heart of international law: for example, in a politico-theological manner.[18] Nor are all practitioners necessarily so equipped to handle this situation, at least according to Koskenniemi.

The present chapter suggests that certain ways of applying the law may seem so self-evident that one does not acknowledge the aforementioned void and the value positions one actually falls back on. In actuality, one feels – or has felt until now – rather equipped to apply the law. For it is possible to see the change that Koskenniemi identifies as a kind of calling into question of the unflinching authority with which the international legal community, despite everything, has expressed itself for a long time about religion and its place in human life, including when it comes to managing and circumscribing religious diversity. To be sure, this authority has itself presupposed a kind of transcendence, at the very least 'the alleged transcendental righteousness in the name of which it operates'.[19] However, until now the transcendence did not require explicit acknowledgement. It was possible to tone it down, suppress it, and perhaps overlook it altogether.

[17] ibid 8.

[18] See in general JD Haskell, 'Political Theology and International Law' (2018) 1(2) *Brill Research Perspectives in International Legal Theory and Practice* 1–89, for an insightful overview and analysis. For the purposes of his article, Haskell stipulates that 'political theology might be most usefully viewed as a rhetorical mechanism, or species of disciplinary sub-genre, that generates certain types of arguments in an attempt to reconcile anxiety-producing contradictions that animate the various doctrinal positions and thematic of international law itself – or even more modest, not of international law broadly, but simply those of us who identify as international law academics'. Haskell, ibid, 6–7.

For his part as well, Koskenniemi points out that a theological frame of reference may actually play a role in decision-making. But it is not something acknowledged earlier, or something one continues to tone down in favour of emphasising (absolute) openness as to how justice might materialise in law. 'In the absence of a formal discussion of "virtue" in global governance today … legal professionals [are left] in a bind: [with the options] either to espouse an openly [broadly conceived] theological understanding of the 'ultimate ends' to which legal practice looks, or to face an existentialist predicament where the gap between what they *know* and what they *should do* appears only as a void'. Koskenniemi (n 3) 7–8.

[19] U Soirila, 'The Law of Humanity Project: An Immanent Critique' (LLD thesis, University of Helsinki, 2018). See also eg M Koskenniemi, 'International Law as Political Theology: How To Read the *Nomos der Erde*?' (2004) 11 *Constellations* 492, 507. For a recent study with a focus somewhat related to but also different from the present chapter, see: C McCrudden, *Litigating Religions: An Essay on Human Rights, Courts, and Beliefs* (Oxford, Oxford University Press, 2018). McCrudden points to both 'ideological' and 'institutional' reasons for the tensions which he identifies as having resulted in a rise in conflicts between 'the human rights system' and 'organized religions'.

Steven D Smith has noted that, despite the presence of faith in a multitude of forms, 'a "secular" worldview' has dominated particular areas of life, and that judicial discourse has taken place in a 'cage of secular discourse'.[20] A cage can be a prison, but we can also think about a cage as offering protection and a clear framework. But now the (self-) description of law and legal practice, the embedded preferences, have been destabilised, the cage has been 'shaken'. As John Haskell has phrased it: 'the claimed non-partisan/non-confessional disposition of international law's cosmopolitan spirit' has been challenged.[21]

III. SHAKING THE CAGE

What has happened? In a discussion of the concept of 'post-secularism', Zachary Calo calls attention to the altered circumstances for making statements about what is meaningful, a situation in which what he terms the 'post-secular condition', among other things, 'refers to a fragmentation in meaning that undermines the universal aspirations of the secular'.[22] We can ask: is it not the case that we also earlier have lived in a world consisting of different universes of meaning, so that the difference with the situation we face today is simply that the balance of power between different normative perspectives and epistemic metrics has shifted?

Among other things, what has surely played a role when it comes to 'shaking the cage' are the ways in which critics in a multifaceted way have stripped international human rights law of its facade of neutrality. Such critics have unveiled the limits of 'sober', 'dispassionate' reasoning,[23] exposing hereby spaces of anxiety and indeterminacy as well as the ways in which the 'void' actually is being filled with meaning.[24]

One example of this dismantling can be found in the work of Helge Årsheim, who discloses the different understandings of religion that contribute to the political and legal ordering of freedom in the United Nations committees

[20] SD Smith, *The Disenchantment of Secular Discourse* (Cambridge, Harvard University Press, 2010) 23.

[21] Haskell (n 18) 5.

[22] Z Calo, 'Religion, Human Rights, and Post-Secular Legal Theory' (2011) 85 *St John's Law Review* 495, 506.

[23] Terminology borrowed from Smith (n 20) 8.

[24] In her recently published book *Liberalism's Religion*, Cécile Laborde observes that the self-understanding of 'liberal egalitarian theory', including as it pertains to governance of religion through law, is being attacked on several fronts, historical and/or contemporary. The contemporary critique has taken the form of 'the *semantic* critique' (the term religion), 'the Protestant critique', and 'the *realist* critique'. Cécile Laborde, *Liberalism's Religion* (Cambridge, Harvard University Press, 2017) 6. See ibid, ch 1, for a more in depth analysis of these critiques, and an assessment of their relevance. David Decosimo, for his part, identifies five types of criticisms directed at 'religions freedom *as such*': 'the *incoherence* criticism', 'the *systemic bias* criticism', 'the *tool of oppression* criticism', 'the *ideology* criticism', 'the *essentialist* criticism'. Decosimo (n 4) 7–8.

tasked with offering authoritative interpretations of key treaties.[25] The titles of recent works reveal the contours of this dismantling: *The Politics of Religious Freedom*,[26] *Beyond Religious Freedom*,[27] *The Impossibility of Religious Freedom*[28] and others. These works expose in particular the distinctive character and special interests of an allegedly liberal perspective[29] as far as the conceptualisation of codified religious freedom is concerned, including how this codified religious freedom is circumscribed for reasons of safeguarding, for example, 'public order'.

> [L]egal and political enforcement of rights to religious freedom and other related regimes of management, including toleration and accommodation of religious diversity necessarily involve a dividing of legal religion from illegal religion – good religion from bad religion. Those separations are effected along an ongoing set of unresolved and competing dichotomies dividing religion as individual or communal, private or public, spiritual or material, belief or practice, chosen or given, Protestant or Catholic, Western or Eastern, peaceful or violent, utopian or locative, universal or particular.[30]

The criticised legal regimes are understood to privilege the former at the expense of the latter, for example, the individual at the expense of the communal and the private at the expense of the public.[31] Thus, according to the critics, what has been considered and portrayed as neutrality comes across instead as partially-selective blindness, 'subtly encoded with … biases', like 'the strict separation between private and public spheres' and 'the emphasis on individual rights at the expense of communal duties'[32] and so on. Or, as Haskell has put it in the context of examining international legal scholarship: what is exposed is an approach that 'ultimately tends to rely on extremely parochial, if not metaphysical,

[25] H Årsheim, *Making Religion and Human Rights at the United Nations*, Religion and Society 67 (Berlin, DeGruyter, 2018).

[26] WF Sullivan, ES Hurd, S Mahmood and PG Danchin (eds), *The Politics of Religious Freedom* (Chicago, The University of Chicago Press, 2015).

[27] ES Hurd, *Beyond Religious Freedom: The New Global Politics of Religion* (Princeton, Princeton University Press, 2015).

[28] WF Sullivan, *The Impossibility of Religious Freedom* (Princeton, Princeton University Press, 2005).

[29] '[F]reedom of religion has often been seen as a core liberal right and part of the liberal architecture of neutrality as to conceptions of the good'. AA Jamal, 'Considering Freedom of Religion in a Post-Secular Context: Hapless or Hopeful?' (2017) 6 *Oxford Journal of Law and Religion* 433, 439.

[30] WF Sullivan, ES Hurd, S Mahmood and PG Danchin, 'Introduction' in WF Sullivan, ES Hurd, S Mahmood and PG Danchin (eds), *The Politics of Religious Freedom* (Chicago, The University of Chicago Press, 2015) 7.

[31] Decosimo (n 4) 14. See also eg Hurd (n 27) 13.

[32] JD Haskell, 'The Religion/Secularism Debate in Human Rights Literature: Constitutive Tensions between Christian, Islamic, and Secular Perspectives' in M Koskenniemi, M García-Salmones and P Amorosa (eds), *International Law and Religion: Historical and Contemporary Perspectives*, The History and Theory of International Law (Oxford, Oxford University Press, 2017) 144. cf Decosimo (n 4) 12–13.

arguments – what we might term, "transcendental nonsense" – that reinforces the authority of distinctly Western, liberal, institutional actors'.[33]

Cécile Laborde, Daniel Steinmetz-Jenkins and Udi Greenberg have recently pointed out that we should not 'confuse genesis with justification'.[34] Nevertheless, the critique has also included a historical turn as a destabilising move. This turn can be seen in the work of Peter Danchin,[35] Marco Duranti,[36] the late Saba Mahmood,[37] Samuel Moyn[38] and Linde Lindkvist,[39] among others. Such scholars have argued that '[t]he conceptual artifice and implementation of secular liberal rule of law [including in relation to freedom in matters spiritual] is deeply enmeshed in [among other things] the colonial experience, and maintains its past inequalities, conceptually and materially'.[40] Besides, we should not forget that legal frameworks and institutions other than domestic Western ones are also being revisited.[41]

Critical remarks such as those described in this section have themselves not gone unquestioned. They have been criticised, for example, for being very theoretical, discursively analytical and too preoccupied with the legal texts that

[33] Haskell (n 32) 136, referring for the term 'transcendental nonsense' to F Cohen, 'Transcendental Nonsense and the Functional Approach' (1935) 35 *Colombia Law Review* 809, in the context of describing how international legal scholarship approach 'secularism' and 'religion' as far as human rights are concerned.

[34] Laborde points out in responding to the critical legal theorists that at least some of them tend to exactly 'confuse genesis with justification'. Yet, according to her, 'a *historical* critique' cannot 'serve as a *philosophical* critique of liberalism'. Laborde (n 24) 16. See also U Greenberg and D Steinmetz-Jenkins, 'The Cross and the Gavel' (2018) 65 *Dissent* 2 106, 112–13; Decosimo (n 4) 15–16. For another in-depth assessment of different scholarly pursuits to critically investigate religious freedom discourses, which he jointly labels 'a new genealogy of religious freedom' and subject to a so-called 'immanent critique', see Decosimo, ibid. See also eg JT Mauldin, 'Contesting Religious Freedom: Impossibility, Normativity, and Justice' (2016) 5 *Oxford Journal of Law and Religion* 457; JA Springs, 'Tentacles of the Leviathan? Nationalism, Islamophobia, and the Insufficiency-yet-Indispensability of Human Rights for Religious Freedom in Contemporary Europe' (2016) 84 *Journal of the American Academy of Religion* 903.

[35] eg PG Danchin, 'The Emergence and Structure of Religious Freedom in International Law Reconsidered' (2007/2008) 23 *Journal of Law and Religion* 455.

[36] M Duranti, *The Conservative Human Rights Revolution: European Identity, Transnational Politics, and the Origins of the European Convention* (Oxford, Oxford University Press, 2017).

[37] eg S Mahmood, *Religious Difference in a Secular Age: A Minority Report* (Princeton, Princeton University Press, 2015).

[38] eg S Moyn, *Christian Human Rights*, Intellectual History of the Modern Age (Philadelphia, University of Pennsylvania Press, 2015).

[39] L Lindkvist, *Religious Freedom and the Universal Declaration of Human Rights*, Human Rights in History (Cambridge, Cambridge University Press, 2017).

[40] Haskell (n 32) 144.

[41] See, eg Y Sezgin and M Künkler, 'Regulation of "Religion" and the "Religious": The Politics of Judicialization and Bureaucratization in India and Indonisia' (2014) 52 *Comparative Studies in Society and History* 448; B Schontal, *Buddhism, Politics and the Limits of the Law: The Phyrric Constitutionalism of Sri Lanka* (New York, Cambridge University Press, 2016); JL Neo, 'Definitional Imbroglios: A Critique of the Definition of Religion and Essential Practice Tests in Religious Freedom Adjudication' (2018) 16 *International Journal of Constitutional Law* 574; T Moustafa, *Constituting Religion: Islam, Liberal Rights, and the Malaysian State*, Cambridge Studies in Law and Society (Cambridge, Cambridge University Press 2018).

articulate a codified religious freedom. While their critique of the failures of law to address matters of faith is considered partially convincing, the limited analytical emphasis which is likely to examine 'law on the books' rather than 'law in action'[42] is viewed as generating reductive readings of what actually happens when matters of faith are negotiated through law.[43] In another context, the present author has called for

> [a]n in-depth, comprehensive and contextual understanding of the purposes, issues and perspectives that are afforded significance in adjudication processes and decision-making in individual cases would be key so as to – in the words of Jason A Springs – counteract 'excessive discursive analytical tendencies'.[44]

This does not mean, however, that the critique has not struck a chord. To summarise, we could perhaps say that a reading of freedom in questions of faith stands out as ambiguous and generates an ambivalent response – to the extent that it does this – because one has earlier considered the law's way of approaching matters of faith, and one's own way of adjudicating such matters, as positive: if not entirely, then at least overwhelmingly so. There has not been hesitation with regard to what is the goal (of adjudication) is, or the correct course of action, and instances of spaces of anxiety as far as religious freedom is concerned have not been recognised.[45]

Certainly, for others the ambiguities have been evident for a long time, if not always, for example, based on their perspective and/or based on the experience

[42] See, eg J Witte Jr and JA Nichols, '"Come Now Let Us Reason Together": Restoring Religious Freedom in America and Abroad' (2017) 92 *Notre Dame Law Review* 427, 436.

[43] Årsheim and Slotte (n 13) 18–19; Springs (n 34). However, see also Sullivan, Hurd, Mahmood and Danchin (n 30), at 9 where this critique is implicitly countered: 'The present volume [shows] …, through the work of various scholars working in a variety of geographical regions, that the meaning and practice of a right to religious liberty varies and shifts depending on the particular configuration of state-religion accommodation and the impact of other historical and transnational forces. Far from being able to be reduced to a question of compliance or noncompliance with a stable, uncontested norm that is being progressively disseminated globally (despite occasional setbacks), promoting a right to religious freedom shapes political and religious possibilities in particular ways, though always differently in different contexts'.

[44] Årsheim and Slotte (n 13) 19; Springs (n 34) 3 and 4.

[45] In a certain sense, this unveiling results in a simultaneous disclosure of authority and undermining of the same, an authority that may constitute a disquieting fact. As David Kennedy observes in his new book *A World of Struggle* (here in the words of Samuel Moyn), 'international lawyers have interpreted their own plight and kept the reality of the power they exercise as experts at length'. S Moyn, 'Knowledge and Politics in International Law' (2016) 129 *Harvard Law Review* 2164, 2176; D Kennedy, *A World of Struggle: How Power, Law, and Expertise Shape Global Political Economy* (Princeton, Princeton University Press, 2016) 172. Moyn notes: 'Even when international lawyers insist doggedly on the reality of international law, Kennedy says, they are loath to view their own expertise as a form of authority that inevitably privileges and distributes. "Rather than seeing the hand of power in the glove of law, mainstream international lawyers focus on the glove," Kennedy writes: "They see law acting everywhere in the world and celebrate the ability of civil society organizations, individuals, or national judges to participate in global rule making. Where the outcomes are not desirable or when bad things happen in the name of law, they prefer to see the misrule of power dressing itself in legal justification."' Moyn, ibid, 2176, quoting Kennedy, ibid, 240.

that the outcomes of legal processes have constantly been unfavourable to them. One example of such unfavourable outcomes are those for certain religious minority positions before the European Court of Human Rights. Law has become a source of distrust. Moreover, all this is not to say that an 'internal' critique vis-a-vis the treatment of religion on part of international law and the international legal profession has not previously existed.[46]

IV. RESPONDING TO THE CHALLENGES OF LEGAL GOVERNANCE OF RELIGION

What follows from this recognition of the ambiguities of freedom in a state of diversity (including concerning what is true, good and right) is a different thing. Clearly, the critique that I have outlined above calls for fresh approaches. One alternative might be to insist on more persuasive reasoning, including with regard to that which has earlier been hidden from view. To paraphrase Samuel Moyn: what once could simply be asserted, now has to be argued.[47] You may still be able to make a case for a particular ordering of society, but you are pushed to justify it in a way you have not had to before.

In relation to this kind of alternative, Haskell has noted that, if inevitably at stake are choices that ultimately could be called 'personal and often discrete', then the goal is 'to become self-reflective of one's particularity, to practice rigorous hermeneutics of suspicion that is aware of its subjective limitations and that knowledge requires openness, whether it comes in the form of cultural expressions, new ideas, and so forth'.[48]

> Between competing fantasies within the human rights regime, the role of the international lawyer is to develop an analytic set of tools that is built out of an attention to the blind spots and margins of law or political manoeuvers, of their risks and unexpected consequences, and which can encourage more active inclusion and participation in legal decision-making and exercise responsibility to others as the conditions of reason itself (discussed in terms, such as 'margin of appreciation',

[46] See eg D Kennedy, 'Images of Religion in International Legal Theory' in MW Janis and C Evans (eds), *Religion and International Law* (The Hague, Martinus Nijhoff Publishers, 1999) 145–53; D Kennedy, 'Losing Faith in the Secular: Law, Religion, and the Culture of International Governance' in MW Janis and C Evans (eds), *Religion and International Law* (The Hague, Martinus Nijhoff Publishers, 1999) 309–19. See also Karen Engle for an analysis of what she takes to be an 'increasing tendency toward self-critique' within the human rights movement, an analysis in which the work of David Kennedy also figures. K Engle, 'Self-Critique, (Anti) Politics and Criminalization: Reflections on the History and Trajectory of the Human Rights Movement' in JM Beneyto and D Kennedy (eds), *New Approaches to International Law: The European and the American Experiences* (The Hague, TMC Asser-Springer, 2012) 41–73.

[47] Moyn (n 45) 2172.

[48] Haskell (n 32) 145.

> 'dialogical intersubjectivity', 'responsibility to others'). International legal practice becomes a reflective balancing act that is receptive and mediates competing fantasies, interests, and passions.[49]

What is required is refined reasoning that takes seriously the spaces of anxiety and in an at least partly novel way clarifies the substantive values, criteria and conceptions of freedom in matters of faith upon which choices and decisions are made. The project of Eva Brems and others, which has involved a close reading and re-reading of judgments and decisions from supranational human rights monitoring bodies, can be viewed as a way to advocate precisely this kind of reasoning.[50]

Another way to respond to and handle the ambiguities could be the way in which the European Court of Human Rights and the European human rights system more generally, and for some time now, has pondered the division of labour between contracting states and the European Court of Human Rights as far as the interpretation of freedom of religion or belief and also other rights is concerned. The question here is: who is best equipped with the contextual sensibility that is called for?[51]

Even so, it is important to keep in mind the distinction between questions of jurisdiction per se and what could be viewed as bad-quality judgments.[52] Sometimes the object of critique is such bad judgments, whereas, for example, the authority of a particular court per se is not questioned. At other times, however, the critique that the uncovering of ambiguities triggers is of a more foundational kind. What this suggests is that we need to seriously reflect on what we wish to make an object of judicial decision-making in the first place. For by making such a move, we authorise certain instances and meaning is 'closed down' in certain respects. As Smith points out, the end result is a 'binary conclusion' with one party to a conflict as the winner, and the other as the loser.[53]

Of course, we cannot but note, for example, as Hans Lindahl does in *Authority and the Globalisation of Inclusion and Exclusion*, that it is impossible to

[49] Haskell (n 32) 145; referring to N Berman, '*Legalizing Jerusalem*, or, of Law, Fantasy, and Faith' (1996) 45 *Catholic University Law Review* 823. This is, as Haskell also observes elsewhere, a salient focal point of both American Legal Realism and so-called Critical Legal Studies: 'every right or principle or value or rule is always matched with a countervailing right or principle or value or rule. The judge is required to balance these competing claims, which ultimately becomes a thing of discretion, of policy. Exactly what legal reasoning is supposed to guard against. And more often than not, between equal rights, force decides'. Haskell (n 18) 74, referring to D Kennedy, 'The Critique of Rights in Critical Legal Studies' in W Brown and J Halley (eds), *Left Legalism/Left Critique* (Duke University Press 2002) 199–218.

[50] E Brems (ed), *Diversity and European Human Rights: Rewriting Judgments of the ECHR* (Cambridge, Cambridge University Press, 2012), see in particular Part III.

[51] See also McCrudden (n 19) 85–88.

[52] See, eg Laborde (n 24) 7–8.

[53] Smith (n 20) 11. Whether or not it is possible at a general level to distinguish between what can or cannot be made the object of judicial decision-making, is a separate question beyond the scope of this chapter.

have global law without exclusion. Every attempt to formulate an understanding of law, every legal concept, includes inevitable contextualisation (which also means that the critique has to be contextual in order not to become too general and blunt). Every legal order will always be 'bounded' and simultaneously inclusive and exclusive.[54] Such is also the case with human rights vocabulary, which in its legal form aspires in theory to capture that which is foundational for all 'decent' human life, provided we will be able to continue calling it 'human'.[55]

Still, the situation has provoked the question of whether it is meaningful to regulate religion in law, including treating religion as a special category when it comes to legal protection. Obviously, the question is not new. However, the discussion has been rather intense in recent years, with positions both for and against.[56]

At least for some, this question relates to the difficulty of ascertaining in the first place what religion is. If religion has no clear-cut meaning, is it then reasonable to ascribe special legal status to it? What is it that we consider worthy of protection in precisely this way? Could we think of more adequate and less ambiguous ways of safeguarding (also) freedom in matters of faith than by means of a tailor-made special legal right? And to do so in ways that do not come across as favouring religious beliefs at the expense of other life views and convictions? In other words, in ways that are more even-handed?[57]

Related to this, Laborde notes in *Liberalism's Religion* that 'not all values can, or indeed should be expressed by the law'. The law can 'put forward an interpretative notion' of, for example, the value of religion, but cannot in any way capture 'the whole of the value of religion'.[58] According to Laborde, what we seek to protect when it comes to faith could be protected via other fundamental rights and freedoms such as freedom of association and freedom of opinion and

[54] See, eg H Lindahl, *Authority and the Globalisation of Inclusion and Exclusion* (Cambridge, Cambridge University Press 2018) 189. See also, eg Haskell (n 18).

[55] See, eg P Slotte, *Mänskliga rättigheter, moral och religion: Om de mänskliga rättigheterna som moraliskt och juridiskt begrepp i en pluralistisk värld* (Turku, Åbo Akademi University Press 2005) 129–30.

[56] See, eg C Eisgruber and L Sager, *Religious Freedom and the Constitution* (Cambridge, Harvard University Press 2007); MA Hamilton, *God vs the Gavel: The Perils of Extreme Religious Liberty* 2nd edn (New York, Cambridge University Press, 2014); A Koppelman, *Defending American Religious Neutrality* (Cambridge, Harvard University Press, 2013); Laborde (n 24); B Leiter, *Why Tolerate Religion?* (Princeton, Princeton University Press, 2013); A Sarat (ed), *Legal Responses to Religious Practices in the United States: Accommodation and its Limits* (Cambridge, Cambridge University Press, 2014); M Schwartzman, 'What if Religion Is Not Special?' (2012) 79 *University of Chicago Law Review* 1351; Sullivan (n 28); Witte and Nichols (n 42).

[57] For example, ways that, when taking a stand on what is allowed, do not take into account the fact that one is dealing explicitly with *religious* belief. See H Strandberg, 'Livsfrihet i stället för religionsfrihet' in J Modée and H Strandberg (eds), *Frihet och gränser: Filosofiska perspektiv på religionsfrihet och tolerans* (Stockholm, Brutus Östlings Bokförlag Symposium, 2006) 244.

[58] Laborde (n 24) 31. Laborde finds that we should not get fixated upon the category of 'religion', nor confuse semantics and interpretation. ibid, 202.

expression.[59] James Nickel adopts a similar position in his 2005 article entitled 'Who Needs Freedom of Religion?'.[60] The question arises: to what extent does this kind of 'disaggregation' – to borrow Laborde's terminology – neutralise ambiguity? Even though one does not seek to endorse a special right of religious freedom, the conceptualisation and legal ordering of relations and freedom will include making distinctions and setting limits. Ambiguity, as well as the ambivalent response it may generate, is not excluded.

V. CONCLUDING REMARKS

I do not intend here to give further examples of ways to seek to respond to the ambiguities to freedom in matters of faith, but I will simply return now to the metaphor of a cage as constraining and simultaneously offering protection, and as a frame (a structure). Agrama describes secularism in a somewhat similar fashion. With reference to Wittgenstein, he explains secularism as a picture that holds us captive with its categories, with what it identifies as being at stake as being meaningful questions and solutions.[61] The picture itself can limit our understanding of it, so that even when we question it – if we question it, for example, following the realisation that it is ambiguous – 'all we end up introducing is the negative. The assumptions that frame the picture remain the same, and we remain beholden to it'.[62] Hence, we 'remain captive to its own image which draws us away from thinking outside the possibilities its framework provides, or more importantly, the modalities of power that the framework articulates'.[63] This is something Haskell also critically highlights as something to be aware of in relation to those positions that underline the need for self-reflection and refined reasoning.[64]

When they contemplate codified freedom in matters of faith, some new openings stay closer to the original picture or cage, some seek to keep more distance, some perhaps unreservedly endorse the original. What is certain is that in the effort to give the desire to institutionalise freedom[65] new forms in a (politically) relevant fashion, we are dealing with restructuring of power rather than

[59] C Laborde, 'Religion in the Law: The Disaggregation Approach' (2015) 34 *Law and* Philosophy 581, 594.

[60] JW Nickel, 'Who Needs Freedom of Religion?' (2005) 76 *University of Colorado Law Review* 941.

[61] Agrama talks of secularism as 'a problem-space'. Agrama (n 13) 28.

[62] ibid 24.

[63] ibid 25.

[64] Haskell (n 32) 146.

[65] Paraphrasing Samuel Moyn in a different context. Samuel Moyn, 'Human Rights in Heaven' in A Etinson (ed), *Human Rights: Moral or Political*? (Oxford, Oxford University Press, 2018) 75.

the setting of absolute confines to it.[66] Returning to what has been said above: laws and judgments convey standpoints. Or, as Koskenniemi has put it:

> You need to choose the law that will be yours; you need to vindicate a particular understanding, a particular bias or preference over contrasting biases and preferences. The choice is not between law and politics, but between one politics of law, and another.[67]

The question is: in this process, 'in the thick of history and politics',[68] who are the new 'bedfellows'?

[66] Soirila (n 19), referring to E Jouannet, 'What Is the Use of International Law – International Law as a 21st Century Guardian of Welfare Essay' (2006) 28 *Michigan Journal of International Law* 815, 854. I am not here using 'power' in an evaluative sense. Exercises of power can be judged both positively and negatively, that power is exercised as such, however, is an inescapable feature of human life. As Decosimo puts it, eg: 'Any act of defining is an act of power'. Decosimo (n 4) 40.

[67] M Koskenniemi, 'International Law in Europe: Between Tradition and Renewal' (2005) 16 *European Journal of International Law* 113, 123. See also, eg Haskell (n 18) 58: 'the necessity of coercion and faith … grounds and sustains any system of governance. We cannot escape serving a master, and we cannot avoid coercion. We are always already coerced into an order that does not need to be so. Freedom is not from coercion, but to have clarity in how violence is appropriated and toward what ends'.

[68] Moyn (n 65) 78.

2

Freedom of Religion in Sweden from a Historical Perspective

JOAKIM NERGELIUS

I. INTRODUCTION

As is probably well-known, Sweden was a Catholic country until the Reformation in the early sixteenth century, when the Protestant ideas of Martin Luther spread to the Nordic countries. The simultaneous birth of the modern Swedish State in 1523 did not alter the constitutional development of Sweden as such,[1] but King Gustaf I (Gustaf Vasa), the national unifier, was instrumental in turning Sweden into a Protestant country, arguing until his death in 1560 that Protestantism was in fact the true, pure Christian belief, superior but not radically opposed to or different from the allegedly 'untrue' Catholicism.[2] Catholics and other non-Protestant believers were, however, considered to be heretics and were forced to leave Sweden if they refused to give up their faith.[3]

In the years surrounding Gustaf Vasa's death in 1560, Sweden thus became a Protestant Evangelical Lutheran state, though this was not formally decided until 1593, at a historically important meeting held in Uppsala ('Uppsala möte'). Here, important rules concerning the relationship between the Church and the State that would determine future developments were laid down.

This meeting held a particular historical significance, since Gustaf Vasa's grandson Sigismund, who had been King of Poland since 1587, had succeeded his father Johan III as King of Sweden in 1592. However, Sigismund was a Catholic, and thus had to accept the decision at Uppsala in 1593 as a condition

[1] For further details on this, see J Nergelius, *Constitutional Law in Sweden* (Alphen aan den Rhijn, Wolters Kluwer, 2011) 13 ss. See also J Nergelius, *Religion and Law in Sweden* (Alphen aan den Rhijn, Wolters Kluwer, 2016).

[2] Needless to say, the reasons for his actions may not only have been religious, but also political and economic. This is, however, not the place to analyse such historical factors.

[3] See J Nergelius, *Religion and Law in Sweden* (n 1), with further references.

for finally being crowned as King of Sweden in 1594. However, he was not a Protestant at heart, so he was in conflict with his uncle Karl (Karl IX), who took over the throne in 1599. Thereafter, Sigismund, who had retired to Catholic Poland, fought a number of unsuccessful wars in order to try to win back the Swedish Crown (and possibly unite the two States). These conflicts played an important role in the developments that led to the Thirty Years' War in Europe from 1618–48.

Since then, and formally since the crowning of Karl IX as King of Sweden in 1604,[4] the relationship between the Protestant Church and the State has been close. The Church of Sweden was thus officially Protestant (Evangelical-Lutheran) from 1593 to 1995 or possibly even 2000, when the concept of an official State Church was abolished, as will be explained below. In 1604, it was decided that the heir to the throne had to be Protestant, a requirement that oddly enough still applies, for both political and religious reasons. Naturally, Karl IX wanted to ensure that it was impossible for Sigismund's descendants to claim any future rights to the Swedish throne. At the same time, this strengthened and underlined the position of Protestantism as the undisputed Swedish faith/religious order.

This was also emphasised in Swedish politics and policies on religious matters in the century that followed. At that time, the Church performed many important public administrative tasks, such as keeping registers on the population, and was thus closely linked to the State. Foreigners were only allowed into the country provided that they refrained from any public (non-Protestant) religious activities. Converts to Catholicism lost their right to inherit property. Religion was also the reason used to justify the many wars against, for example, Catholic Poland and Orthodox Russia, although religious tensions were slightly reduced after the Peace of Westphalia in Europe in 1648.

During the eighteenth century, however, things gradually changed. As a reaction to a minority Protestant group who wanted to meet for informal religious ceremonies outside the Church, a harsh law banning any such ceremonies was introduced in 1726.[5] However, when further steps in this somewhat authoritarian direction were taken in 1735, a discussion on the importance of greater religious freedom started to grow. This can be seen in the light of the beginning of the Age of Enlightenment in Europe, but was also due to purely economic and commercial reasons, since immigration was suddenly seen as positive for the economy. Thus, moves in this direction were made in 1741 and freedom of religion finally introduced in 1781 under King Gustaf III, who as a Francophile was very inspired by the ideas of the Enlightenment.[6]

[4] He was then succeeded, after his death in 1611, by his more well-known son Gustaf II Adolf, founder of Gothenburg and leader of protestant Sweden in the Thirty Year's War until his death in the battle of Lützen, Germany in 1632.

[5] The so-called *konventikelplakatet*.

[6] While this law only included Christian believers, Jews were given similar rights in 1782.

Nevertheless, the Constitution of 1809 meant further progress was made in this area, thus introducing more liberal views into freedom of religion. As opposed to modern laws, the rather hastily written and quickly enacted Constitution suffered from a certain lack of written sources, which meant that the real significance of its rules was frequently contested.[7] This was also true regarding the rule on basic or fundamental rights in Article 16. Discussions on this Article were more than just theoretical in nature, since this was in fact the only rule in the Swedish Constitution that covered any fundamental rights outside the scope of the Freedom of Press Act until 1974.[8] Bearing in mind that the European Convention on Human Rights (ECHR) was not incorporated into Swedish law until 1995, the importance of the former Constitution's Article 16 becomes even clearer.

Using rather antiquated language, the Article covered personal freedom and some crucial procedural guarantees, and then also explicitly guaranteed freedom of conscience (ie religious belief) and a free exercise of all religions, provided that this did not cause any disruption to the public peace or social order.[9] Among the issues that were contested were, initially, whether it really protected every kind of religious belief or just Christian and Jewish ones and, also, whether it was possible for Swedish citizens to leave or abandon the Swedish State Church in favour of other religious communities. Gradually, liberal interpretations were to prevail in both respects, in particular when new legislation was enacted in 1873.[10]

In 1951, the Freedom of Religion Act was passed (1951:680). This was the first time that the State declared its wish to stay neutral in matters relating to the religious beliefs of individuals.[11] The right not to be a member of any religious community was thus explicitly stated. In the *travaux préparatoires*, the right to belong to other religious communities than the Swedish Church without losing any rights was also stressed.[12] Moreover, the rules on and conditions for membership of the Church of Sweden were clarified; it was thus stated that children born in Sweden would become members of the Church if their parents were already members, but not otherwise, and that foreign Protestant believers coming to live in Sweden would automatically become members of the Church

[7] For an in-depth discussion, see among others A Brusewitz, *Studier över 1809 års författningskris* (Uppsala, Akademiska Bokhandeln, 1917) and R Karlbom, *Bakgrunden till 1809 års regeringsform* (Gothenburg, Elander, 1964).

[8] For a comparison, see J Nergelius, *Media Law in Sweden* (Alphen aan den Rhijn, Wolters Kluwer, 2015).

[9] A thorough and somewhat authoritative interpretation of the significance of the rule was made in 1938 by the Constitutional Committee of the Swedish Parliament; see KU 1938:16. An almost classical contribution from the legal doctrine was made by CA Reuterskiöld, 'Vår Regeringsforms Magna Charta' (1897–99) *Statsvetenskaplig tidskrift* 282 ss.

[10] For further details, see V Enkvist, *Religionsfrihetens rättsliga ramar* (Uppsala, Iustus, 2013) 55 ss.

[11] See Swedish government official report (SOU) 1949:20.

[12] See Government bill (proposition) 1951:100 p 47 ss.

from the day that they acquired Swedish citizenship. In other words, this law may be seen as a kind of practical, concrete enforcement and elaboration of Article 16 in the former Constitution of 1809.

Since then, however, two important changes have taken place. First, the rule on freedom of religion in the Swedish Constitution was amended and modernised – but perhaps not clarified very much – with the new Constitution, the Instrument of Government of 1974. And second, in 1995, a decision was made by the Swedish Parliament to separate the Church from the State. This separation finally took place in 2000, based on a law enacted in 1998 (1998:1593). This did not, however, happen 'overnight', but only after in-depth discussions starting in the 1950s. The Church Act was enacted in 1992, and replaced the old act from 1686 (at that time it was the oldest Swedish law in force). Finally, in 1998, the current laws were enacted.[13]

II. CURRENT REGULATIONS

In Chapter 2 Article 1, paragraph 6, freedom of religion or worship has been described as 'the freedom to practice one's religion alone or in the company of others' since 1974, as further explained below. For the period between 1974 and 1998 (or 2000), certain elements or aspects of the legal regulation of freedom of religion were slightly unclear. According to a transitional provision to the main Swedish constitutional act, the Instrument of Government (IG) or *Regeringsformen* of 1976 (page 3), the rules on membership of the Swedish Church described above continued to be in force, regardless of the wording in Chapter 2, Article 1, paragraph 6. The modalities and procedures for leaving the Church, should someone wish to do so, were at that time described in Articles 11 and 12 in the Act of 1951 (which required a personal application from the individual). This transitional provision was subsequently abolished in 1998, thus at the same time as the separation between the Church and State took place.

Finally, the somewhat obsolete rules on the monarchy and its freedom of religion shall be presented here. This leads us to the Act of Succession, the most outmoded of the four fundamental laws, in its language as well as in its contents. According to IG Chapter 1, Article 5, Section 2, the provisions of IG that relate to the King shall apply to the Queen should a Queen be head of State. This reform, aiming primarily at gender equality in society in a more general sense, was introduced in 1979, since the firstborn of the current King Carl XVI Gustav was a girl (Crown Princess Victoria). At the same time, changes were also introduced into the Act of Succession. Under its first Article, the right of succession to the throne of Sweden is vested in the male and female descendants of

[13] For *travaux préparatoires* where this development has been discussed, see Swedish government official report 1994:42, KU 1995/96:12, Swedish government official report 1997:41-47, KU 1997/98:20 and KU 1998/99:5. For an overview, see also Enkvist (n 10) 64 ss.

King Carl XVI Gustaf, with precedence for older siblings and their descendants over younger siblings and their respective descendants. And under Article 2, all provisions of the Act of Succession relating to the King shall relate to the Queen should she be head of State.

The rather outmoded nature of some of the provisions that still relate to the monarchy may be illustrated by Article 5 of the Act of Succession according to which a prince or princess of the Swedish Royal Family may not marry unless the government has given its consent thereto upon an application from the King; should a prince or princess marry without such consent, he or she will forfeit the right of succession for him or herself, his or her children and their descendants. In addition, according to Article 7, the heir to the throne may not undertake any travel abroad without the knowledge and consent of the King.

Still, the most outdated rule of the Swedish Constitution, all the four fundamental laws included, is without any doubt Article 4 of the Act of Succession, according to which the following applies in relation to the religious activities of the Royal Family:

> In accordance with the express provision of article 2 of the Instrument of Government of 1809 that the King shall always profess the pure evangelical faith, as adopted and explained in the unaltered Confession of Augsburg and in the Resolution of the Uppsala Meeting of the year 1593, princes and princesses of the Royal House shall be brought up in that same faith and within the Realm. Any member of the Royal Family not professing this faith shall be excluded from all rights of succession.

In more contemporary language, this means that all the members of the royal family who wish to keep their right to inherit the throne must profess the pure Evangelical (ie Protestant) faith. Thus, no freedom of religion exists for the Royal Family.[14] Apart from that regrettable fact, the still valid provision expresses values and attitudes that are simply not in line with contemporary attitudes in Swedish society. For that reason, it is surprising that the committee preparing a constitutional reform in 2010 was not given the task of looking into those or any other rules related to the monarchy. It ought to be possible for such a committee to discuss changes to some apparently obsolete rules without putting the monarchy as an institution into question (which the main political parties agreed not to do in 1971, in a well-known compromise).[15]

This particular Article on freedom of religion has recently been discussed at length after the birth of the young Princess Leonore – daughter of Princess Madeleine – in New York on 20 February 2014. Two questions have emerged, namely what will happen should she remain in the USA and spend her childhood

[14] It may of course be called into question whether members of the Royal Family enjoy other human rights like the freedom of speech or the right to vote. A correct statement would seem to be that the Royal Family is not deprived of such rights, but does not use them due to tradition; see eg, W Warnling-Conradsson, H Bernitz, L Sandström and K Åhman, *Statsrättens grunder* 6th edn (Stockholm, Nordstedts juridik, 2018) 190 s.

[15] The so-called *Torekovskompromissen*.

there (and thus not be brought up 'within the Realm') and what will be her religion, given that her father, Mr Chris O'Neill, is a Catholic. While the first question is probably easy to resolve should she come to Sweden in time to start school at the age of six, the second question seems more difficult. What is absolutely clear, however, is that she will lose her right to the throne – for which she is now number five in line – the very second she 'comes out' as a Catholic or is baptised in the Catholic Church. Needless to say, these rules seem very old-fashioned in an otherwise rather progressive society.

In the Swedish Constitution of 1974, the rules on fundamental rights are to be found in Chapter 2. Freedom of religion, or freedom of worship as it is called in the official translation, is thus to be found in Chapter 2, Article 1, paragraph 6, as far as the positive right to worship or exercise of a religion is concerned, and in Chapter 2, Article 2 concerning the so-called 'negative right to religion' (ie the right to not to have to reveal your faith). This second kind of freedom of religion is, in many ways, easier to identify and describe. As the wording in Chapter 2, Article 2 stipulates, this means that no one shall in their contacts with public institutions be coerced into divulging an opinion on a religious or other (political, cultural) such connection.[16] Nor may anyone in their contacts with public institutions be coerced into participating in a meeting for the shaping of public opinion or a demonstration or other manifestation of an opinion, or to belong to a religious community or other association for an opinion.[17]

In Chapter 2, Article 1, paragraph 6, freedom of religion or worship is described as 'the freedom to practise one's religion alone or in the company of others'. Here, no definition has been attempted concerning what constitutes a religion, which is a problem since it was hardly the intention of the 'Fathers' of the IG to protect any kind of spiritual or allegedly religious movements; in that case, even sectarian movements who worship their leaders and/or brainwash their members would be constitutionally protected, but that seems wholly unrealistic. Still, the question of how to interpret freedom of religion in this context is even more important given that according to Chapter 2, Articles 23 and 24, freedom of religion may never – as opposed to the other *freedoms of opinion* mentioned in Chapter 2, Article 1 – be limited, for any reason whatsoever. It is thus a so-called *absolute right* in Swedish law, which formally puts it alongside the right to life or the right not to be tortured. But what does this actually mean?

The closest thing to a definition can be found in one of the *travaux préparatoires* to the IG from the 1970s, where the Minister of Justice clarified that

[16] Before 1998, it was, unsurprisingly, sometimes put into question whether this provision was compatible with the Freedom of Religion Act of 1951, with its rules on automatic membership of the Church of Sweden and the difficulties leaving it involved for members (see eg Government bill 1975/76:209 p 117). See for a defence of the old system G Bramstång, 'Den s.k. negativa religionsfriheten och medlemskap i svenska kyrkan. Ett diskussionslägg' (1978) 1 *Förvaltningsrättslig Tidskrift* 27–35.

[17] Official translation, The Constitution of Sweden – The Fundamental Laws and the Riksdag Act, Sveriges Riksdag, Stockholm 2012.

freedom of religion included the freedom to hold a certain religious conviction, as well as a freedom of worship including the right to practise it, by spreading its message, organising and/or participating in sermons, and to join or found religious associations. At the same time, however, it was also stipulated that the limitations that might occur in and be applied to the other freedoms of opinion (ie the freedoms of speech, information, assembly, manifestation and association) according to Chapter 2, Articles 23 and 24 would apply also when those latter freedoms were being used in various religious contexts. For example, meetings may be forbidden during an epidemic outbreak, and that must also apply to religious meetings. Moreover, limitations to the freedom of speech regarding libel or racism will also apply to religious texts or messages.[18]

Thus, other freedoms will not enjoy stronger protection simply because they are being used for religious purposes, and otherwise criminal or punishable deeds, such as bigamy, the killing of animals or use of drugs, will not be legal by simply being justified with religious arguments. At the same time, however, laws that directly target specific religions are forbidden[19] and as was shown in the much publicised *Åke Green* case of 2005 further mentioned below, the simultaneous use of freedom of speech and freedom of religion may put the speaker in a rather privileged position, at least when the ECHR is also being invoked.[20] Thus, the fact that freedom of religion enjoys a stronger constitutional protection than other freedoms of opinion is not legally insignificant. From a historical perspective, it is perhaps best understood as an attempt by the constitutional legislators in the 1970s to avoid the type of situation that was commonplace at least until 1951, where other religions other than Protestantism were placed in a far inferior legal position. The message from the IG that this may never happen again without constitutional change is very clear.[21]

Generally speaking, freedom of religion is of course closely related to freedom of association, which is as such very strongly protected in Swedish law. The rule on freedom of association in Chapter 2, Article 1, Section 1, paragraph 5 IG, protects the freedom to associate with others for private or public purposes, including associations that are mainly commercially oriented. This freedom may under other rules in Chapter 2 in fact only be restricted in respect of organisations whose activities are of military or quasi-military nature, or constitute the persecution of a population group of a particular race, colour or ethnic origin. Thus, this right is probably more difficult to restrict than most other rights in Chapter 2 IG, with the sole exception of freedom of religion. The strong protection that those two rights together offer for religious communities was clearly

[18] See Government bill 1975/76:209 p 40.

[19] cf J Nergelius, *Svensk statsrätt* 4th edn (Lund, Studentlitteratur, 2018) 145 ss.

[20] See NJA 2005 p 805, particularly when compared with NJA 2006 p 467, where some Neo-Nazis who had used less harmful language than Rev Green were found guilty of libel, as opposed to him.

[21] cf T Bull and F Sterzel, *Regeringsformen – en kommentar* 2nd edn (Lund, Studentlitteratur, 2013) 72.

shown in a case in 2017, when Jehovah's Witnesses were granted the status of a religious community, with the right to receive state support by the Supreme Administrative Court, despite the fact that the government had a different view.[22]

III. RELIGIOUS COMMUNITIES AND PROTECTIONS OF THE INDIVIDUAL – PROTECTION OF PRIVACY

The issue of protection of privacy has been quite frequently discussed in Sweden in recent years, but mainly in relation to electronic surveillance and various problems related to the internet.[23] In relation to religion, the topic has led to less discussion, but two issues stand out as important from this particular point of view.

The first one is abortion, which is still a sensitive issue in many European countries but less so in Sweden, where it has been recognised and legal since 1974. In fact, it became legal as a method already in 1938, but only when it was necessary for medical reasons or when the pregnant woman had been raped or otherwise violated. Since 1974, it has been generally legal for every woman in the first 18 weeks of pregnancy, regardless of her reasons for wanting to do so (unless it entails a severe medical risk for the woman). After 18 weeks, an abortion is only possible if the competent medical authority (*Socialstyrelsen – The National Board of Health and Welfare*) grants special permission, which it will not do if the foetus looks healthy; on the other hand, a very late abortion may take place should this be required in order to protect the health and wellbeing of the mother.[24] Thus, the Swedish legislation can only be regarded as liberal. It is also important to note that there is no mention of "human dignity" or similar wording in the Constitution that could be used by anti-abortion groups to argue against the operation which is performed quite frequently.[25] Public opinion against abortion is weak. In Parliament, it is only the Christian Democrats and the nationalist party the Sweden Democrats that sometimes argue in favour of stricter rules. In 2017, the Swedish Labour Court (Arbetsdomstolen) concluded that the right to freedom of religion was not violated when a midwife, who

[22] HFD 2017 ref 4.

[23] For a survey of these issues, see Swedish government official report 2008:3, Skyddet för den personliga integriteten – Bedömningar och förslag.

[24] See Abortlag (1974:595).

[25] Approximately 38,000 abortions are carried out every year, according to the competent public authority; see www.socialstyrelsen.se/statistik/statistikefteramne/aborter. There has been some discussion in recent years on the right for midwives not to assist in abortions, should this go against their religious beliefs. See Resolution 1763 (2010) The Council of Europe – The right to conscientious objection in lawful medical care. No such legal right exists at the moment, but the Christian Democrat Party argued in favour of such a right in 2015. See also K Zillén, 'Conscientious Objection to Abortion in Sweden – A Commentary on the Swedish Case of Ellinor Grimmark, AD 2017 nr 23' (2017) 4 *Giornale di Diritto del Lavoro e di Relazioni Industriali* 791–811.

refused to participate in abortions due to her religious beliefs, was refused a position at a State-run hospital.[26]

As regards religious slaughter or ritual slaughter, this is probably the most sensitive issue in Swedish law that concerns the activities of religious communities and their relation to other laws (in this case preventing not the rights of humans but the so-called rights of animals). According to the Swedish Animal Welfare Act (*Djurskyddslagen*, 1988:534), Article 13 and in particular Article 14, animals must be unconscious before they are slaughtered, unless they have to be slaughtered immediately for medical reasons.[27] Despite this, both Jews and Muslims have practised ritual methods of slaughter (kosher, halal or dhabh), according to which the animal must lose its blood before slaughter, for a long time. How is this at all possible?

First of all, this kind of slaughter must be considered as a practice of religion, under Chapter 2, Article 1, paragraph 6 IG as well as Article 9 ECHR.[28] This has also been acknowledged by the Swedish authorities. According to IG, no limitation is at all possible (although this might be allowed under the ECHR). Apart from this very legal and formal answer, you could also add that these religiously motivated ways of slaughtering animals have been accepted in Sweden for a very long time and that it would thus be highly controversial should new legislation change and put an end to this. It is also important to note that the European Court of Human Rights (ECtHR) acknowledged ritual or religiously inspired slaughter as such as a religious practice in the *Cha'are Shalom ve Tsedek v France* case in 2000.[29]

Another important question is circumcision (female genital mutilation), which is generally forbidden for girls but allowed for boys, on religious grounds. In 1982, a special law declared the operation or incision illegal with regard to girls and adult women, qualifying it as a crime (*könsstympning – genital mutilation*).[30] For boys under 18, on the other hand, it is allowed and regulated in a special law from 2001.[31] The law stipulates that circumcisions may be performed with the consent of the boy's parent(s) or custodian(s), but not against the boy's own will – which is of course impossible to establish concerning very young boys. As regards the operation itself, it may only be performed by a qualified medical practitioner (or by a person who has been specially licensed by Socialstyrelsen, the National Board of Health and Welfare, upon request from a religious community, which is normally the Jewish Synagogue) and the

[26] AD 23:17. The case has been referred to the ECtHR.

[27] This requirement seems to be stricter than in most other European countries; see Enkvist (n 10) 165 s for a comparative survey.

[28] cf Enkvist (n 10) 134 ss and on 143 ss for a historical perspective.

[29] *Cha'are Shalom ve Tsedek v France* App no 27417/95 ECHR 2000-VII 231 (ECtHR 27 June 2000).

[30] See lag (1982:316) med förbud mot könsstympning av kvinnor.

[31] Lag (2001:499) om omskärelse av pojkar. (NB While the law forbidding this incision on girls has the word women (kvinnor) in its title, this law uses the word boys (pojkar)).

child shall be given a local or general anaesthetic. Should a surgical error occur during the operation, Socialstyrelsen may revoke such a licence with immediate effect, but the decision to do so may be appealed before an administrative court.

Circumcision must, in the same way as religious slaughter, be seen as a religious practice. The special law, with its rather precise medical requirements, is a clear limitation of the totally free exercising of this religious tradition, of a kind that is formally not allowed according to Chapter 2, Article 1, paragraph 6 IG (but probably under Article 9 ECHR).[32] On the other hand, this law may be seen mainly as a way of ensuring that a particular unusual medical operation – which is thus permitted as such – is being performed in a medically safe way. This was the line of reasoning used by the government in the *travaux préparatoires* for the law,[33] and it is rather convincing to a certain extent.

IV. CONCLUDING REMARKS

Thus, freedom of religion has a strong position in Swedish constitutional law. Of all the fundamental rights mentioned in Chapter 2 IG, few are so strongly protected and hard to limit as the one on freedom of religion. As shown above, this fundamental right can also quite easily be adapted to modern conditions and a highly secularised society, without losing its essence.

[32] cf Enkvist (n 10) 182 ss.
[33] See Government bill 2000/01:81 and Ds 2000:5.

3

The Significance of Religion for Swedish Labour and Social Legislation

REINHOLD FAHLBECK*

I. OVERTURE

WHAT IS THE significance of religion for Swedish labour and social legislation? Bluntly speaking, the answer is that religion is of negligible overall significance for labour and social legislation in Sweden. The cynic might even feel tempted to say that there is no justification for attributing any significance at all to religion in these two fields of the law. The realist would not really disagree.

In the decades after World War II, religion gradually disappeared from the public room. Ironically, the enactment in 1951 of the Freedom of Religion Act can be seen as the harbinger of that disappearance. By and large, religious organisations took on a defensive attitude or even went into quasi-oblivion. Public education was purged of its previously strong Christian character with mandatory confessional teaching and likewise mandatory attendance at confessional morning prayers. The judicial system was gradually cleared of religious

* The present text was originally presented at the conference 'Religion, Werte und Recht', organised by the German Gesellschaft für Rechtsvergleichung, at Universität Bayreuth in September 2015. The text is a reprint from the comprehensive conference volume 'The Significance of Religion for Today's Labour and Social Legislation', edited by professors Ulrich Becker (München), Sebastian Krebber (Freiburg) and Achim Seifert (Jena), and published by Mohr Siebeck, Tübingen 2017. Mohr Siebeck has kindly expressed its assenting understanding of this reprint and so have the editors.

Unfortunately, it has been necessary to change formalities in the footnotes, such as abbreviations, formatting, punctuation and referencing, in order to accord with Hart's 'Publishing Style Guidelines'. Though these changes have resulted in deviations from common practice in legal texts, they have no bearing on the substance of the original notes.

An Addendum is attached. It contains translations into English of quotes in German in two footnotes. A clarification is added to footnote 30. The Addendum also briefly highlights recent attitudinal changes within Sweden towards overt religious manifestations.

elements, eg bibles in court rooms and oaths of a religious character. By and large, religious manifestations became limited to the privacy of churches and other places of worship. A leading Swedish daily triumphantly proclaimed: 'God is dead'.[1] The newspaper and large segments of Swedish society agreed that God as a being – if such a being had ever existed or could even be envisaged – was indeed dead. Religion exited from the public room.

The decades after World War II saw the coming into existence of the Swedish social welfare system and its modern employment law system. This happened in a social and existential environment where religion by and large had become non-existent or at least politically and socially irrelevant.

The last two decades have seen the resurrection of God, as it were. Not only that but also a return of religion to the public room. Religion is again at the focus of attention. Immigration of Muslims predominantly accounts for that. Overt Muslim religious practices have raised awareness not just of Islam but also of the Christian foundation of our society. Prevailing Western notions and practices concerning freedom of religion and thought as well as freedom of speech have come under attack by Muslims. Freedom of conscience based on religious or secular ideas has become one of the hottest topics in recent years, primarily in connection with medical practice; cf Section V below.

Still, despite the return of religion as a factor of importance in social life, religion continues to be a factor without any significance in the legislative process. Its role is rather to be eliminated wherever it still has a role!

The pivotal example in this particular respect is the 2010 School Act with its radical removal of anything that smacks of religious confession from the curriculum in public schools. However, one significant exemption to this tendency of removal of religion from statutory law is the 2008 Discrimination Act.[2] Religion is one of the protected grounds of the act. The Discrimination Ombudsman has proved very zealous indeed in bringing offenders (actual or purported) to justice.

II. SOURCES OF THE LAW ON RELIGION

Religious law in Sweden has two basic sources: external and internal. External sources are of international origin, primarily the Convention for the Protection of Human Rights and Fundamental Freedoms (henceforward the European Convention or ECHR), adopted in 1950 by the Council of Europe. Internal sources are domestic – national – law, ie constitutional and sub-constitutional,

[1] The liberal newspaper *Dagens Nyheter* (Today's News). The proclamation did not accord with Nietzsche's identical statement since it lacked all metaphysical content, being meant as a statement of a simple, literal fact.

[2] The official Swedish designation of the 2008 Act is in fact the 'Discrimination Act'. The agency in charge of implementing the legislation is called the 'Discrimination Ombudsman'. Both designations can easily lend themselves to confusion and misunderstanding. What is meant is the opposite, ie anti-discrimination. The act aims at preventing discrimination and to remedy acts of discrimination.

ordinances by competent administrative agencies (eg the Work Environment Agency), court-made case law and, finally, decisions by administrative agencies (eg the Discrimination Ombudsman).

The European Convention is binding upon Sweden in three ways: (1) as a ratified international convention under public international law; (2) as part of the law of the European Union; and (3) as a Swedish statute, transposed and incorporated into Swedish law in 1994. The Convention has primacy over domestic national Swedish law, including constitutional law.[3] The European Union (EU) also has legal rules on religion. However, the ECHR is part of EU law. Furthermore, a process is under way for the EU to become a member of the Council of Europe and consequently a formal signatory to the ECHR. If and when that happens, rulings by the European Court of Human Rights (henceforward the European Court) will be legally binding upon the EU.

The Swedish 1951 Freedom of Religion Act was repealed in 1998, effective from 2000, with no substantive replacement. The vacuum thus created was remedied by the simultaneous adoption of the 1998 Communities of Faith Act. The act points at the freedom of religion regulation in the core Swedish constitutional act (the 1974 Instrument of Government) and the ECHR. Those are, today, the two legal instruments for freedom of religion in Sweden.

Included in its chapter on fundamental rights and freedoms, the 1974 Instrument of Government contains articles on the freedom of religion, positive and negative.[4] The articles are limited to the relationship between the public realm and members of society. Though they can be invoked in legal proceedings, they are of little impact in actual life. They are only rarely referred to in legal affairs and no body of case law exists on it.[5]

[3] The 1974 Instrument of Government (the core Swedish constitutional law):

Ch 2 art 19: 'No act of law or other provision may be adopted which contravenes Sweden's undertakings under the European Convention for the Protection of Human Rights and Fundamental Freedoms'.

Ch 12 art 10: 'If a public body finds that a provision conflicts with a rule of fundamental law or other superior statute, or finds that a procedure laid down in law has been disregarded in any important respect when the provision was made, the provision shall not be applied'.

[4] The 1974 Instrument of Government: Ch 2 art 2: 'No one shall in his or her relations with the public institutions be coerced to divulge an opinion in a political, religious, cultural or other such connection. Nor may anyone in his or her relations with the public institutions be coerced to participate in a meeting for the shaping of opinion or a demonstration or other manifestation of opinion, or to belong to a political association, religious community or other association for opinion referred to in sentence one'.

Ch 2 art 1: 'Everyone shall be guaranteed the following rights and freedoms in his or her relations with the public institutions: … 6. Freedom of worship: that is, the freedom to practise one's religion alone or in the company of others'.

[5] One exception is the much publicised ruling by the Swedish Supreme Court in 2005 in a case dealing with a sermon by a pastor. He spoke very negatively of homosexual people and of homosexual practices. Prosecuted for hate speech under the Swedish Criminal Act he was acquitted by the Trial Court but found guilty by the Court of Appeal. The Supreme Court also found him guilty under that statute. The Court found no basis for acquittal in Swedish constitutional law, ie the 1974

Of importance in national law is any legislation aimed to combat discrimination. The focal statute is the 2008 Discrimination Act. One of the grounds for discrimination is 'religion'. However, the Act and its *travaux préparatoires* do not elaborate on the meaning of the word 'religion'. They limit themselves to stating that the word 'religion' shall be used in accordance with its customary meaning without elaborating on what that meaning is!

The Discrimination Ombudsman is in charge of the implementation of the Discrimination Act. A very substantial body of administrative case rulings exists, including religious discrimination. However, so far no decision by the Discrimination Ombudsman regarding purported religious discrimination has been examined by a court of final instance. Employers found guilty of discrimination on grounds of religion have preferred to pay the penalty imposed by the Discrimination Ombudsman, thus getting rid of the matter once and for all. As a consequence, it is not clear whether the legal standards and practices adopted by the Discrimination Ombudsman in cases involving religion would pass scrutiny by the courts of final instance. The Discrimination Ombudsman applies a definition of and standards for 'religion' that seemingly go beyond what is protected as 'religion' and 'religious discrimination' under the European Convention.[6]

Thus, the European Convention, the ECHR, is *the* legal basis in Sweden for freedom of religion and religious practices. The ECHR is a living legal instrument. A body of case law exists and it grows as the European Court tries new cases.

Religious communities create internal rules and regulations of a legal character for their activities. Examples are Catholic Canon law and Islamic Sharia law. Such rules and regulations fall outside the scope of this article. They are distinct from Swedish national law. The reason is that they have no legal standing or authority per se under Swedish national law. They may be invoked in legal proceedings but they have no specific legal authority.

This is also the case with the rules and regulations of the Church of Sweden. Until 2000 a State church, it is now separated from and independent of the State.[7] It no longer enjoys a special position under constitutional law. However, as distinct from other religious communities, it is dealt with in a statute separate from the 1998 Communities of Faith Act for all other religious communities.

Instrument of Government as quoted in the previous footnote. Ultimately, the Court turned to the ECHR for guidance. It studied Arts 9 (freedom of religion) and 10 (freedom of speech). It came to the conclusion that a verdict of guilt would probably constitute a non-acceptable infringement of the pastor's rights under the ECHR, so he was acquitted.

[6] On the one and so far only court case concerning discrimination on religious grounds a district court of first instance deliberately set aside the ECHR and fashioned a definition of its own of 'religion'; Hässleholm trial court, case T 1370-13, judgment of 4 April 2015. The ruling looks like an archetypical example of 'armchair law'!

[7] Beginning in the 1520s, the Protestant Reformation took hold in Sweden. The country became firmly rooted in Lutheran Protestantism. The principle that all subjects should follow the religion of the Head of State (*cujus regio ejus religio*) was enforced with the utmost severity.

To a very limited extent, that separate statute equals the Church of Sweden with public law bodies. Apart from that, its rules and regulations are of private law character. Membership is now radically voluntary but a majority of Swedes still belong to it. Membership entitles members to certain coveted church services, eg marriage ceremonies and baptism.

III. THE JUDICIARY AND RELIGION

When the then newly enacted Common Law of the Realm of 1734 went into effect in 1736 it was decided that it should be prefaced with a set of moral rules. To some extent, the rules form the religio-philosophical basis of the 1734 Statute Book. Generally referred to as the *Rules for Judges (Domarregler)*, they are commonly ascribed to Olaus Petri, one of the persons that brought Protestant Christianity to Sweden in the first part of the sixteenth century.[8] They are thought to have been written – or compiled – in their present form around 1540 but go back to medieval times. To a great extent, they are based on canon law. Some 43 maxims spell out the norms of proper judicial behaviour. The initial statement starts with the following:

> A judge shall first consider that he holds God's command and that his office belongs to God and not him and for that reason the judgement that he pronounces is God's … and is for sure God's judgement and not that of men.[9]

These rules are still printed in the annual, semi-official, publication of core Swedish statutes.[10] Though reference to them by courts is very rare today and has been so for decades, the rules are nevertheless known by all legally trained people in Sweden. They enjoy a prestige that borders reverence.

What is of importance in the present context is that these rules point at the close historical relationship between religion, the law and the judiciary. Today that relationship has been severed virtually in its totality, but that is of fairly recent date.

The Christian cross has not been part of the fittings of Swedish court rooms, at least not in modern times.[11] Prayers or other acts of faith have not been part

[8] See, eg G Schmidt, *Die Richterregeln des Olavus Petri* (Göttingen, Vandenhoeck & Ruprecht, 1966).

[9] My translation. For a German version see previous note.

[10] Sveriges Rikes Lag (The Law of the Realm of Sweden), published since the 1860s by Norstedts Publishing House (now Norstedts Juridik, part of Karnov Group). The publication is traditionally edited by a judge of the Swedish Supreme Court (serving or retired).

[11] cf, eg, the ruling by the German Constitutional Court (Bundesverfassungsgericht), BVerfGE 35, 1 BvR 308/69, 17 July 1973, in a case dealing with complaints by Jewish persons that the presence of a Christian cross in the court room violated their rights under Art 4 (freedom of religion) of the German Federal Constitution since it forced them to conduct their case 'under the Cross' ('Verhandlungen unter dem Kreuz', on p 376). The Court agreed. See also eg BVerfGE 93, 1 BvR 1087 /91,

of court procedures in modern times either, but bibles were present in court rooms until quite recently.

Religious oaths were very much indeed part of court room procedures until quite recently. Two examples: judges took an oath upon being sworn in as judges. That oath resonated of the *Rules for Judges* – and still does today. Witnesses also had to take an oath. In both instances this was done with one hand on the Bible and with express reference to 'Almighty God and His Holy Word'.[12] Both oaths were secularised as recently as in 1975. Oaths are 'taken', not 'sworn'.[13]

Another remnant of previous customs was 'the court divine service', also known as 'the court sermon'. The 1686 Church Act prescribed that each year of the district court procedures was to begin with a divine service. The prescription was in force until 1990. A divine service still takes place in various courts on a voluntary basis. The Svea Court of Appeal, the oldest (1614) and most prestigious of the courts of appeal, discontinued the custom as recently as in 2008.

IV. WORKING TIME

A. The Ecclesiastical Year and the Secular Year

As in all 'Christian countries' the secular year has been heavily influenced by the ecclesiastical (or liturgical) year, even mirroring it. First and foremost, the Christian seven-day weekly calendar is also the secular calendar. Second, the Christian Sunday celebration-*cum*-rest is reflected in Sunday as the traditional secular rest day. Third, Christian religious feasts have traditionally been celebrated as secular holidays as well, often as days off from work. In previous centuries the number of holy days was quite substantial. A gradual reduction has been in progress since at least the Church Ordinance of 1571 and in particular the holiday reform of 1772. The latest holiday to be thus de-sanctified was the Whit-Monday, ie Monday following Whitsunday (2005). Other holidays have been moved to the nearest Saturday, eg All Saints Day (1953).

16 May 1995 (C II.2 a) on p 18, ('einen Rechtsstreit unter dem Kreuz zu führen'). No similar case is recorded in Sweden.

[12] An illustration: during my time as clerk of a district court ('Referendar') in the mid-1960s I often administered the swearing of oaths. It was done in the most formal and solemn way imaginable. We – my fellow recording clerk and I – were formally dressed, stood at attention in front of the witness, asked the witness to reciprocate, looked the witness straight in the eyes and ordered the witness to reciprocate, ordered the witness to lay his/her right hand on the Bible and take the oath as pronounced by me. Not a few witnesses found it difficult to do so in a clear and strong voice!

[13] The admonition by Christ in the Sermon on the Mount (Matthew 5, verses 33–37), not to 'swear' any oaths was discussed when the religious reference was abolished in 1975. However, Swedish case law has no equivalent to the 1972 decision by the German Constitutional Court on refusal to 'swear' oaths; Bundesverfassungsgericht, 11 April 1972, 2 BvR, 75/71 (Eidesverweigerung aus Glaubensgründen). The 1734 Common Law of the Realm obliged judges to 'swear' the oath and to 'promise and swear' to follow the commandment of the oath but today the obligation is secularised and only obliges to 'promise and assure'.

As of 2015, only a few Christian feast days fall on weekdays (Christmas Day, if it falls on a weekday, Good Friday, Easter Monday and Ascension Day). They are observed as secular holidays in the sense that they are days off from work. In addition, work on the days before these religious feast days often ends at noon or in the early afternoon.

Unless compensatory time off from work is introduced, the de-sanctification of holidays results in an increase in the total yearly working time. This was avoided in 2005 when Whit-Monday ceased to be a work-free Christian feast day. It was replaced by June 6, the National Day, which became a work-free holiday.

The Christian Lent is not reflected in statutory rules or in collective agreement regulations. One reason probably is that strict fasting is no longer practised by Christians at large.

B. Working Time Legislation

The 1977 Annual Holidays Act is strictly religion-neutral. Religion is not a factor in any sense in the structure of the act or its administration.

The 1982 Working Time Act is a piece of framework legislation. The Act represents something of a hybrid between public and private law since it can be replaced wholly or in part by collective agreements. This has also happened to a great extent. Of interest in the present context is whether and to what extent religion has influenced the legislation (and collective agreement regulations).

The ecclesiastical year to a great extent rules the Working Time Act, though religion per se has no impact whatsoever on present-day working time legislation. The seven-day week is the unit for computing standard (normal) working time. Overtime work computation depends to some extent on the seven-day week as well (though the month – non-ecclesiastical unit – is of greater importance).

In accordance with EU law – but antedating it by decades – employees are entitled to a weekly rest period. Under the 1982 statute (and its predecessors) that rest period must be at least 36 hours. As far as possible, this weekly rest shall be scheduled for weekends. Derogation by means of a collective agreement is possible. However, weekly rest falls on weekends for the overwhelming majority of employees.

Of course, the fact that the weekend and the Christian Sunday coincide is not coincidental. However, that concurrence has by and large lost its religious character. Social life at large today explains why the weekend is still the weekly rest period for most employees. This lost connection between religion and the weekend rest is vividly illustrated by the legislative history of the 1982 Working Time Act. In its bill to Parliament (1981/82:154) proposing a new working time legislation, the government discusses working time issues at great length. However, not even one single time are words like 'religion', 'church service', 'church attendance' or 'prayer' found. The bill is clinically free of any religious allusions.[14] On the other hand, the word 'veckovila' ('weekly rest') figures no less than 99 times.[15] A person not privy to knowledge of Sunday as the Christian day of worship can find no explanation why the weekend has been chosen as the period for the weekly rest!

Unless limited by rules in collective agreements, employers are at liberty to order work on Sundays. What would happen if an employee refuses to perform work on a Sunday (or any other day considered holy by the employee)? To the best of my knowledge, no Swedish court has ever been faced with this situation. By all likelihood the refusal would constitute just cause for dismissal under the 1982 Employment Protection Act, unless legally mitigating factors would dictate otherwise. The reason is that the employee would be held to be in breach of his/her contractual obligations. Furthermore, Article 9 of the ECHR has been held not to protect such refusals and a Swedish court – if it were aware of the holdings in question – would no doubt consider domestic Swedish law corroborated by those holdings.[16]

C. Leave of Absence/Time Off

Some 20 statutes grant time off to employees, eg parental leave, friends and family care, family reasons and studies. No statute provides for time off for reasons related to religion.[17]

[14] The same is true for all subsequent bills with changes and amendments to the statute. That includes the implementation of Working Time Directive 2003/88/EC; see s IV.C below.

[15] It is tempting in this connection to refer to case C-84/94 *United Kingdom v Council of the European Union* [1996] concerning Council Directive 93/104/EC (ECR I-5755). The case dealt with aspects of the organisation of working time, eg the weekly rest. The directive required that the rest period had to, in principle, include Sunday. That requirement was questioned by the UK. The Court concurred, stating that 'the Council has failed to explain why Sunday, as a weekly rest day, is more closely connected with the health and safety of workers than any other day of the week' (para 37). Similarly, the Swedish government failed to explain why it was necessary, in principle, that the weekly rest under the 1982 Working Time Act be scheduled to fall on weekends, ie primarily on Sundays. However, as the Government Bill to Parliament indirectly makes dear, it can be stated for certain that in 1982 such scheduling was not considered necessary for reasons relating to religion!

[16] See in this respect two cases dealt with by the (former) European Commission of Human Rights under Art 9 of the ECHR. The first case is *Konttinen v Finland* App no 24949/94, (ECtHR 3 December 1996) concerning a member of the Seventh-Day Adventist Church. Citing religious concerns, Mr Konttinen refused to work after sunset on Friday. His dismissal was considered to be caused not 'because of his religious convictions but for having refused to respect his working hours'. The second case is *Louise Stedman v the United Kingdom* App no 29107 /95 (ECtHR, 9 April 1997). Ms Stedman was ordered to work on Sundays. She declared that she was not willing to work on Sundays, which she – as a Christian – considered 'should be devoted to non-commercial, family and religious activities'. She was dismissed. However, the Commission declared that Ms Stedman 'was dismissed for failing to agree to work certain hours rather than her religious belief as such'.

[17] See generally R Fahlbeck, *Bed och arbeta. Om religionsfrihet i arbetsliv och skola* (Malmö, Liber, 2011) ss 6.3.4. See very succinctly also R Fahlbeck, 'Ora et Labora – On Freedom of Religion at Work Places. A Stakeholder cum Balancing Factors Model' (2004) 20 *International Journal of Comparative Labour Law and Industrial Relations* 57 et seq.

EC Working Time Directive 2003/88 specifically points at 'workers officiating at religious ceremonies in churches and religions communities'.[18] Swedish law has no equivalent provision. The 1982 Working Time Act is silent in this respect. So are the *travaux préparatoires*.[19]

The liturgical year of other religions has so far had no influence on Swedish labour law or social legislation. No statutory rules have been introduced to accommodate the faithful of other religions and no such rules are envisioned. Also, there is no generally accepted practice for dealing with requests by employees of such religions for leave from work in order to meet the requirements of their religion. Calls for the introduction of statutory (or case law) rules to that effect are unheard of. Collective agreements sometimes contain provisions but only rarely so. The ECHR imposes an obligation on employers to try to accommodate employee wishes. Under the ECHR, employers are obliged to observe the positive obligation to promote the exercise of freedom of religion.[20] However, it is definitely true that most Swedish employers are unaware of that obligation. By all likelihood, the Work Environment Agency, in charge of overseeing working time legislation, also lives in benign ignorance of any such obligation!

The Jewish community is partly accommodated since Saturdays are work-free at most places of work. Time off for the Muslim Friday prayer is de facto granted only at the discretion of employers. Still, collective complaints by Muslims concerning the absence of provisions for time off for Friday prayer are not heard of. The Muslim *Ramadan* is a factor of practical importance at many places of work. Strict fasting during all daylight hours may pose a work safety problem. Ad hoc solutions will have to be found. One possibility is to schedule the annual holiday to coincide with *Ramadan*.

D. Store Opening Hours

Under the 1966 Store Opening Hours Act (and its predecessors) commercial retail was allowed only within specified time limits. The Act elapsed by the

[18] Art 17(1) (c).

[19] See eg Government Bill 1995/96:162 and Government Bill 2003/04:180, both on the implementation of the EC Working Time Regulation. The Government Report SOU 1995:92 preparing for the 1995/96 Government Bill refers to Art 17 of the Directive. However, it does not mention the provision concerning religious ceremonies. This omission conveys the impression that that provision was deliberately ignored. Disregarding the need for time off of non-Christian religions officiating persons at days other than Sundays is remarkable, perhaps reprehensible.

[20] See in this respect *X v The United Kingdom* App no 8160/78 (Commission decision, 12 March 1981), 'the Muslim teacher's case'. It illustrates the situation under Art 9 ECHR. A Muslim teacher at a public school applied for time off to attend Friday prayer. Under its obligation to promote the exercise of freedom of religion of its employees, the school had actively tried to accommodate the teacher. The Commission found that the teacher's absence to attend prayers caused 'serious difficulties' for the school to fulfil the statutory requirements of the education system. For this reason and because the teacher had accepted employment without reservation for his wish to attend Friday prayer, the Commission came to the conclusion the school had not failed to 'give due consideration to his freedom of religion'. The ruling and its underlying legal premises is virtually unknown in Sweden.

end of 1971 and was not replaced by new rules. This had the deliberate consequence of introducing full freedom for retailers. Thus, no particular days, no particular hours of the 24-hour day and no particular period of the year were exempted. Critics talked of the substitution of 'the law of the jungle' for 'the rule of law'. During the 1971 deliberations in Parliament references to religion as a factor weighing against complete freedom were virtually non-existent. The report of the parliamentary committee in charge of the matter did not discuss it at all, limiting itself to mentioning in passing hesitation by some political groupings.[21]

The radical deregulation by the 1971 Act persists. Today no one seriously advocates statutory limitations. Collective agreements specify additional pay for working hours considered inconvenient, such as evening and night hours as well as work on weekends. Such payment makes these working hours attractive to many employees. For that reason there is no general employee opposition to Sunday work, not even work on days such as Christmas Day or Good Friday. Nor are there any qualms of ethical or religious character about work being performed on Sundays among the population at large, not even work on Sunday mornings when church services are customarily held.[22] No restrictions – voluntary or otherwise – exist on the sale of food, beverage or other merchandise that might be considered offensive on Sundays or religious holidays, such as Good Friday.[23]

In actual practice most stores are closed on Sundays. However, shopping malls tend to be open on weekends as are most stores selling food and beverages.

V. THE DUTY TO WORK. WORK TASKS. CONSCIENTIOUS OBJECTIONS

The main aspects of an employee's duty to work relate to *what*, *when*, *where* and *how* work is to be performed. Of interest in the present context are the issues of *when* and *what*. The *when* issue relates to working time. It has been discussed above. The *what* issue relates to the work tasks that employees can

[21] Trade and Industry Committee (*Näringsutskottet*) report 1971:53.

[22] As is well known, the German Constitutional Court (*Bundesverfassungsgericht*) in a ruling of 1 December 2009 (1 BvR 2858/07), found regulations in the Federal State of Berlin (*Bundesstaat Berlin*) allowing stores to stay open for certain hours on all four Sundays in Advent in violation of the 1949 Federal Constitution. The 1949 Federal Constitution in this respect has taken over Article 139 of the 1919 Weimar Constitution. It states: 'Der Sonntag und die staatlich anerkannten Feiertage bleiben als Tage der Arbeitsruhe und der seelischen Erhebung gesetzlich geschützt'. Swedish working time regulation knows of nothing like 'seelische Erhebung'. The very notion of *spiritual edification* is utterly alien to present time public mentality and thinking in Sweden and has been so for several decades, probably for the entire post-World War II period.

[23] The one and only exception is the sale of alcoholic beverages in the State liquor monopoly stores. Opening hours are limited by statute, late Saturday afternoons and evenings as well as Sundays being precluded as a rule. However, that regulation is exclusively based on considerations concerning public health. Religion is of no import.

be assigned and are obliged to perform. By and large this issue has no religious implications. Most work tasks have no moral implications.

However, certain work tasks may have moral and religious implications. The issue in this respect is to what extent moral or religious misgivings can serve as excuses to perform certain work tasks. This is an issue that has attracted little attention in Swedish labour law and social security regulation.[24] The traditional legal response has been that employees (and social security applicants) are obliged to perform all work which meets two criteria: it must fall within the employer's natural area of activity and within the employee's (applicant's) professional ability. This *litmus test* affords little or indeed no room for religious misgivings.

A well-established, unwritten, principle of general application is that employees are not obliged to perform work contrary to public policy, *contra bonos mores*. This principle would easily lend itself to the area of ethical or religious misgivings. So far, however, no instance where that has happened has been recorded.

As was mentioned in Section I, the last decades have seen the return of religion to the public room. One consequence of this is a development resulting in religious misgivings being increasingly voiced. However, nothing substantial has been attained to clarify the legal consequences of such misgivings at places of work or within the social security system. No domestic statutory or case law exists.

Article 9 of the ECHR presents the overriding norm. That norm is directly applicable at places of work, even private ones. Under Article 9, paragraph 2, a balance must be struck between the competing interests at stake, primarily the employee's interest not to have to perform work that infringes upon his or her ethical or religious beliefs, the employer's interest to have all workplace work tasks performed and the interests of the persons affected by the work performance refusal of the employee, be they clients, customers, patients, students or other persons concerned.

No domestic regulation exists, statutory or otherwise. Case law is non-existent as well. Article 9 ECHR rules. Consequently, the legal situation in Sweden does not differ from any other Member State of the Council of Europe. Case law is scarce under the ECHR.[25] It is non-existent under the Swedish

[24] See generally a discussion regarding Sweden in Fahlbeck, *Bed och arbeta* (n 17) ss 6.3.5. See very succinctly also Fahlbeck, 'Ora et Labora' (n 17) at 58 et seq.

[25] Case of *Eweida and others v the United Kingdom* App nos 48420/10 (Ms Eweida), 59842/10 (Ms Chaplin), 51671/10 (Ms Ladele) and 36516/10 (Mr McFarlane) (ECtHR, 15 January 2013) provides the best illustration. Ms Ladele refused, for reasons of her Christian faith, to be designated as a registrar of civil partnerships and Mr McFarlane for the same reason refused to provide psycho-sexual counselling to same-sex couples. The European Court found the opposing interests of others to be outweighing their religious misgivings. Also, since the policy pursued by the employer was considered to have a legitimate aim and to be proportionate there was no indirect discrimination under Art 14 either. No corresponding court cases exist in Swedish case law. The Ms Eweida and Ms Chaplin cases concern the wearing of a visible Christian cross; cf s VI below.

application of the ECHR. A few cases have been decided without reference to the ECHR.[26] The decisions are of an ad hoc character. No principles have been established.

The notion and reality of 'conscientious objection' was part of the social fabric during the Cold War as conscientious objection to military service occurred, albeit fairly rarely. With the end of the Cold War awareness of the notion subsided. Today the situation is completely different. The issue has attracted enormous attention in recent years. That attention has focused almost solely on medical work, virtually exclusively on abortion. Unlike most European countries Sweden today does not allow for medical personnel being excused from participating in work relating to abortion. The *travaux préparatoires* to the present 1974 Abortion Act specifically provide for conscientious objection and so do several subsequent parliamentary reports.[27] However, the statements to that effect seem to have been forgotten or are being deliberately overlooked. The 2010 Resolution (1763) by the Parliamentary Assembly of the Council of Europe on '[t]he right to conscientious objection in lawful medical care' is well known but derided and belittled as non-binding.[28] The call in Parliamentary Resolution 1928 (2013) to 'ensure the right to well-defined conscientious objection in relation to morally sensitive matters, such as … services related to health care' is ignored.[29] A much publicised case concerning conscientious objection is now before a district court. It concerns a midwife who refuses all participation in work related to abortion.[30]

Feelings are running very high indeed on the subject, in particular among those opposing conscientious objection. It has even gone so far in some circles as to hail unhindered availability of abortion as something of a higher moral

[26] eg Labour Court case 2005 no 21, the eldercare case. A Jehovah's Witness refused to perform certain work that was part of her regular work assignment. She was dismissed. She claimed that she had been indirectly discriminated against. The Court disagreed. It took the position that any person with the same work assignment, who, regardless of reason, was to refuse to perform the specific work in question, would be treated in the same way. Refusal to perform the work, not religion, was the reason for her dismissal, according to the court. Cf rulings by the (former) European Commission based on the same rational quoted in n 16.

[27] See eg Government bill to Parliament 1974:70 proposing what became the 1974 Abortion Act, on p 76 et seq. See also the report on that Government bill submitted by the Social Committee of Parliament 1974:21, on p 40. For reiterations see eg reports by the same parliamentary committee 1983/84:3, on p 16, 1984/85:11, on p 17, 1986/87:5, on p 11, or 1987/88:2, on p 2. More recent reports by the committee ignore those previous statements and take the position that there is no excuse for conscientious objectors.

[28] Ironically, the initiative to a resolution on the issue came from Swedish assembly members. Their intention was to attain a resolution banning conscientious objections to participating in abortions. The initiative backfired. Sweden has actively – but so far unsuccessfully – worked to have the resolution revoked.

[29] Resolution 1928 (2013), Safeguarding human rights in relation to religion and belief, and protecting religious communities from violence, para 9.10.

[30] Örebro tingsrätt (Örebro District Court), case T 1781-14, *Ellinor Grimmark v the Administrative Board of the County of Jönköping* (Landstinget i Jönköpings län). The District Court ruled against the midwife. The case is now before the Labour Court (a court of final instance).

order than conscience generally. There is an urgent need for a cooling down of sentiments. A ruling by the ECHR might settle the issue, perhaps in favour of conscientious objection in accordance with the 2010 Resolution 1763.

VI. RELIGIOUS DRESS AND ORNAMENTS AT PLACES OF WORK

Religious dress (or 'religious garb') and religious ornaments have emerged as legal issues only recently. Immigration accounts for that, primarily of Muslims. In the three or four decades after World War II, dress and religious ornaments were considered private matters. Apart from places of work specifically calling for dress codes, employees were at liberty to dress as they chose, all within the boundaries of decorum. No statutory rules existed and case law dealt with practical matters, such as the necessity at specific places of work for special clothes, eg for safety reasons, and the responsibility to provide and pay for such clothes.

Today the situation is totally different. Religiously motivated garb and ornaments have become common. The situation has become very sensitive indeed.[31]

The European Court once declared that '[s]chools should not be the arena for missionary activities or preaching'.[32] Though the Court has not been called upon to pronounce itself on the role of religious garb at workplaces, it seems fair to believe that the Court would come to the same conclusion.

On the other hand, freedom of religion and the concomitant right to manifest one's religion under Article 9 of the ECHR applies to workplaces as well. A recent case concerned a private workplace in the UK (British Airways). An employee wished to wear a cross visibly on a necklace and to deliberately manifest her religious beliefs in that way. The European Court stated:

> As previously noted, this is a fundamental right: because a healthy democratic society needs to tolerate and sustain pluralism and diversity; but also because of the value to an individual who has made religion a central tenet of his or her life to be able to communicate that belief to others.[33]

A body of ECHR case law on the matter has emerged. It primarily concerns Muslim attire, the Muslim headscarf and the Muslim burka. The European

[31] For a thoughtful discussion on religious garb see eg R Robson, *Dressing Constitutionally: Hierarchy, Sexuality, and Democracy from Our Hairstyles to Our Shoes* (New York, Cambridge University Press, 2013), in particular ch 6, 'Dressing Religiously'. Though the discussion is limited to the US, the issues and problems discussed are universal. For a discussion regarding Sweden see Fahlbeck, *Bed och arbeta* (nb 17) ss 6.3.8. See very succinctly also Fahlbeck, 'Ora et Labora' (n 17) at 60 et seq.

[32] *Lautsi v Italy* App no 30814/06 (ECtHR, 3 November 2009) unanimous Chamber ruling, para 47(c). The ruling was reversed on appeal by the Grand Chamber, 18 March 2011. Though the statement of the Chamber has not been repeated by the Grand Chamber, the general character of its ruling conveys the same message.

[33] *Eweida and others* (n 25) para 94.

Court has always found bans on such attire acceptable, despite the infringement on the religious freedom of the bearer that such bans (might) represent.[34] The *Eweida* case just referred to dealt with a Christian cross. The Sikh turban and the Jewish kippa have not been dealt with under the ECHR in a workplace context (or in the context of social security).

Sweden has not developed any rules of its own regarding religious attire or ornaments at workplaces. Case law is non-existent. So is regulation in collective agreements. No labour market standards have developed either.[35] This means that the case law of the European Court is the prime source of law. At the same time, Sweden enjoys a wide margin of appreciation to fashion its own rules. The reason is that there is no consensus among the Member States concerning religious attire and religious ornaments at the workplace.[36]

Public opinion is divided and vacillating between acceptance, reluctance or downright hostility. However, that does not apply to the treatment of women. Unequal treatment of women vis-à-vis men and female oppression is very much indeed frowned upon. Most Swedes would wholeheartedly agree with the European Court when it stated the following in a 2001 ruling:

> In those circumstances, it cannot be denied outright that the wearing of a headscarf …, as the Federal Court noted, is hard to square with the principle of gender equality. It therefore appears difficult to reconcile the wearing of an Islamic headscarf with the message of tolerance, respect for others and, above all, equality and non-discrimination that all teachers in a democratic society must convey to their pupils …

and

> the advancement of equality of the sexes is today a major goal in the member States of the Council of Europe. This means that very weighty reasons would have to be advanced before a difference in treatment on the ground of sex could be regarded as compatible with the Convention.[37]

[34] The rulings concern primarily France and Turkey. In these countries secularism – or *laïcité*, as it is referred to in France – is part of basic national law. It is not at all certain that the outcome will be the same if and when the European Court is confronted with the same issue in countries with no or little similar basic traits, for example Sweden. Cf in this respect the much publicised ruling by the German Constitutional Court (*Bundesverfassungsgericht*) concerning Ms Feresta Ludin, a teacher; BVerfGE, 2 BvR 136/02, 24 September 2003). Ms Ludin had been refused employment at a public school since she insisted on wearing a Muslim headscarf even in the classroom. The Constitutional Court found the, refusal unacceptable since it lacked the necessary legal authority in the law of the federal state in question (Baden-Württemberg). Thus, the Court did not rule out a ban as an unconstitutional infringement per se of the constitutionally protected freedom of religion.

[35] Swedish school authorities have been quite permissive with regard to student attire but no similar development can be recorded for universities. The issue of attire by teachers in public schools has not been addressed.

[36] For comments by the European Court concerning the margin of appreciation in matters of religious attire and ornamentation see eg *SAS v France* App no 43853/11 (ECtHR 1 July 2014) para 129.

[37] *Dahlab v Switzerland* App no 42393/98 ECHR 2001-V, 447 (15 February 2001) para 43 et seq. The reference to the Federal Court concerns Switzerland. Statements to the same effect as in Dahlab

Most Swedes would also wholeheartedly agree with the blistering criticism expressed in the Council of Europe Resolution 1464 (2005), *Women and Religion in Europe*, on the way religion is sometimes invoked to justify differing treatment of women. Paragraphs 5 and 6 inter alia state the following:

> Freedom of religion cannot be accepted as a pretext to justify violations of women's rights, be they open or subtle, legal or illegal, practised with or without the nominal consent of the victims – women.[38]
>
> It is the duty of the member states of the Council of Europe to protect women against violations of their rights in the name of religion and to promote and fully implement gender equality. States must not accept any religious or cultural relativism of women's human rights.[39]

On the other hand, there is also a widespread reluctance to interfere with the behaviour of others. This is particularly the case with regard to immigrants. There is a widespread fear of being considered hostile to immigration or even racist if reacting in a negative or condescending way to the customs and behaviour of immigrants. Coupled with this is an attitude of indifference to all things religious prevailing among large segments of the Swedish population. This indifference is probably the main reason why the public attitude towards religious attire and ornamentation – though by and large loathed – is very permissive.

This all would point in the direction of permissiveness to religious attire and other religious manifestations at workplaces. However, by and large this is not the case. Religious manifestations at workplaces are quite rare. One reason for this is perhaps that many feel embarrassed and uncomfortable, even annoyed, by overt religious manifestations regardless of what religion is manifested. They are frowned upon. By and large, religion is still considered a private matter and should be kept private. Another reason – and perhaps the strongest – is the marked reluctance on the part of employers to accept religious manifestations at their workplaces. The prevailing employer attitude is that workplaces are no arenas for religious manifestations and should not be.

All things considered, religious manifestations have so far given rise to precious little public discord in actual working life. As far as is known, open workplace conflicts are very rare indeed. Resort to the courts is unheard of. No court case is recorded. Still, the situation is very sensitive indeed.

The conclusion so far is that from a domestic legal regulatory point of view the whole area of religious manifestations at workplaces is something of a *terra incognita*, and has been so for the entire post-World War II period.

are common in the case law of the European Court. For a recent statement see eg *SAS v France*, ibid, upholding the ban on wearing a burka in public places in France. The Court reiterated in this connection 'that the advancement of gender equality is today a major goal in the member States of the Council of Europe ...'; para 119.

[38] Para 5.

[39] Para 6.

However, returning to overriding international norms the picture is changing somewhat. Article 9 of the ECHR applies. Case law from the European Court provides guidance on the principal level. As was said in Section V a balance must be struck between the legitimate wishes of the employee concerned and legitimate opposing interests. The methodology presented by the European Court in the *Eweida* case applies.[40] As the reasoning of the Court in that case demonstrates, no simple yardsticks are available. The necessary balance has to be struck on an ad hoc basis, taking into account the circumstances of the situation at hand.

As was pointed out in Section II, the 2008 Discrimination Act deals with religious discrimination. The Discrimination Ombudsman is very active in combating discrimination. This also applies to religious discrimination. As was also pointed out, employers found guilty by the Ombudsman have consistently refrained from taking those decisions to court, preferring to pay the penalty imposed by the Ombudsman, thus getting rid of the matter once and for all. As was also pointed out, it is far from certain that decisions by the Ombudsman would always be upheld by courts if brought before them. It seems fair to say that a legal sub-culture exists here that ought to be tested by the courts. The sub-culture is characterised by a very permissive attitude towards religiously motivated attire and behaviour. This is in particular the case with regard to Muslims. For example, the Muslim scarf is consistently considered to be a religious manifestation. No attention is paid to the possible infringement of the negative freedom of religion of others that such wearing might constitute or to other effects that the wearing of such a scarf might have, eg the employers' interest to create and convey a certain corporate image. Nor is any attention paid to the highly controversial issue whether the scarf is the result of female oppression. The 2010 Council of Europe Resolution 1464 (2005), *Women and Religion in Europe*, with its blistering criticism of religions for the subjugation of women, has never been referred to. It is taken for granted that female attire is based on genuine rather than nominal consent. The stated policy of the Discrimination Ombudsman is that religious manifestations take precedence over gender equality, at least as far as Muslim manifestations are concerned. This policy is justified as a means of promoting integration into Swedish society. Some observers are critical to this policy since, in their view, it represents integration by means of segregation.

[40] N 25 above. Reference can also be made to a ruling by the German Federal Labour Court (*Bundesarbeitsgericht*), 2 AZR 472/01, 10 October 2002 (Vol 103, 2004, p 111). It concerns the dismissal of a saleswoman who wished to wear a Muslim headscarf. The Court here presents a well thought-out model for striking the necessary balance. The model is in perfect harmony with the ECHR and the subsequent *Eweida case* but it is more elaborate than *Eweida*.

VII. EMPLOYMENT POLICY PROGRAMMES AND EMPLOYMENT POLICY MEASURES

Full employment is a cherished social value. It has been a lodestar of public policy throughout the entire post-World War II period.

The Socialdemokratiska Arbetarepartiet (SAP, the Social Democratic Party) defined itself as 'the workers' party' and was originally built on a constituency of manual workers. Full employment has been the mantra of the SAP for the entire post-World War II period. Since the SAP had been in power uninterruptedly between 1945 and 1976 (and again for approximately half of the time since then), the full employment idea has been the single strongest feature of post-World War II labour politics and social engineering. Enormous administrative efforts have been undertaken to achieve the goal and enormous amounts of money have been spent. Active labour market policy has been a hallmark of post-World War II Swedish society and one of the most prominent features of Swedish social fabric.

The National Labour Marker Board was in charge of implementing efforts to achieve that goal. Various unemployment benefit schemes have been available for the unemployed. Robust, voluntary and active public employment exchange has been an important ingredient. So have various schemes for work-experience placement of the unemployed and referral to specific jobs that are available.

The reverse side of all these schemes is – and has consistently been – the obligation of the unemployed to participate in efforts to find and accept work and/or work-experience placement. Central in this respect is the obligation to accept 'suitable work' or 'suitable work-experience placement'.

General reference in this respect can be made to rules adopted by the ILO, namely the 1988 Convention No 168 concerning Employment Promotion and Protection against Unemployment.[41]

The overriding Swedish statute is the 1997 Unemployment Insurance Act. The statute replaced a 1973 predecessor. Words such as 'religion' or 'faith' are non-occurring in the *travaux préparatoires* of either of them.

At present, a public Directive of 2012 on what constitutes 'suitable work' is in force.[42] It has several predecessors. Section 4 of the 2012 Directive states that if the person in question 'cannot accept available work due to personal

[41] Art 21 para 2 of the Convention reads: 'In assessing the suitability of employment, account shall be taken, in particular, under prescribed conditions and to an appropriate extent, of the age of unemployed persons, their length of service in their former occupation, their acquired experience, the length of their period of unemployment, the labour market situation, the impact of the employment in question on their personal and family situation and whether the employment is vacant as a direct result of a stoppage of work due to an on-going labour dispute'. The 1988 Convention replaced several predecessors, eg the 1934 Unemployment Provision Convention and Recommendation.

[42] Directive on suitable work, issued by the Inspectorate for the Unemployment Insurance, IAFFS 2012:1.

conditions or circumstances that are acceptable under this Directive, such person must as soon as possible take measures to eliminate such obstacles, whenever possible'.[43] Failure to do so will result in the withdrawal of benefits. To some extent the Directive specifies acceptable excuses. They all deal with practicalities. The labour market authorities retain a wide margin of appreciation and have done so during the entire post-World War II period. It seems justified to say that the present Directive is very strict indeed. In this respect it does not differ in principle from its post-World War II predecessors, although the strictness of predecessors has differed somewhat depending on the economic situation.

What is of relevance here is that the 2012 Directive does not make any reference to conscientious objections or objections of a religious nature. This may seem reprehensible, perhaps even shocking. No room for spirituality, no room for conscience? However, the structure of the Directive is perhaps not surprising after all since Article 21 of the 1988 ILO Convention (see note 39) makes no reference to religion or conscience either.

An ongoing court case at the time of this writing illustrates the situation.[44] A Jehovah's Witness refused, for religious reasons, to come to a work-experience placement interview at a company that promotes and sells lotteries to private organisations. His refusal was considered non-acceptable by the labour market authority so he was barred from further assistance. He appealed. The Administrative Court of first instance ruled in his favour, citing freedom of religion. The labour market authority appealed. The Administrative Court of second instance upheld the bar. The Court rook the position that the refusal did not enjoy protection in terms of 'religion' under Article 9 of the ECHR. Nor was it justified for any other reason. The position offered was considered to be 'not unsuitable' so the refusal was unacceptable. That ruling by the Administrative Court of second instance stands since the Supreme Administrative Court in 2015 declined to hear the case.

To conclude: neither religion nor faith has played any role whatsoever for the structure and administration of the single most important work-related social security system in Sweden.

VIII. THE SOCIAL SECURITY SYSTEM AT LARGE

The concluding remark in Section VII on employment policy was that neither religion nor faith had played any role whatsoever for the structure and administration of the single most important work-related social security system in Sweden.

[43] My translation of the Swedish original.

[44] The Administrative Court of first instance (Förvaltningsrätten i Göteborg), case no 6207-14, judgment of 4 July 2014. The Administrative Court of second instance (Kammarrätten i Göteborg), case no 4254-14, judgment of 22 April 2015.

What about other social security systems? The Swedish social security system has attracted worldwide attention. Sweden has even been looked upon as something of a model. The notion that Sweden is the *People's Home* is cherished and is indeed often used to characterise Sweden as a nation. Swedes are supposed to take pride in that and it seems fair to say that during the first three to four decades after World War II – the heydays of 'the Swedish Model' – a good proportion of the population actually did feel this way.

Examples of social security systems other than the employment policy system are schemes for financial social assistance to individuals in need, housing allowance (rent allowance), free medical care (including free-of-charge abortion) and family/child allowances. These schemes all cost huge amounts of money.

What is the role of 'religion' or 'faith' – positive or negative – in the structure and administration of these schemes? The answer is that religion plays no role whatsoever in any of these schemes. It is true that they are all built on notions of solidarity and brotherhood. However, confessional religion or creed played no role whatsoever.

IX. COLLECTIVE LABOUR LAW

The law on collective bargaining, freedom of association, the right to organise, labour market unions, collective agreements, industrial actions and industrial democracy/co-determination forms the core of collective labour law. Sweden has a mighty body of collective labour law. Its origins and basic legal structures date to times before World War II but its present statutory dress dates primarily from the 1970s. Has religion played any role in the formation of this body of law?

The answer is negative. Collective labour law as a social and legal phenomenon has deep roots in the Swedish social fabric. That fabric lost most of its confessional religious character already before the advent of the collective labour movement. The labour movement distanced itself from religion, indeed by and large repudiated it. No Christian unions were formed. No overtly Christian political party emerged until long after the formation of collective labour law. Mainly for these reasons, confessional religious elements were never part of the development of collective labour law.

Religious communities such as churches or parishes have always enjoyed the same rights under collective labour law as all other collective legal entities. The degree to which they have taken advantage of it has depended on the internal policies of those very communities and not on the legal system per se. No vestiges of religious communities can be found in collective labour law.

Religious bodies acting as employers have always enjoyed the same rights as non-religious employers. They have also always been subjected to the same requirements as non-religious bodies, e.g. the duty to bargain. They have never enjoyed any immunities, e.g. from industrial actions.

Collective labour law cases with religious elements involving religious bodies are virtually non-existent. Some rare exceptions do exist.

One much publicised case concerned the Plymouth Brethren. Part of the religion is a refusal to sign agreements. A company owned by members of the religion refused to sign a collective agreement. The union decided to boycott the company in order to force the company to sign such an agreement. The Labour Court ruled against the union. However, the reason had nothing to do with religion. The word 'religion' does not even figure in the ruling. The Court found that the company enjoyed immunity from industrial action with the declared aim under the 1976 Co-Determination Act for the one and only reason that it was a family business. As such it was protected from industrial actions of the kind under investigation.[45]

X. CONCLUDING REMARKS. RELIGION AND SWEDISH SOCIETY IN THE POST-WORLD WAR II PERIOD

As said in Section I, the decades after World War II saw the coming into existence of the Swedish social welfare system and its modern employment law system. In both respects, Sweden has often been looked upon as a model. In both respects, the build-up represents a mighty feat of social engineering. That engineering was very determined. It was primarily conducted by the ruling Social Democratic Party (SAP) in power in the forming decades of 'the Swedish Model'.[46] The survey of the significance of religion for Swedish labour and social legislation presented here amply demonstrates that religion has played virtually no role whatsoever in that social engineering.

Would it be appropriate to finish this survey on that note? No, most definitely not, I would say. This is my answer.

It is true, as was said in Section I, that the post-World War II body of labour and social legislation was created in a social and existential environment where religion by and large had become non-existent or at least politically and socially irrelevant. It should be pointed out that no party of a Christian character existed, quite unlike in Central and Southern Europe. It should also be pointed out that Sweden was not exposed to the social thinking of the Catholic Church.

It is equally true that the very idea that religion should be of significance in the build-up of the welfare-*cum*-employment law systems was frowned upon, if such an idea was at all considered (which, by and large, it most definitely was not).

However, this ascertainment is not the appropriate endnote. One has to consider the social ethics prevailing in post-World War II Sweden. The efforts of the ruling SAP were based on ideas such as equality and solidarity between all

[45] Arbetsdomstolen (Labour Court) 2008 no 5.

[46] The party was in power uninterruptedly between 1945 and 1976 and much of the time since then.

members of society, equal rights for and equal treatment of women and men, social security for all members of society, collectivism in solidarity and equal sharing, the right to work and the right to enjoy a meaningful working life. Though little or no reference was made to ideas of a religious nature the prevailing social ethics had a strong flavour of secular religiosity akin to confessional religion. Catholic social thinking played no overt part but the ruling SAP was familiar with it, primarily through its contacts with the German trade union movement.

A present-day observer might in fact be tempted to say that the building stone of the social engineering in the first post-World War II decades was 'The Golden Rule'. In biblical terms, that rule is phrased as an exhortation to '[d]o to others whatever you would like them do to you'.[47]

ADDENDUM

Translation of German quote in footnote 22: 'Sundays and State approved Holy Days are protected as days for work-rest and spiritual advancement'.

Footnote 30. The Labour Court ruling 2017 no 23 went against the midwife. For scathing criticism of the ruling see eg Fahlbeck, Reinhold, Barnmorskedomen – politiken vann, juridiken förlorade (the midwife ruling – politicising won, the rule of law lost), Juridisk Tidskrift 2017/18 p 218.

Translation of German quote in footnote 45: 'A good man, in his inmost yearning, is well aware of virtue's path'. The conversation between *Der Herr* (God) and Mephistopheles is part of the prologue in Himmel (ie in Heaven).

The years since the article was written in 2015 have seen a hesitant and reluctant, but growing, acceptance of certain overt Muslim religious manifestations in the public arena and at places of work. However, the situation is still legally floating and highly controversial. Ideas to introduce legislation to curb such manifestations are ventilated, in particular when they entail gender inequality or gender based differentials in comportment or treatment.

[47] Luke chapter 6 verse 31, Matthew chapter 7 verse 12. A German observer might be tempted to recall what Der Herr said to Mephistopheles in the opening Prolog im Himmel in Goethe's *Faust*: 'Ein guter Mensch in seinem dunklen Drange / Ist sich des rechten Weges wohl bewusst'. This is not to say that the architects of the post-war social engineering worked in the dark. Quite the contrary. They were most conscious about what they were doing. It can, however, perhaps be said that they did so in their 'dunklen Drange' from the point of view of a confessional religious perspective!

Part II

4

EU Law and Religion: Protecting a Privileged Position for Majority Faiths?

RONAN McCREA

I. INTRODUCTION

REGULATING THE POSITION of religion in society is difficult and inherently controversial. In the West, predominant ideas of religion encompasses two elements each of which calls out for very different treatment of the law. Religion is difficult because it is both a set of beliefs people hold that can change over time that are akin to political and other beliefs and is a form of largely fixed cultural identity akin to one's race, ethnicity or gender. Similarly, in relation to its role in public life, a religion can either be seen as a controversial worldview which the state should avoid appearing to endorse or, given the blurred boundary between religion and culture, a necessary element of a rooted communal identity. The truth is that religion is *both* a form of identity and a series of beliefs. The trick is to work out when it is appropriate to treat it as belief and when it is appropriate to treat it as identity.

For a number of reasons, religion is particularly controversial. As writers like Cécile Laborde have noted,[1] many religions deal in matters of supreme importance such as eternal salvation, religion is linked to sensitive matters of identity and because of its all-encompassing nature can feel threatening to those who value autonomy in matters of sex, life, death and family.

Given this controversial nature and given that the EU was founded on a model of 'functional integration' that sought to avoid entangling the integration project with emotionally and symbolically fraught matters, it is not surprising that the Union's desire to stake out a distinctive approach to issues of religion, law and state has major limits. This is reflected in its commitment in

[1] C Laborde, *Liberalism's Religion* (Cambridge, Harvard University Press, 2018).

Articles 17(1) and 17(2) of the Treaty on the Functioning of the European Union which states:

1. The Union respects and does not prejudice the status under national law of churches and religious associations or communities in the Member States.
2. The Union equally respects the status under national law of philosophical and non-confessional organisations.[2]

On the other hand, the Union has to adopt an approach to these matters to some degree for two main reasons. One is that, in exercising its law and policy-making competence, the Union inevitably regulates religion to some degree. From agricultural policies that are relevant to ritual slaughter to employment law competences relevant to discrimination on grounds of religion,[3] the EU must adjudicate upon the claims made by religions and must shape the role played by religion in European societies to some degree thus either directly or indirectly articulating a vision of religion's role in its constitutional order, including on issues of the degree of influence religion may be permitted to exercise over this law and the degree to which religious freedom, especially for the purposes of this chapter, collective religious freedom, should be accommodated by EU law.[4]

II. RELEVANCE OF RELIGION TO EU LAW

Although the Union lacks competence to regulate the relationship between religion and the state at Member State level and needs, as a matter of political prudence, to show considerable deference to Member State choices in this area, it also needs to set out, and to some degree impose, constraints on the kind of relationship between religion and state Member States may have.

It is clear that being a fundamental-rights-respecting liberal democracy is a requirement of EU membership. Article 2 of the Treaty on European Union states that 'The Union is founded on the values of respect for human dignity, freedom, democracy, equality, the rule of law and respect for human rights'. The Copenhagen Criteria governing accession of new members require that applicant states respect fundamental rights, democracy and the rule of law. Article 7 of the Treaty on European Union envisages loss of voting rights for Member States found to be in serious breach of the principles referred to in Article 2. There are, of course, issues in relation to the high political hurdles that must be overcome before Article 7 may be invoked, but the principle that adherence

[2] Treaty on the Functioning of the European Union [2008] OJ C115/47, art 17.

[3] See Council Regulation 1099/2009 of 24 September 2009 on the protection of animals at the time of killing OJ L 303, 18/11/2009 P 001-0030 and Council Directive 2000/78/EC of 27 November 2000 establishing a general framework for equal treatment in employment and occupation OJ L 303, 02/12/2000 P. 0016 – 0022.

[4] R McCrea, *Religion and the Public Order of the European Union*, paperback edition (Oxford and New York, Oxford University Press, 2013) ch 1.

to liberal democracy is required of EU Member States is clear. Even when it has proved impossible to trigger the Article 7 procedure, failure to respect liberal democratic norms, such as the rule of law, may trigger a refusal to grant the mutual recognition of judicial decisions of a Member State that EU law normally requires.[5]

This means that, although religion–state relations are not a matter of direct EU competence, because an appropriate relationship between religion and state is recognised as a key element of liberal democracy, the Union must ensure that the relationship between religion, law and state must not be such as to place into question the status of a Member State as a fundamental-rights-respecting liberal democracy.[6] In addition, the interpretation of EU law in a range of areas, particularly employment law, may have knock-on consequences for religion-state relations at Member State level.

The contention of this chapter is that the EU system for regulating religion, in relation to religious influence over law and the rights of collective religious freedom, does provide or reflect a degree of privilege for culturally entrenched faiths. I will show that the Union's commitment to separation of religion and law-making does not preclude culturally entrenched faiths from exercising a degree of indirect influence over law that minority 'outsider' faiths cannot exercise and that the privileges granted to religious organisations also privilege to some degree, culturally established faiths. However, in the final section, I question whether any other approach is possible for the Union, partly because absolute religious neutrality is simply not an attainable goal for almost any legal order and may be better seen as something to be aimed for rather than something that can ever be fully achieved.

III. THE UNION'S SECULARISM

The EU has committed itself to requiring limits on the degree of influence exercised by religion over law and politics in the Member States. When Romania criminalised homosexuality after a campaign by the Orthodox Church in the late 1990s, the Commission and Parliament made it clear that this law would have to be repealed if Romania was to join the EU.[7] When Turkey announced plans to criminalise adultery in 2004, the Commission stated that it could not introduce 'Islamic elements' into its legal system if it wished to join the Union.

[5] See for example the Art 267 reference made by the Irish High Court querying whether an individual could be surrendered to Poland under a European Arrest Warrant in the light of the doubts over respect for the rule of law in Poland: 'High Court Judge Seeks EU Ruling on Effect of Polish Law Changes' *The Irish Times* (20 March 2018) www.irishtimes.com/news/crime-and-law/courts/high-court/high-court-judge-seeks-eu-ruling-on-effect-of-polish-law-changes-1.3424530.

[6] McCrea (n 4) ch 6.

[7] ibid.

By 2007 the then Enlargement commissioner was stating explicitly that what he called 'democratic secularism' was a condition of membership.[8] This approach complemented European Court of Human Rights (ECtHR) case law. In *Refah Partisi v Turkey* the Strasbourg Court made it clear that theocracy was incompatible with the Convention.[9]

There is some degree of privileging of insider faiths perhaps to be seen in the contrasting approaches of EU institutions to Romania and Turkey. It is notable that although the Romanian anti-gay law was introduced at the behest of the Orthodox Church, the EU characterised the issue only as one of LGBT fundamental rights while in relation to Turkey, the question of adultery was seen in terms of a systemic problem in relation to the role of Islam. In other words, EU institutions more readily perceived a threat to the secular political order when it came from Islam than Christianity. I don't want to overstate the point but this approach does, to some degree, come up in relation to the Union's own legislation, to which I now turn.

IV. LAW-MAKING: INDIRECT INFLUENCE BY REFORMATTING AS CULTURE

The EU, as an organisation of attributed competence, clearly lacks authority to legislate to impose religious norms. It is unthinkable that the recital of a directive, for example would quote biblical injunctions in favour of the relevant legislation. The degree to which the EU's legal order allows Member States to rely on religious justifications in their implementation of EU law (particularly in terms of derogating from it) is interesting.

The Court of Justice has never had to explicitly rule on a religiously-justified derogation from EU law by a Member State. The closest it has come was in the case of *Commission v Poland*[10] where it was faced with a derogation claimed by Poland that aimed to restrict the movement on genetically modified organisms. Halfway through proceedings Poland changed its case from one that cited potential harm to health and the environment to one that cited 'a Christian conception of life' and 'Christian and Humanist social principles'. The Court found it was unnecessary to rule on whether and to what extent Member States may rely on religious or ethical arguments as it found on the facts that these arguments were not actually the ones Poland relied upon. The Court did certainly hint that purely religious arguments may not be acceptable.[11]

However, the Court's case law on issues such as gambling or Sunday trading rules does allow indirect religious influence over law provided that such religious

[8] ibid.
[9] *Refah Partisi v Turkey* (2003) 37 EHRR 1.
[10] Case C-165/08 *Commission v Poland* [2009] ECR I-06843.
[11] McCrea (n 4) preface, xv–xviii.

influence is repackaged as part of a wider public morality or claim to cultural autonomy. Thus, the Court was willing to recognise the 'moral, religious or cultural' aspects of gambling to uphold restrictions (*Sjöberg* and *Schindler* cases).[12] Similarly, a decision to restrict trading on Sundays was upheld as an instance of 'certain political and economic choices [that aim to ensure that] working and non-working hours are arranged as to accord with national or regional socio-cultural characteristics'.[13]

Religious values, in other words, repackaged as part of a broader public morality or as national culture, can, to a degree, be accommodated by EU law. This is a source of indirect influence denied to 'outsider' faiths whose large-scale presence in Europe is more recent and who are less likely to be able to have formed national culture or public morality. A Christian-influenced attempt to restrict Sunday trading, therefore, may be accommodated by EU law without triggering restrictions on religious influence over law as such an attempt can be repackaged as part of national culture. An Islamically-influenced attempt to ban alcohol or pork cannot be similarly repackaged and could not therefore be similarly accommodated. To be fair, an openly-Christian-influenced attempt to change a secular status quo in relation to Sunday trading could fall outside of the parameters of national cultural tradition and so may struggle for acceptance within the EU legal order. However, given the long history of Christianity as the dominant faith in almost all Member States, religiously-influenced traditions are more likely to reflect Christianity than any other faith so the point that Christianity retains a degree of indirect privilege within the EU legal order stands.

V. MAINTAINING, BUT LIMITING, EXISTING PRIVILEGE

Accommodation of the cultural and institutional role of culturally entrenched religions is also seen to some degree in EU rules around exemptions from anti-discrimination laws for religious employers (or as the relevant directive, Directive 2000/78, says, 'organisations the ethos of which is based on religion or belief').[14] The Directive in Article 4(2) allows such organisations to impose a difference of treatment based on religion or belief where 'by reason of the nature of these activities or of the context within which they are carried out, a person's religion or belief constitute a genuine, legitimate and justified occupational requirement having regard to the organisations' ethos' taking account of Member State

[12] Case C-275/92 *Her Majesty's Customs and Excise v Gerhart Schindler and Jörg Schindler* [1994] ECR I-01039 and Joined cases C-447 & 448/08 *Criminal proceedings against Otto Sjöberg and Anders Gerdin* [2010] ECR I-06921.

[13] Case C-145/88 *Torfaen Borough Council v B & Q plc* [1989] ECR I-3851.

[14] Council Directive 2000/78/EC of 27 November 2000 establishing a general framework for equal treatment in employment and occupation OJ L 303, 02/12/2000 P. 0016 – 0022, art 4.

constitutions and the General Principles of EU law.[15] The Directive also allows religious employers to require 'individuals working for them to act in good faith and with loyalty to the organisation's ethos'.[16]

The Court of Justice has required that any discrimination on grounds of religion, motivated by the desire of employers to protect their ethos, must satisfy a proportionality test including showing an objective link between the job in question and religious functions such as taking part in the determination of the ethos of the church or participating in its evangelising mission. In the *Egenberger* case, a woman was refused a contract to write a report for the German Protestant church on the basis that she was not of the Protestant faith.[17] The Church did so relying on German legislation that allowed religious employers to determine for themselves, subject only to plausibility review by the courts, whether a role needs to be subject to a religious test. Ms Egenberger argued that providing such a wide scope for religious employers to discriminate on grounds of religion was contrary to Directive 2000/78. The Court of Justice agreed. Although the text of the Directive did not impose a requirement that any ethos-based discrimination be proportionate, the Court relied on the Charter and general principles of law to read in a proportionality requirement, thereby significantly limiting the scope of the opt-out granted to religious bodies by German law.[18]

Similarly, in *JQ v IR* the Court of Justice found that the imposition of a greater duty of loyalty to an employer's ethos on a Catholic employee of a Catholic hospital in Germany ('JQ' had been fired from his post as a doctor in a Catholic hospital for remarrying after his divorce) needed to satisfy a proportionality test and, while acknowledging that factual matters were ultimately for the national court, openly doubted whether adhering to the Catholic notion of marriage could be seen as being necessary for a person in JQ's role.[19]

Thus, the CJEU has now ruled twice that EU law requires restriction of the scope granted by German law to religious employers to discriminate in order to maintain their ethos. In both cases it made it clear that it regards the commitment in Article 17 of the Lisbon Treaty[20] to respect the status of religious bodies in national law not as a mandate to exempt the legal privileges of religious bodies from review for their compliance with EU legal norms but as a statement of the EU's neutrality in relation to the different ways in which Member States

[15] ibid, Art 4(2).

[16] ibid.

[17] Case C-414/16, *Vera Egenberger v Evangelisches Werk für Diakonie und Entwicklung eV* Judgment of the Court (Grand Chamber) of 17 April 2018.

[18] See E Frantziou, 'Mangold Recast? The ECJ's flirtation with Drittwirkung in Egenberger' *European Law Blog* (24 April 2018) https://europeanlawblog.eu/2018/04/24/mangold-recast-the-ecjs-flirtation-with-drittwirkung-in-egenberger/ and R McCrea, 'Salvation Outside the Church? The ECJ Rules on Religious Discrimination in Employment' *EU Law Analysis Blog* (18 April 2018) http://eulawanalysis.blogspot.com/2018/04/salvation-outside-church-ecj-rules-on.html.

[19] *JQ v IR* Case C-68/17 Judgment of the Grand Chamber, 11 September 2018.

[20] Treaty on the Functioning of the European Union [2008] OJ C115/47, art 17.

organise their relations with churches and religious bodies. The Union therefore provides a degree of privilege to religious organisations but it also limits the degree to which Member States can exempt religious bodies from non-discrimination rules. The EU's commitment to non-discrimination may ensure that only exemptions that pass a proportionality test can be granted.

Interestingly, the carve out from anti-discrimination law granted by Directive 2000/78, whose scope was restricted by the ruling in *Egenberger*, takes the form of an optional standstill clause allowing Member States where religious organisations have historically acted as important providers of services such as healthcare and education, to allow religious bodies to continue to play this role. Such an approach would not benefit a state that, for instance, decided to revamp its laws in order to grant new exemptions to religious organisations in order to accommodate the views of a recently arrived and rapidly growing Muslim population or which decided to grant new exemptions to religious employers as part of a Fidesz-style campaign to re-Christianise the country. The exemption aims at protecting pre-existing religious structures in the market as they take the form not of a freestanding right of religious organisations but rather they have the form of a standstill clause that gives a right but not a duty of Member States to maintain such privileges in national law. Again, therefore we see that, to some degree, religious claims are repackaged as national cultural claims with knock on privileges for culturally-entrenched faiths that already held established privileges before Directive 2000/78 came into force.

VI. IMPOSSIBILITY OF NEUTRALITY

The picture I have painted is of a system that does operate more favourably towards majority, culturally-entrenched faiths. The Union has been more vigilant in detecting threats to secularism when they come from Muslim than from Christian sources. Limits on religious influence over law and politics allow culturally-entrenched religions to gain a degree of influence denied to outsider faiths by translating their claims into claims on behalf of national culture, employment law exemptions from non-discrimination rules are designed to allow states where certain faith groups have traditionally played a large role in healthcare and education to maintain that role.

However, I think that the EU framework is, by and large, doing about as much as it can be expected to do. The Union has limited legitimacy. It has no authority or indeed ability to sweep away differences in relationships between religion, state and law in the Member State or to require Member States to be entirely religiously neutral. For one thing, absolute religious neutrality is something that is unattainable, even if the EU had much greater legitimacy than it currently has. After all any conceivable arrangements will be easier for adherents of some faiths to adhere to than others. This is particularly the case in relation to arrangements or symbols that reflect national histories.

Although the idea of being 'national' is counter intuitive for universalist religions such as Christianity and Islam, particular religions have exercised such disproportionate and formative influences over national cultures that historically-resonant symbols are likely to bear some imprint of those religions. The Swedish flag clearly has some kind of Christian imprint as do festivals such as Christmas or Saint Patrick's day. Expunging any symbol or arrangement that bore the imprint of a particular faith would mean the end of meaningful national cultures that have any connection with the idea of a shared past needed to constitute the 'imagined community' of a country.

This doesn't mean that the idea of religious neutrality must be discarded. Rather that it should be seen as a desirable goal to be pursued, even though we know that it can never be entirely achieved. Absolute equality will never be achieved either but that does not mean that the state should not pursue it to the maximum degree compatible with other valuable goals.

The EU actually makes a valuable contribution in this regard. It is committed to avoiding religious domination of politics and the dangers which that can bring (though it would be interesting to consider, given the weakness of the Article 7 TEU procedures shown in dealings with Poland and Hungary, whether the Union could effectively combat the embrace of theocracy by an existing Member State). The Union's law is committed to equal protection of religious and non-religious world views, something that is absent in US constitutional law, and even more so in many countries in the Middle East and South Asia where atheists and apostates from Islam are persecuted. Its law recognises and facilitates the right of religious organisations to play a broad role in society but ensures that this role cannot disproportionately restrict other important rights such as the rights of employees to privacy and equal treatment thus protecting freedom from religion to a significant degree.

The fact that EU law does not step in and impose what people view as ideal solutions is more of a reflection of a healthy degree of doubt than anything else. Europe is undergoing changes in its religious make up that are without precedent. For centuries, the vast majority of Europeans were Christian. We are moving to a situation where in the space of a few decades the majority of Europeans are likely to be non-religious with a large, intensely religious Muslim minority in many countries. This is a change of such magnitude that it is simply impossible to know how it is going to turn out. Things may work out fine or they may not. But it is certain that there will be enormous unanticipated outcomes, positive and negative, and significant issues to deal with along the way. We simply don't know what is the best way to manage this changing religious situation. Both countries with integrationist approaches and countries with multiculturalist approaches have their problems. It would represent an extraordinary degree of confidence (and I would suggest, blinkered thinking) for the EU to think it could identify and impose a single ideal approach for all its states. Much more sensible is for the Union to allow Member States to experiment with different approaches but to ensure that in doing so, the states remain within the bounds of basic liberal democratic, egalitarian norms.

Thus, in relation to religious influence over law and politics, the EU probably has to allow religions a degree of indirect influence over law by allowing them to form national cultural preferences that the Union then accommodates. This approach prevents religious domination of politics by excluding laws based solely on religious norms but also accommodates the historical reality of the disproportionate influence of particular faiths over national cultures while also allowing 'outsider' religions to play a gradually increasing role as they make their mark on European societies over time.

This limited, but valuable role can also be seen in relation to discrimination on grounds of religion by religious employers. EU anti-discrimination law, has granted significant privileges to religious employers while ensuring that such privileges do not curtail non-discrimination rules in a disproportionate way, thus protecting freedom from religion as well as freedom of religion. The same mix of control mixed with significant latitude to Member States has been seen in relation to litigation in relation to rules restricting the wearing of religious symbols at work where the Court of Justice has upheld the validity of neutrality requirements while ensuring that individual religions cannot be selectively targeted by supposedly 'neutral' rules. In the recent rulings in the cases of *Bougnaoui*[21] and *Achbita*[22] on restrictions on headscarves at work, the Court held that Member States can choose whether it is desirable to allow all religious symbols at work or to exclude all such symbols but could not restrict Islamic symbols alone. This did not go as far as some commentators would like but to my mind it shows a healthy level of doubt on the part of the Court of Justice in relation to its ability to identify and impose ideal or comprehensive solutions.[23]

Europe is living through unprecedented religious change. At this early stage no-one knows how this rapid increase in religious diversity will best be managed. Both French-style approaches under which everyone is expected to hold off on expressing their religious identity in certain contexts and British-style approaches under which people are permitted to express their full identity in a wider range of situations have their admirers and detractors. It is simply not yet clear what approach works best and in these circumstances, it is prudent for the Court of Justice to have doubts about its ability to identify and impose an

[21] Case C-188/15 *Asma Bougnaoui and Association de défense des droits de l'homme (ADDH) v Micropole SA*, Judgment of the Court (Grand Chamber) of 14 March 2017.

[22] Case C-157/15 *Samira Achbita and Centrum voor gelijkheid van kansen en voor racismebestrijding v G4S Secure Solutions NV*, Judgment of the Court (Grand Chamber) of 14 March 2017.

[23] E Spaventa, 'What is the Point of Minimum Harmonization of Fundamental Rights? Some Further Reflections on the Achbita case' *EU Law Analysis Blog* (21 March 2018) http://eulawanalysis.blogspot.com/2017/03/what-is-point-of-minimum-harmonization.html; but in favour of the ruling see R McCrea, 'Faith at Work: the CJEU's Headscarf Rulings' *EU Law Analysis Blog* (17 March 2018).

ideal solution across the board. What is certain is that ideas of neutrality and secularism can be used instrumentally by those such as the Front National in France who had little love for secularism before discovering that it could be used to pursue an exclusionary agenda. In these circumstances, by rendering it much more difficult to use ideas of religious neutrality to selectively target the symbols of one faith, the Court of Justice has made a significant contribution.

One thing that is likely is that law, and EU law, will remain sites of conflict in relation to religious matters. Given that the EU is, above all, a community of law a challenge that EU law and the law in general is likely to face in coming years is the increasing legalisation or juridification of matters of religion. Increased religious diversity means that shared cultural and social expectations about religion and its role in society are decreasing. This means that dealing with these matters by means of social convention rather than law becomes less feasible and the law takes over. It is noticeable how, in Europe in recent years, matters which were not really regulated by the law have been juridified. In short, the law is being used to achieve tasks previously assigned to society.

This is dangerous for the EU as its laws across a range of areas are likely to be more and more frequently dragged into the kind of culture war that the Union has been keen to avoid becoming embroiled in. In these circumstances, the approach to date which recognises the reality of the predominant historical role of particular faiths while ensuring that this role does not become oppressive of minority and individual rights, seems to be a sensible way to proceed.

5

What's in a Scarf? On the Ripple Effect of the ECtHR's Case Law

PATRIK BREMDAL

I. INTRODUCTION

In recent years, the European Court of Human Rights (ECtHR) has dealt with questions concerning different types of Islamic clothing for women in a number of cases. The cases tend to originate from some kind of ban on religious clothing, for instance the Islamic headscarf.

As will be shown below, these cases have ruled in favour of the ban, most often with a reference to the margin of appreciation and the national interpretation of the principle of secularism.[1] Although this is in itself an interesting topic for research, this chapter will not deal with that issue. Instead, I intend to discuss how the Court attributes certain characteristics to the Islamic headscarf and how this characterisation affects the conclusions drawn by the Court and its subsequent case law.

The hypothesis of this text is that the case of *Dahlab v Switzerland* in particular started a ripple effect that has had a major impact on the development of subsequent case law.[2] It can be compared to a stone thrown into the water. At first, there is at big splash and then there are ripples on the surface that expand to include more and more of the surface.

First, I will take a closer look at the *Dahlab* case and examine the conclusion drawn by the court. Thereafter, I will analyse how the *Dahlab* case has affected subsequent case law by examining the cases in which there is a direct or indirect reference to *Dahlab*, and the impact that that reference has had on the conclusions of the Court. Finally, I will discuss my findings and critically discuss the Court's methods in these cases.

[1] The only exception is *Lachiri v Belgium*, App no 3413/09 (ECtHR, 18 September 2018).
[2] *Dahlab v Switzerland*, App no 42393/98, (ECtHR, Decision on admissibility, 15 February 2001).

This chapter is essentially a case study and therefore the material consists primarily of cases concerning the Islamic headscarf. Some additional cases, relevant to the discussion on the Court's stance on religious clothing, as well as articles relating to the cases at hand, will supplement the study.

This chapter is not an analysis of what the Islamic headscarf represents or how it is perceived by others. The aim of this contribution is to analyse the impact that different characterisations made by the Court have had on subsequent case law, and whether or not it is suitable for the Court to make these characterisations.

II. THE STARTING POINT – *DAHLAB v SWITZERLAND*

In this chapter, the starting point is the *Dahlab v Switzerland* case. The applicant was a primary school teacher in Geneva. She was a Swiss national who had converted from Catholicism to Islam and consequently had started to wear an Islamic headscarf in class as part of her religious beliefs. She had worn her headscarf since 1991, without any complaints or comments from parents.

In 1996, the applicant received a letter from the Director General of primary education requesting that the applicant stop wearing her headscarf while teaching, because it was in violation of Section 6 of the Public Education Act. This particular legislation stated, amongst other things, that the religious beliefs of the pupils and parents should be respected and that it should be possible for members of all faiths to attend State schools without being affected in any way in their freedom of conscience or belief. The applicant appealed the prohibition but it was upheld by the Swiss courts.

The question before the ECtHR was whether or not the prohibition was an interference with the applicant's rights according to Article 9 of the ECHR, and, as I will elaborate further below, the Court's reasoning focused on whether or not the action taken by the Director General was justified and necessary in a democratic society.

The Court began by underlining the importance of freedom of religion as 'one of the foundations of a democratic society within the meaning of the Convention'.[3] In addition, it stated that the specific right also includes the freedom to manifest your religion. The Court stated that there had been an interference concerning the applicant's rights according to paragraph 1 of Article 9 and the question was whether or not it was justified under paragraph 2. According to the Court, the interference was prescribed by law and pursued a legitimate aim, namely the protection of the rights and freedoms of others, public safety and public order.

[3] ibid, para 1, 11.

With that out of the way, the Court focused on the matter at hand, namely whether the interference was necessary in a democratic society. It pointed out that the applicant had been teaching with the headscarf on without any objections from parents and without rendering any action from the head teacher or the schools inspectorate. The Court stated:

> The Court accepts that it is very difficult to assess the impact that a powerful external symbol such as the wearing of a headscarf may have on the freedom of conscience and religion of very young children. The applicant's pupils were aged between four and eight, an age at which children wonder about many things and are also more easily influenced than older pupils. In those circumstances, it cannot be denied outright that the wearing of a headscarf might have some kind of proselytising effect, seeing that it appears to be imposed on women by a precept which is laid down in the Koran and which, as the Federal Court noted, is hard to square with the principle of gender equality. It therefore appears difficult to reconcile the wearing of an Islamic headscarf with the message of tolerance, respect for others and, above all, equality and non-discrimination that all teachers in a democratic society must convey to their pupils.[4]

The Court concluded by stating that in weighing the right of the applicant to manifest her religion against the need to protect the pupils 'by preserving religious harmony' the State had acted within their margin of appreciation and the measures taken were 'therefore not unreasonable'.[5] The application was deemed manifestly ill-founded and therefore inadmissible.

It is important to note that the deciding factor in this case was the relationship between a teacher and his or her pupils. The Court emphasised the young age of the children and stated that pupils of such a young age 'wonder about many things and are also more easily influenced than older pupils'. That meant that the interest of protecting children from undue influence from their teacher prevailed over the teacher's freedom to manifest her religion.

The paragraph from the ruling quoted above lies at the centre of this text and is the stone thrown into the water, starting the ripple effect. In its statement, the Court not only characterised the headscarf as a 'powerful external symbol' but also as a symbol so powerful that it might have a proselytising effect on the pupils. It was also a symbol that was 'difficult to reconcile … with the message of tolerance, respect for others and, above all, equality and non-discrimination'. These claims were made by the Court without any support or evidence that this was actually the case.[6] On the contrary, the only actual 'proof' presented by the Court was that the applicant had been teaching the pupils while wearing the headscarf for five years prior to the prohibition without any complaints.

[4] ibid, para 1, 13.
[5] ibid, para 1, 13.
[6] For a discussion on the lack of evidence in *Dahlab*, see D Lyon and D Spini, 'Unveiling the Headscarf Debate' (2004) 12 *Feminist Legal Studies* 333–45.

III. THE FIRST RIPPLES – CASE LAW REFERRING TO *DAHLAB* v *SWITZERLAND*

The first real ripple of the *Dahlab* case came with the case of *Leyla Sahin v Turkey*.[7] The case concerned an applicant who had been prohibited from wearing her Islamic headscarf during lectures at Istanbul University. The applicant claimed that her right to freedom of religion prescribed by Article 9 of the Convention had been violated and that the interference was not justified according to paragraph 2 of Article 9.

When discussing the general principles applicable in the case, the Court stated that freedom of religion was one of the foundations of a democratic society but that not every act motivated by religion was protected under the Convention. The Court also stated that it was incompatible with state neutrality to assess the legitimacy of ways in which a person's beliefs are expressed. State neutrality requires the state 'to ensure mutual tolerance between groups'[8] and the role of the State authorities 'is not to remove the cause of tension by eliminating pluralism but to ensure that the competing groups tolerate each other'.[9]

In its reference to *Dahlab* in the discussion on general principles, the Court cited the paragraph above in the case in this way:

> In Dahlab, which concerned the teacher of a class of small children, the Court stressed among other matters the 'powerful external symbol' which her wearing a headscarf represented and questioned whether it might have some kind of proselytising effect, seeing that it appeared to be imposed on women by a religious precept that was hard to reconcile with the principle of gender equality. It also noted that wearing the Islamic headscarf could not easily be reconciled with the message of tolerance, respect for others and, above all, equality and non-discrimination that all teachers in a democratic society should convey to their pupils.[10]

Even though the Court mentioned that the case concerned 'the teacher of a class of small children', the emphasis on the age of the children in contrast to older pupils was no longer part of the quote. This meant that there was a shift in the focal point, from the interest of protecting young children to the proselytising effect of the headscarf. The nuance made by the Court in the *Dahlab* case had been lost.

The Grand Chamber referred to the judgment by the Chamber that stated that gender equality was recognised by the Court 'as one of the key principles underlying the Convention'.[11] The Chamber emphasised the Turkish context where the Islamic headscarf might have a negative impact on those who chose not to bear it because it was perceived as a compulsory religious duty to wear it.

[7] *Leyla Sahin v Turkey* App no 44774/98 (ECtHR 10 November 2005).
[8] ibid, para 107.
[9] ibid, para 107.
[10] ibid, para 111.
[11] ibid, para 115.

The Chamber also added that it could not 'lose sight of the fact that there are extremist political movements in Turkey which seek to impose on society as a whole their religious symbols and conception of a society founded on religious precepts'.[12]

The Grand Chamber concluded, by referring to the margin of appreciation, that the university was in principle better placed than an international court to 'evaluate local needs and conditions'.[13] Therefore, the Court found the interference justified 'in principle' and proportionate, and consequently also that there had been no violation of Article 9.[14]

Even though there is no direct reference to *Dahlab* in the Court's line of reasoning in the specific case, it was cited as a part of the general principles that were applied in the case. As mentioned above, there was a shift in the focal point of the Court's findings in the *Dahlab* case. This shift makes it easier to draw the conclusion made by the Chamber and the Grand Chamber, namely that the Islamic headscarf is a powerful external symbol that affects its surroundings. In the *Dahlab* case, it was the young children, in *Leyla Sahin*, women who have chosen not to wear a headscarf. In the latter case, it is also to protect Turkish society against extremist Islamic movements.[15]

A couple of months after the ruling in *Leyla Sahin*, the Court decided in the case of *Kurtulmus v Turkey*.[16] This case was a follow-up to *Leyla Sahin* in that it concerned a prohibition of the Islamic headscarf at a Turkish university, but in this case, the prohibition concerned teachers wishing to wear religious clothing while teaching. This case was, in other words, a mixture between *Dahlab* and *Leyla Sahin*, and consequently these were the two most referenced cases.

The Court found that the application was manifestly ill-founded and therefore inadmissible. The deciding factor in the case was the principle of neutrality in the State education system combined with the margin of appreciation.

The decision in the *Kurtulmus* case was a logical consequence of *Dahlab* and *Leyla Sahin*. In *Dahlab*, the Court deemed it to be in line with the margin of appreciation to prohibit a teacher who taught young children from wearing the headscarf because of the proselytising effect the headscarf might have. When deciding the *Leyla Sahin* case, the Court expanded the scope of application to include the impact the headscarf had on older students when a fellow student wore the Islamic headscarf. It was thus logical that the effect the headscarf had on older students when their teacher wore the headscarf was included in the scope of application.

[12] ibid, para 115.
[13] ibid, para 121.
[14] ibid, para 122.
[15] For a critical discussion on the interpretation of pressure in *Leyla Sahin*, see S Langlaude, 'Indoctrination, Secularism, Religious Liberty, and the ECHR' (2006) 55 *International and Comparative Law Quarterly* 929–44.
[16] *Kurtulmus v Turkey* App no 65500/01 (Decision on admissibility 24 January 2006).

IV. A SECOND SET OF RIPPLES – EXPANDING THE MARGIN OF APPRECIATION

The next ripple in the ECtHR case law is the case of *Dogru v France* in 2008.[17] The case concerned an 11-year-old pupil at a secondary school in France who had been expelled because she had refused to remove her headscarf during PE. According to France, the ban on wearing a headscarf during PE was mainly justified for safety reasons and on public health grounds although the State also referred to the principle of secularism. The Court ruled that there had been no violation of Article 9 of the Convention with reference to the principle of secularism and the margin of appreciation.

As in the previous cases, the Court cited the *Dahlab* case, first by stating that the Court in *Dahlab* held that in a democratic society, it was necessary to prohibit a teacher from wearing a headscarf whilst teaching young children amongst other things with regard to secularism. The Court stated:

> The Court stressed [in *Dahlab*] the 'powerful external symbol' represented by wearing the headscarf and also considered the proselytising effect that it might have seeing that it appeared to be imposed on women by a religious precept which was hard to square with the principle of gender equality.[18]

Once again, there was a shift in the wording from 'it cannot be denied outright that the wearing of a headscarf might have some kind of proselytising effect' (*Dahlab*) via 'questioned whether it might have some kind of proselytising effect' (*Leyla Sahin*) to 'also considered the proselytising effect that it might have' (*Dogru*). This evolvement of the wording makes it possible to include even more situations where a ban on wearing a headscarf does not violate Article 9 of the Convention.

In the *Dahlab* case, the focus was that it could not be ruled out that the young children would be affected by the headscarf. The justification in the Court's line of reasoning in *Dahlab* was to protect children from undue pressure. In *Dogru*, the justification in the Court's reasoning was that the wearing of a headscarf should not 'take on the nature of an ostentatious act that would constitute a source of pressure and exclusion'.[19] This meant that the scope of possible limitations to Article 9 concerning headscarves was widened.

In the *Dogru* case, the Court did not confine the possibility of banning headscarves to reasons of safety and public health in reference to PE, but widened the scope when instead it referenced the principle of secularism. The effect of this reasoning became clear in the case of *Aktas v France*[20] where the applicant had been expelled from her school because she had refused to remove her headscarf

[17] *Dogru v France* App no 27058/05 (ECtHR 4 December 2008).
[18] ibid, para 64.
[19] ibid, para 71.
[20] *Aktas v France* App no 43563/08 (Decision on admissibility, 25 May 2010). The decision is only available in French.

in class. In that case, the ban on headscarves was not limited to PE but applied to all classes. The Court stated that a ban on 'all conspicuous religious symbols'[21] could be justified under the principle of secularism within the margin of appreciation. The Court stated that it was up to the State to decide, within the margin of appreciation, whether a religious symbol exerted pressure on others.

What links the *Dogru* and *Aktas* cases to the *Dahlab*, *Kurtulmus* and *Leyla Sahin* cases is that the reasoning of the Court was focused on characterising the headscarf. It was labelled as a 'powerful external symbol' with a proselytising effect. It was deemed not to be compatible with the principle of gender equality and could not be reconciled with a 'message of tolerance, respect for others and, above all, equality and non-discrimination'. The headscarf also had a negative impact on the women who chose not to wear it, because it was perceived as a compulsory religious duty to wear it. The Court also stated that the headscarf was a symbol of 'extremist political movements'. The headscarf was also, according to the Court, an ostentatious and conspicuous religious symbol that exerted pressure on others.

In other words, with every new case that dealt with this issue, the headscarves were given more and more labels at the same time as there was a shift in the wording of the Court when it cited previous cases. All this combined rapidly extended the margin of appreciation and, consequently, the scope of application permitted for limitations of Article 9 of the Convention.

V. AN ALL-INCLUSIVE APPROACH?

If you were to continue chronologically, the next key case would be *SAS v France*.[22] In this case, the Court was faced with assessing a blanket ban on concealing one's face in public, a ban that especially affects women who wear a full-face veil. There are certain aspects that distinguish this case from the ones examined above. First, this case did not deal with the Islamic headscarf but the full-face veil. Second, the ban is not specifically aimed at the Islamic veil but at all clothing that covers the face, although the ban mainly affects Muslim women.

This case has been discussed extensively elsewhere, and I will not analyse the case in this context.[23] This is because my focus is primarily on the characterisation

[21] ibid, para 2. In French: 'tout les signes religiuex ostensible', translation by the author.

[22] *SAS v France* App no 43835/11 (ECtHR, 1 July 2014).

[23] See eg, Y Hakeem, 'SAS v France: Supporting Living Together or Forced Assimilation' (2014) 3 *International Human Rights Law Review* 277–302; E Brems, 'SAS v France: A Reality Check' (2016) 25 *Nottingham Law Journal* 58–72; SL Wade, 'Living Together or Living Apart from Religious Freedom: The European Court of Human Right's Concept of Living Together and Its Impact on Religious Freedom' (2018) 50 *Case Western Reserve Journal of International Law* 411–35; J Marshall, 'SAS v France: Burqa Bans and the Control or Empowerment of Identities' (2015) 15 *Human Rights Law Journal* 377–89 and S Trotter, '"Living Together", "Learning Together", and "Swimming Together": Osmanuglu and Kocabas v Switzerland (2017) and the Construction of Collective Life' (2018) 18 *Human Rights Law Review* 157–69.

of the Islamic headscarf, while the Court's reasoning in the *SAS* case was focused on the effects of a full-face veil on social interaction. Although it is an interesting discussion, it is not relevant to the topic of this text. On the other hand, you have to be aware of the importance of the *SAS* case on the continuous development of the Court's view on Islamic clothing in general, which also affects future case law on the headscarf.

For the purpose of this text, it is sufficient to note that the Court in the *SAS* case constructed a new understanding of the legitimate aim of protecting the rights of others in Article 9.2. The Court accepted the concept of social interaction or 'living together' as a legitimate aim and took into account that the face plays an important role in social interaction and that concealing one's face would create a barrier for interpersonal relationships.

It is interesting to note that the Court seemed to take a somewhat different stance regarding arguments on gender equality when it comes to bans on certain religious clothing. The Court in *SAS* stated:

> The Court takes the view, however, that a State Party cannot invoke gender equality in order to ban a practice that is defended by women – such as the applicant – in the context of the exercise of the rights enshrined in those provisions, unless it were to be understood that individuals could be protected on that basis from the exercise of their own fundamental rights and freedoms.[24]

Seemingly, this is a step away from the statement made in *Dahlab* that the headscarf is hard to reconcile with the principle of gender equality. Could this constitute a shift in how the Court assesses Islamic clothing?

As the ripple effect of the *Dahlab* case widens, more and more arguments from the States are accepted as limitations on Islamic clothing for women under Article 9.2 of the Convention. Another example of this is the *Ebrahimian v France* case in which the Court accepted that a ban on Islamic headscarves did not have to be limited to the special context of employees in state education but could apply to all civil servants.[25]

In the *Ebrahimian* case, the Court cited both *Dahlab* and *Leyla Sahin* to conclude that 'the State is entitled to place restrictions on the wearing of the Islamic headscarf if it is incompatible with the pursued aim of protecting the rights and freedoms of others and public order'.[26] The Court also cited *Kurtulmus* stating that as public servants representing the State, their appearance was required to be neutral 'in order to preserve the principle secularism and its corollary, the principle of neutral public service'.[27]

In the case at hand, the Court observed that the applicant, a social assistant in a public hospital, had not been accused of 'acts of pressure, provocation or

[24] *SAS v France* (n 22), para 119.
[25] *Ebrahimian v France* App no 64846/11 (ECtHR, 26 November 2015).
[26] ibid, para 57.
[27] ibid, para 57.

proselytism with regard to hospital patients or colleagues'.[28] Despite this, the Court stated that the fact that the applicant wore her headscarf was perceived 'as an ostentatious manifestation of her religion'[29] and was deemed incompatible with the neutrality of public service.

The Court stated in its judgment that the ban on wearing the headscarf was linked to the question of equal treatment. According to the Court, 'the neutrality of the public hospital service may be regarded as linked to the attitude of its staff, and requires that patients cannot harbour any doubts as to the impartiality of those treating them'.[30] With regard to the margin of appreciation, the limitation of the applicant's freedom of religion was considered proportionate to the aim pursued.

When it comes to characterising the headscarf, it is repeatedly referred to as an ostentatious symbol, which is similar to the reasoning in the *Dogru* case. The Court also seems to hold the view that you cannot be perceived as neutral when wearing an Islamic headscarf. On the contrary, it is 'incompatible with the neutrality of public service'.[31] In light of these statements, the Court concluded that prohibiting public servants from wearing the Islamic headscarf was not a violation of Article 9 of the Convention.

VI. TO SUM UP – WHERE ARE WE TODAY?

Let me start by recapping the evolvement of the case law of the Court. In the first case, the deciding factors were the context of State education and the relationship between a teacher and young children. As the ripple effect spread, the context in which a State was awarded a margin of appreciation expanded to include the relationship between fellow students at a university and between a teacher at the university and his or her students. In this expansion, the Court moved away from the protection of small children to the protection of others.

In subsequent case law, the scope expanded even further to first include participation in PE and then on to include all teaching activities before it finally left the context of education and applied the reasoning on all civil servants. To summarise, the Court's focus in the discussion on when it is justified to limit a person's right to freedom of religion, has thus gone from protecting young children from undue pressure to protecting all citizens from doubts concerning the impartiality of civil servants.

If you skip all the cases in between, the Court takes quite a leap from *Dahlab* to *Ebrahimian*. In slowly adding new meaning to the headscarf and how it is perceived by others, the Court has been able to move the boundaries of what

[28] ibid, para 62.
[29] ibid, para 62.
[30] ibid, para 64.
[31] ibid, para 62.

constitutes a justified interference of a person's right to manifest his or her religion, in this case the wearing of a headscarf.

As stated, the Court has been able to justify its reasoning by attributing certain meaning to the Islamic headscarf. This has been done without any supporting evidence that the headscarf actually represents these values or that the Islamic headscarf is actually perceived in the manner described by the Court.[32] On the contrary, the evidence presented in the different cases rather proves the opposite. Take *Dahlab* for instance. There had been no complaints from students or parents regarding her capability as a teacher, although she had worn her headscarf in class for five years. The same goes for *Ebrahimian*, who had worked at the hospital without any complaints concerning her abilities as a social assistant.

The Court has labelled the Islamic headscarf as a 'powerful external symbol', and as such, it has a proselytising effect according to the Court. The headscarf has also been described as ostentatious and conspicuous, and as such, exerts pressure on others. When worn by a student at a university it has a negative impact on those who choose not to wear it and the headscarf is also associated with extremist political Islam. All these assertions have been made by the Court without any support or evidence to back them up.[33]

It is interesting to compare the reasoning by the Court in cases concerning the Islamic headscarf with the reasoning in the case of *Lautsi and others v Italy* even though the circumstances of the cases differ substantially.[34] The case concerned the question of whether or not it was permitted to have a crucifix hanging on the wall of classrooms in Italy. When deciding the case, the Grand Chamber did not agree with the reasoning of the Chamber. In its decision, the Chamber stated that a crucifix constituted a 'powerful external symbol' within the meaning of the decision in *Dahlab*. It concluded that it was not justifiable to allow a crucifix on a classroom wall.

The Grand Chamber disagreed and considered that the decision in Dahlab 'cannot serve as a basis in the present case because the facts of the two cases are entirely different'.[35] The Court instead took the stance that 'a crucifix on a wall is an essentially passive symbol'[36] and that there was no evidence in the case suggesting that the presence of a crucifix had had a negative effect on the applicants' children.

Even though, as the Grand Chamber pointed out, the *Lautsi* case concerned an entirely different situation than the headscarf cases, the difference in approach is still striking. The Court offered no explanation as to why a crucifix

[32] For a discussion on this issue, see M Adrian, 'The Principled Slope: Religious Freedom and the European Court of Human Rights' (2017) 45 *Religion, State & Society* 174–85.

[33] See eg, S Garahan, 'A Right to Discriminate? Widening the Scope for Interference with Religious Rights in Ebrahimian v France' (2016) 5 *Oxford Journal of Law & Religion* 352–58 or Adrian (n 32).

[34] *Lautsi and others v Italy* App no 30814/06 (ECtHR, 18 March 2011).

[35] ibid, para 73.

[36] ibid, para 72.

on a wall was a passive symbol, while an Islamic headscarf was a powerful external symbol. You could also question why the Court in the *Lautsi* case focused on the lack of evidence, when no evidence supported the claims made in the cases of the Islamic headscarf.

So, where do we stand today in the case of Islamic headscarves? States enjoy a very wide margin of appreciation in determining the need for limitations on religious expression. In all the cases on the Islamic headscarf, the Court accepted the reasoning of the state and upheld the prohibitions. As I have shown, in each case the Court has widened the scope of application of Article 9.2 of the Convention.

This development has been made possible by the small shifts in the categorisation of the headscarf and in how previous cases have been cited. As I have shown, the different ways of citing *Dahlab* on the proselytising effect of the headscarf, made it possible to include new situations and contexts within the margin of appreciation.[37]

The Court's claim regarding how the headscarf affects others and how it is perceived has led us to where we are today, and with the ruling in the *Ebrahimian* case the Court seems to claim that the Islamic headscarf is incompatible with a neutral state. According to the Court, it is legitimate for a person who makes use of a public service to question the impartiality of a civil servant on the sole basis of the headscarf she is wearing. This reasoning opens up for a wide range of arguments from the State on the grounds on which you could question the impartiality of a civil servant.[38] Is it justified to call on race, gender or a name, when questioning the impartiality of a civil servant? Where does the Court draw the line?

Another development that opens up to an arbitrary line of reasoning is the unsubstantiated claims made by the Court regarding the headscarf. In the *Lautsi* case, the Court ruled in favour of the State because the applicants had not provided any evidence that the crucifix had affected their children. However, in the cases concerning the headscarf, no evidence was presented to support the Court's claims. Even though the applicants had shown that there had been no interference, proselytising, pressure or even complaints, the Court stated that the headscarf had exerted pressure and had had a negative impact on others. This raises questions regarding the impartiality of the Court.

In its judgment in *SAS v France*, the Court stated several facts about the ban that it had taken into consideration when deciding on the proportionality of the ban. First, the ban would only affect a small number of women (approximately 1700 women). Second, a ban would have a significant impact on the situation of

[37] Hill and Barnes examine the case law on freedom of religion in the ECHR and conclude that the doctrine of margin of appreciation is unpredictable, see M Hill and K Barnes, 'Limitations on Freedom of Religion and Belief in the Jurisprudence of the European Court of Human Rights in the Quarter Century since Its Judgment in *Kokkinakis v Greece*' (2017) 12 *Religion & Human Rights* 174–97.

[38] See eg Garahan (n 33).

women who had chosen to wear the full-face veil for religious reasons. Third, the ban might contribute to a consolidation of stereotypes and encourage intolerance. Fourth, the scope of the ban was broad since it concerned all public spaces. Fifth, the ban mainly affected Muslim women and that the idea of being prosecuted could be traumatising to the women affected and sixth, the ban was a restriction on pluralism.

On the other hand, the Court also pointed out that the punishment for violating the ban was among the lightest possible and that the ban was not expressly aimed at religious clothing but at clothing that conceals the face.

To sum up the Court stated:

> However, for their part, the Government indicated that it was a question of responding to a practice that the State deemed incompatible, in French society, with the ground rules of social communication and more broadly the requirements of 'living together'. From that perspective, the respondent State is seeking to protect a principle of interaction between individuals, which in its view is essential for the expression not only of pluralism, but also of tolerance and broadmindedness without which there is no democratic society … It can thus be said that the question whether or not it should be permitted to wear the full-face veil in public places constitutes a choice of society.[39]

That said, the Court concluded that, with reference to the wide margin of appreciation in the case in question, the ban was proportionate to the legitimate aim of living together as part of the protection of the rights and freedoms of others.[40]

So, in this case, the Court drew up a long list concerning why a ban should not be deemed proportional but in the end these arguments did not matter because the State wished to protect 'a principle of interaction between individuals'. Not even the fact that NGOs, the Parliamentary Assembly of the Council of Europe, the Commissioner for Human Rights of the Council of Europe and the French National Advisory Commission on Human Rights all found the ban disproportionate, could outweigh the fact that wearing a full-face veil was a practice that the State deemed incompatible with the requirements of 'living together'.[41]

VII. THE FINAL RIPPLES? SOME CONCLUDING REMARKS

The question arises as to whether there are any limitations to what a State can do in the name of protecting the rights and freedoms of others. The Court may have

[39] *SAS v France* (n 22), para 153.

[40] A similar ban in Belgium was also upheld by the Court as being within the margin of appreciation of the State with reference to the *SAS* case. Case of *Dakir v Belgium*, App no 4619/12 (ECtHR, 11 July 2017).

[41] After this ruling, the UN Human Rights Committee has ruled that the French ban is in violation of the ICCPR, see CCPR/C/123/D/2747/2016 and CCPR/C/123/D/2807/2016.

answered this question in the cases of *Hamidovic v Bosnia and Herzegovina*[42] and *Lachiri v Belgium*.[43] In the first case, the Court ruled against a ban on wearing an Islamic skullcap during proceedings in a national court. The Court referenced several of the cases mentioned above and concluded that there was a difference between a private citizen and a civil servant where the latter was performing official duties and was therefore bound by a duty 'of discretion, neutrality and impartiality'.[44] The Court also emphasised that the applicant had a duty to appear in front of the court in contrast to people who stay in public spaces. These facts distinguished this case as different from the ones discussed above. Finally, the Court stated that the applicant's skullcap did not interfere with the proceedings before the court. On the contrary, the applicant submitted to the laws before the court and had a respectful attitude.

The judgment in *Hamidovic* was upheld in the *Lachiri* case, where the Court concluded that demanding a Muslim woman to remove her headscarf in court was a violation of her rights according to Article 9. The Court distinguished the situation from the *SAS* case because a headscarf does not cover the face and consequently, the principles set forth in that case did not apply to the *Lachiri* case. Instead, the Court referenced *Hamidovic* and pointed out the difference between a civil servant and a private citizen. Lachiri was not a representative of the State and therefore not bound by the same obligation of discretion concerning religious conviction.[45]

In the cases of *Hamidovic* and *Lachiri*, the Court seems to have established a limit to the expansion of the ripple effect. A line is drawn between private citizens and those who perform public duties. If this is valid, then the case of *Ebrahimian* could be seen as the last ripple concerning the Islamic headscarf. You could argue that the precedent in *Ebrahimian* covers all public servants, and since the headscarf does not cover the face, the principles established in *SAS v France* do not apply.

The Court has dealt with the Islamic headscarf in a brazenly ethnocentric manner. It has attributed meaning and value to the headscarf from a Christian and European perspective, and from this point of view has made claims on how the headscarf is perceived.[46] This ethnocentric standpoint becomes even more obvious in the *Lautsi* case where the crucifix was perceived as a passive symbol in contrast to the headscarf that was a powerful external symbol.

[42] *Hamidovic v Bosnia and Herzegovina* App no 57792/15 (ECtHR, 5 December 2017).

[43] *Lachiri v Belgium* App no 3413/09 (ECtHR, 18 September 2018). The judgment is only available in French.

[44] *Hamidovic v Bosnia and Herzegovina* (n 42), para 40.

[45] In French: 'Dans son évaluation des circonstances de l'affaire, la Cour relève ensuite que la requérante est une simple citoyenne: elle n'est pas représentante de l'État dans l'exercice d'une fonction publique et ne peut donc être soumise, en raison d'un statut officiel, à une obligation de discrétion dans l'expression publique de ses convictions religieuses'.

[46] For a discussion on the impact of a Christian perspective in questions on religious freedom, see L Vickers, 'Religious Freedom: Expressing Religion, Attire, and Public Spaces' (2014) 22 *Journal of Law and Policy* 591–611.

The danger of this ethnocentric approach is that the Court makes false claims on Islamic customs and clothing. It attributes meaning to the headscarf that does not correspond with the actual Islamic perception and does not take into account that the actual meaning of the scarf and how it is perceived differs between individuals. This means that there is a risk that the Court contributes to prejudice and misunderstandings in relation to Islam and Muslims.

In the cases I have discussed in this text, the Court lays down some essential principles on Article 9 of the Convention. The Court states that Article 9 represents one of the foundations in a democratic society and 'the pluralism indissociable from a democratic society'[47] depends on it. In *Leyla Sahin v Turkey* the Court stated:

> The Court … also considers that the State's duty of neutrality and impartiality is incompatible with any power on the State's part to assess the legitimacy of religious beliefs or the ways in which those beliefs are expressed … and that it requires the State to ensure mutual tolerance between opposing groups … Accordingly, the role of the authorities in such circumstances is not to remove the cause of tension by eliminating pluralism, but to ensure that the competing groups tolerate each other.[48]

You could compare these statements with the one made by the Court in *Handyside v United Kingdom*.[49] The Court stated, in connection to Article 10 of the Convention, that the Article is:

> applicable not only to 'information' or 'ideas' that are favourably received or regarded as inoffensive or as a matter of indifference, but also to those that offend, shock or disturb the State or any sector of the population. Such are the demands of that pluralism, tolerance and broadmindedness without which there is no 'democratic society'.[50]

If you were to take these statements literally, how the Islamic headscarf is perceived would not be an issue.[51] Even if the headscarf offends and disturbs, the response should not be to limit pluralism, but to protect the wearing of that headscarf to promote a pluralistic and broadminded democratic society. To paraphrase a quote commonly (and falsely) attributed to Voltaire, I disapprove of what you wear, but I will defend to the death your right to wear it.

[47] See eg *Dahlab v Switzerland* (n 2), para 1, 11.
[48] *Leyla Sahin v Turkey* (n 7), para 107.
[49] *Handyside v United Kingdom* App no 5493/72 (ECtHR, 7 December 1976).
[50] ibid, para 49.
[51] See eg, Adrian (n 32). For an extended discussion on the principles laid down by the Court in relation to the case of *Ebrahimian*, see Garahan (n 33).

6

The Freedom of Religion in Relation to Other Human Rights

KARIN ÅSTRÖM

I. INTRODUCTION

In this chapter, the relationship between freedom of religion and other fundamental freedoms and human rights will be explored and discussed. The backdrop is a completed EU project on hate crime, in which it was discovered that the freedom of religion come in conflict with other human rights or is used as an argument for exemption of criminal responsibility in hate crime cases.[1]

In recent years, groups of Nazis and others with anti-democratic values and beliefs have increasingly expressed their views through demonstrations and in other ways. Their actions have been emphasised in the media and political debates, and have been described as threats to other's human rights as well as the democratic and fundamental principles of the rule of law.[2] They have proclaimed *their* right to express *their* views in accordance with *their* human rights. It has been difficult for the Swedish judiciary to deal with these groups and the way they have expressed themselves in relation to the rights of others. Freedom of expression is a human right with a special position in international and Swedish law, and it therefore enjoys long-term protection. This might lead to other freedoms of opinion, such as the freedom of assembly, including the right to demonstrate, and the freedom of religion being applicable during manifestations that express hate and contempt. The issue of legal boundaries and

[1] "The Lifecycle of a Hate Crime", was a two-year project funded by the EU Directorate-General Justice, in which five European countries examined the application of national hate crime legislation. In this project we interviewed legal professionals, as well as victims and offenders, to capture best practice and limitations in the tools used to combat hate crime.

[2] See R KM Smith, *International Human Rights Law*, 8th edn (Oxford, Oxford University Press, 2018) 316–317, for a further description of how propaganda which incites national, racial or religious hatred is condemned internationally.

the relationship between different freedoms and rights is highly controversial as there are situations when these rights are in conflict or when the restriction of one right interferes with the enjoyment of another.

A starting point for the analysis is the scope and boundaries of these freedoms and rights in different rights complexes. The main question in this chapter is how the freedom of religion is 'used' in relation to the freedom of expression and freedom of assembly in Swedish domestic courts. It will be argued that it is important to enforce all human rights equally and that it is necessary to guarantee each right for the enjoyment of another. This will be discussed on the basis of two judgments; one from the Court of Appeal for Northern Norrland regarding freedom of expression and agitation against national or ethnic groups, and the other from the Administrative Court of Appeal in Gothenburg regarding the right to demonstrate versus the right to religion.[3]

II. HUMAN RIGHTS AND FUNDAMENTAL FREEDOMS

The rights discussed in this text are different fundamental freedoms of opinion, set out in several international instruments, which Sweden has signed and ratified. International treaties are different in design compared to national laws, as they are the product of international negotiations and written as agreements with compromises rather than stated law. This means that the rights and freedoms included in international treaties are not designed to be directly applicable in national courts. Instead, these human rights need to be implemented into national law.

In Sweden, human rights and fundamental freedoms are protected in several rights complexes. The design of the rights and the restriction criteria vary between the different rights complexes and between different rights. The rights complexes also have different standings as legal source in the Swedish legal system. Most international instruments that have been signed and ratified by the Swedish Government are implemented through 'transformation'. That basically means that the rights within a treaty are adjusted and placed where it is deemed that they fit best in the existing legislation. The European Convention has, however, been 'incorporated', meaning that an act has been passed which states that the treaty, or part of the treaty, is Swedish law.[4] The European Convention is also protected in the Swedish Constitution, Instrument of Government Chapter 2 Article 19, creating a system of multiple layers of protection and the complexity of being used as different types of sources.

[3] Case B 428-16, B 490-17, Court of Appeal for Northern Norrland of 08-09-2017 and case 5083-17, 5084-17, Administrative Court of Appeal in Gothenburg of 29-09-2017.

[4] The precise English meaning of 'incorporation' and 'transformation' differ from the Swedish terms 'inkorporering' and "transformation" so the two terms should be used with caution.

Regardless of whether an international treaty has been implemented through transformation and included in existing laws, through incorporation as its own statute or just through confirmation that the treaty is already fulfilled, Swedish courts and administrative agencies shall apply and interpret national law in accordance with the purpose of international treaties. This can be described as the principle of treaty-conform construction.[5] The rights and freedoms included in the European Convention are no different in that regard, the interpretations and the scope of the articles of the Convention are furthermore developed through the practice of the European Court of Human Rights, which should be regarded in cases concerning fundamental freedoms of opinion in national courts.[6]

In addition, the Swedish Constitution includes a catalogue of fundamental rights and freedoms including the right to demonstrate, freedom of expression and freedom of religion. The catalogue of fundamental rights and freedoms is applicable both to the legislator who may not create laws that contradict these rights but also the courts and other authorities that shall interpret and act in accordance with these rights.[7] Even though the catalogue lists the different rights and freedoms included, they are supposed to be interpreted together and they are all to some extent interlinked. This particularly concerns the freedom of expression which may interact with all the other rights listed.[8]

The Swedish constitutional right to demonstrate and the freedom of expression are relative rights that can be limited by law as stated in the Constitution, the Instrument of Government Chapter 2 Articles 21–24. Such restrictions have been made, inter alia through the establishment of the Public Order Act and the provision on agitation against national or ethnic groups, which are discussed further below. Possible limitations are also stipulated in the European Convention regarding freedom of assembly and freedom of expression, and the conditions are rather similar to those in the Swedish Constitution. Freedom of religion can also be restricted in accordance with the European Convention but differs from other freedoms of opinion in the Swedish Constitution, where it is absolute. Freedom of religion may not, according to the Constitution and from a formal perspective, be limited in Swedish law. This creates a complex system of regulations that the Swedish courts have to take into account and master when ruling in matters concerning human rights and fundamental freedoms.

Both these legal sources, the European Convention and the Constitution, will be central to this text. The interpretation and application of these fundamental rights, of rights-limiting legislation and the handling of conflicts between these rights have proved to be problematic. The following sections

[5] I Cameron, *An Introduction to the European Convention on Human Rights* 5th edn (Uppsala, Iustus förlag, 2006) 27 ff.

[6] ibid 19 ff.

[7] T Bull and F Sterzel, *Regeringsformen – en kommentar* (Lund, Studentlitteratur, 2016) 58.

[8] ibid 60 ff.

discuss how Swedish courts have dealt with situations in different ways when religious freedom has been invoked in cases concerning the right to demonstrate and freedom of expression. Particular focus will be on the issue of how the European Convention as an international source of law is applied in relation to Swedish law in cases where these rights and freedoms are apparent.

A. The Freedom of Religion as an Absolute Right

The right to religious freedom is protected in Article 9 of the European Convention stating that everyone has the right to freedom of thought, conscience and freedom of religion. Article 9(1) includes the right for churches and religious communities to operate and for individuals to become members of churches and other religious communities and participate in their activities. The provision also includes the freedom to change religion or belief, as well as the freedom to exercise religion or belief through worship, teaching, customs and rituals alone or in community with others, publicly or individually. As with other articles of the Convention, the state's duty is not limited to permitting religious practice. There is also a positive obligation to ensure that religious practice is protected against interference from those who, for religious or other reasons, wish to seek to prevent a particular religious community from exercising its religious right.

Freedom of religion as it is worded in the European Convention includes not only the right to exercise religion but also the freedom to missionise. The European Court of Human Rights has found that Article 9 includes a right to influence others through religious preaching. This influence may not, however, be done through improper means, such as moral threats.[9] The purpose of religious freedom in the European Convention was originally to protect people from persecution on religious grounds. There was a strong political consensus that it was important to provide adequate protection for the freedom of religion.[10]

In accordance with Article 9(2) of the European Convention, freedom of religion may be limited as regards an individual's manifestation of his or her beliefs or religion if it is prescribed by law and necessary in a democratic society in the interests of public safety, for the protection of public order, health and morals, or for the protection of the rights and freedoms of others. Even though the freedom of religion, in accordance with the European Convention, may be limited it is also absolute in parts where no derogations may be made. The absolute part of the Article concerns the sphere of personal beliefs and religious creeds. The absolute part can however not be stretched further

[9] *Kokkinakis v Greece* App no 14307/88 (ECtHR, 25 May, 1993).
[10] V Enkvist, *Religionsfrihetens rättsliga ramar* (Uppsala, Iustus förlag, 2013) 100.

than to protect from interventions regarding the core of the religious beliefs or religion.[11] Since the freedom to exercise religion or belief through worship, teaching, customs, and rituals is relative, whilst the core of the religious beliefs or religion is absolute, the individual's right to practise a religion must be interpreted with caution.[12]

The freedom of religion is also protected under the Swedish Constitution. The Instrument of Government Chapter 2 Article 1 paragraph 6 states that each person is guaranteed to practise their religion either alone or with others without interference from public institutions. Religious freedom is the only freedom of opinion in the Constitution, which cannot be limited by law. In order to be provided such strong protection, the freedom of religion must be precise and narrowly defined. It is particularly important to determine what falls within and beyond the meaning and scope of the right. The distinctive character, the ultimate core, of the right, which is protected with no limitations available, is described in the preparatory works as the right to believe. All religious acts and manifestations which include one of the other freedoms of opinion, such as the freedom of expression or freedom of assembly, are not considered as the core and shall instead be deemed to lie outside the absolute part of the freedom of religion. They should instead be considered as expressions or gatherings with the protection provided for those freedoms by the Constitution.[13] In other words; limitations that can be made to the freedom of expression, freedom of assembly and the right to demonstrate may also be made when these freedoms are used in religious contexts.[14]

The fact that the freedom of religion has a different design is due, inter alia, to the fact that the legislator found it necessary to establish a strong protection for religious minorities in the light of the persecution of the Jews during the Second World War. At first glance, freedom of religion seems to provide much stronger protection than the other freedoms of opinion, but it is apparent from the above discussion that exercising religious freedom can be seen as an extension of one of the other freedoms of opinion. In the preparatory works prior to the establishment of the freedoms in the Constitution as they are laid out today, it is explained, that limitations that apply to ordinary human acts or human negligence also apply to religious practice.[15] Neither does the fundamental protection of religious freedom mean that what are otherwise punishable acts are legitimate if they are made with religious motives.[16] Such statements imply that the scope of the absolute protection is thus significantly narrower than previously suggested.

[11] H Danelius, *Mänskliga rättigheter i europeisk praxis* 5th edn (Stockholm, Nordstedts juridik, 2015) 446.

[12] Enkvist (n 10) 108 ff.

[13] Government inquiry (SOU) 1975:75, p 132 and p 194. Bull and Sterzel (n 7) 67.

[14] Enkvist (n 10).

[15] Government bill (prop) 1975/76:209, p 48, Government inquiry 1975:75, p 132.

[16] Government bill 1975/76:209, p 114. Bull and Sterzel (n 7) 67. Enkvist (n 10).

In contrast to the narrow scope of the freedom to manifest religion under the Swedish Constitution, the European Court of Human Rights has provided quite a broad scope of religious manifestation in accordance with Article 9(1) of the European Convention. However, it has also taken a broad approach to what is permissible interference with the freedom of manifestation in Article 9(2). The same broad approach concerning the limitations of freedom of religion has granted the Member States a wide range of margin of appreciation.[17] All in all, the freedom of religion is not to be considered as a completely absolute right.

III. FREEDOM OF EXPRESSION

In accordance with Article 10 of the European Convention, freedom of expression includes the right to freedom of opinion and the freedom to receive and disseminate tasks and thoughts without the involvement of public authorities. The scope of Article 10(1) encompasses all forms of expression of opinions and all types of speech and writing. The European Court of Human Rights has recognised the freedom of expression as one of the essential foundations of a democratic society and that it includes a wide range of expressions even those which 'offend, shock or disturb'.[18]

However, according to the second paragraph of Article 10, freedom of expression may be limited by formal provisions, conditions, restrictions or penalties prescribed by law which are necessary in a democratic society with regard to state security, territorial integrity or public security, to prevent disorder or crime, for the protection of health or morals or for the reputation and good name or rights of others. Limitations may also be made to prevent confidential intelligence being disseminated or to maintain the authority and impartiality of the courts. It has been emphasised that the restrictions in Article 10(2) shall be narrowly interpreted and that their raison d'être must be 'convincingly established'.[19] Punishment for discriminatory or belittling statements directed collectively against any particular group of people, nationality or religion is deemed to be in line with the restriction rules in Article 10(2).[20]

Freedom of expression is also regulated in the Swedish Constitution. The Instrument of Government Chapter 2 Article 1 paragraph 1 states that all forms of freedom of expression such as speeches, written matter, artistic expression, information, both commercial and for other purposes, are protected. The contents of the expressions include thoughts, opinions and feelings. Expressions

[17] Cameron (n 5) 120.

[18] *Handyside v United Kingdom* App no 5493/72 (ECtHR, 7 December 1976).

[19] *Observer and Guardian v United Kingdom* App no 13585/88 (ECtHR 26 November 1991) para 59, see also Cameron (n 5) 124.

[20] Danelius (n 11) 495.

that are part of criminal actions are, however, not protected through the provision in the Constitution. In an international comparison, the freedom of expression is exceptionally well protected in Sweden and, in many respects, exceeds what is provided in the European Convention.[21]

The Swedish Constitution also manifests legal possibilities to limit freedom of expression in Chapter 2 Article 20 of the Instrument of Government. These limitations are described as vital for the compliance of the otherwise extensive protection that the Swedish Constitution offers.[22] A more precise set of rules that prescribes how and why the freedom of expression may be limited can be found in Chapter 2 Article 23 of the Instrument of Government, which stipulates that freedom of expression may only be limited with regard to the security of the nation, public security, public order, the reputation of individuals, the privacy of individuals or the prevention and prosecution of crimes and if a particularly important reason calls for it. In addition, Chapter 2 Article 23 provides that when the limitations are being assessed, particular attention shall be paid to the importance of the broadest possible freedom of expression in political, religious, trade, scientific and cultural matters.

A. Agitation Against an Ethnic or National Group

Chapter 16 Section 8 of the Penal Code on agitation against an ethnic or national group is a provision designed to limit the scope of the freedom of expression. The provision prohibits statements of a racist or similar nature, regardless of whether they appear orally, in writing, or via other media such as symbols on clothing or in pictures. Anyone who threatens or expresses contempt in a statement or message that is disseminated, and if that violation can be linked to a group of persons by allusion to race, skin colour, national or ethnic origin, religious belief or sexual orientation, shall be convicted of agitation against an ethnic or national group.

The relationship between agitation against an ethnic or national group and the freedom of expression in line with constitutional and international obligations was discussed in the preparatory works of the provision. It was stated that the meaning of 'contempt' should be interpreted with some caution and that punishment should only come into question when it is *fully established* that the statement exceeded the boundaries of objective and reliable discussion.[23] In a later amendment, the Government stated that even

[21] Besides protecting an individual's right to expression in the Instrument of Government, extensive protection of expressions in print and freedom of expression in the media are included in the Constitutional Acts Freedom of the Press Act, the Fundamental Law on Freedom of Expression. See also Cameron (n 5) 121.

[22] Bull and Sterzel (n 7) 90.

[23] Government bill 1948:80, see also Government inquiry 1944:69.

though the meaning of contempt was not clearly specified, the provision had in practice been widely applied and included in principle all, even indirect, expressions of racism and xenophobia. Even statements that involve ridiculing a group of persons fall within the provision, but at the same time, this is not a punishable crime if it does not exceed the limits of objective criticism.[24]

The provision of agitation against an ethnic or national group was all in all considered necessary in a democratic society and in accordance with the Instrument of Government Chapter 2 Article 20, motivated by the need to counter anti-Semitic propaganda, and to maintain order and security.[25] Even though the reason was to counteract anti-Semitic propaganda, it was considered inappropriate to give a specific group a particular legal protection, as it could be seen as a privilege and it might risk increasing the vulnerability of the group. Instead, the provision aimed at violations of groups of certain descent or creed, including, in addition to Jews, 'gypsies, Sami people, foreigners who have taken refuge in Sweden as well as members of different sectarian groups'.[26]

The application of the provision on agitation against an ethnic or national group is a controversial issue, not least in view of the fact that freedom of expression is considered to be a fundamental right, and restrictions must be made with caution. The reason why the provision on agitation against an ethnic or national group is controversial is partly due to the design of the provision. From some perspectives, it may be considered too narrow in scope and not applicable for its purpose. On the other hand, it may also be considered too wide and it might be implied that the scope of application interferes too much with the freedom of expression where no limitations are considered possible. As regards the application of the provision on agitation against an ethnic or national group, each statement must be put into context and assessed based on that particular context. In Swedish case law, the use of the provision on agitation against an ethnic or national group is used rarely and convictions are even more unusual, indicating that this limiting regulation is used with caution.[27]

B. Hate Preaching – The *Mall Preachers* Case

Hate preaching may constitute a hate crime as an offence of agitation against an ethnic or national group. Hate preaching also lies at the centre of many religions' understanding of the manifestation of their religion, and frequently raises the contentious issue of the regulation of the use of sacred scriptures.[28]

[24] G Granström and K Åström, *Lifecycle of a Hate Crime: Country Report for Sweden* (Umeå, Umeå University, 2017) 25.

[25] Government bill 1948:80, see also Government inquiry 1944:69.

[26] Government bill 1948:80 p 194–96.

[27] Granström and Åström (n 24).

[28] PW Edge, 'Oppositional Religious Speech: Understanding Hate Preaching' (2018) 20(3) *Ecclesiastical Law Journal* 278–89.

In a case called 'the *Mall Preachers* case',[29] plaintiffs X and Y proclaimed messages in public declaring that 'Muslims are to be punished', 'Islam is invading Sweden and raping women', 'homosexuality is sinful and unnatural' and that 'gay men will perish'.[30] The statements of defendants X and Y in the *Mall Preachers* case were also to a certain extent specifically targeted towards passers-by, which may indicate offensive intentions. These statements reached quite a large audience and were recorded and uploaded on YouTube.

On some of these occasions, police were summoned and both X and Y were subsequently charged with agitation against an ethnic or national group according to Chapter 16 Section 8 of the Penal Code. Both X and Y admitted to grossly degrading Muslims and homosexuals, but they argued that their statements were based on the Bible and their Christian faith. The defence argued in the District Court, in accordance with the European Convention and the practice of the Supreme Court, that the plaintiffs could not be convicted of agitation against an ethnic or national group when their expressions were to be considered as them exercising their freedom of religion. Subsequently, the District Court in the Swedish city of Umeå only sentenced X and Y for crimes according to the penal provision on agitation against an ethnic or national group regarding the parts of their statements that could not be linked to a religious text from the Bible.[31]

Using religious freedom as an argument for exemption of responsibility in criminal hearings was long unheard of. But in 2005, the Supreme Court ruled in the notorious case of the Pentecostal Pastor, Åke Green, who in a sermon made offensive and disparaging comments about homosexuals in front of his parish.[32] The Supreme Court ruled that, although the statements objectively fell under the provision of agitation against an ethnic or national group in the Swedish Penal Code, it was not possible to sentence Green considering his rights and freedoms under the European Convention. The Supreme Court acquitted Green in this case, setting a precedent. However, only a year later four young neo-Nazis were prosecuted for agitation against an ethnic or national group after handing out leaflets at a school.[33] The leaflets contained suggestions that homosexuals live promiscuous lives and are responsible for spreading HIV. They were convicted of agitation against an ethnic or national group by the Supreme Court, which in this case argued that the precedent set by the European Court of Human Rights emphasises the need for freedom of expression in a political context, but also the importance of limiting this right when someone imposes the right for illegitimate reasons.

[29] Case B 428-16, B 490-17, Court of Appeal in Upper Norrland of 08-09-2017.
[30] ibid.
[31] ibid.
[32] The Supreme Court of Sweden, NJA 2005 s 805.
[33] The Supreme Court of Sweden, NJA 2006 s 467.

The European Court of Human Rights has concluded that there is an obligation on the Member States to counteract, as far as possible, unnecessary defamatory statements that do not contribute to a public debate.[34] Unlike the *Green* case, the accused had not made their statements in a religious context, so religious freedom as a protected principle was not applicable. However, the discussion regarding limitations of the freedom of expression including unnecessary defamatory statements and restricting possibilities to take advantage of this freedom is applicable even in the *Mall Preachers* case.

The Court of Appeal, like the Supreme Court in the *Green* case, found that the prerequisites of the crime agitation against an ethnic or national group were objectively met, but that it was also important to investigate whether a conviction would constitute an unlawful restriction of Articles 9 and 10 of the European Convention. Here, the Court of Appeal ruled that it was necessary to waive the objective of the national legislation, which had been clarified in the legislative process or case law, when it was required by a treaty-conform interpretation of the European Convention. The Court of Appeal thereby confirmed the verdict of the District Court.

A large part of the legal argument in the *Mall Preachers* case was based on the same arguments and conclusions as in the *Green* case. This is problematic not only because these were not similar circumstances, which will be discussed below, but also because the *Green* case was based on *assumptions* about how the European Court of Human Rights would have ruled, and not an actual judgment. In the *Mall Preachers* case the Court of Appeal emphasised, on the basis of the judgment of the European Court of Human Rights in *Kokkinakis v Greece*, that it may only be possible in rare cases to judge expressions made in a preaching situation as an offence such as agitation against a national or ethnic group. However, the national legislation that was interpreted in *Kokkinakis v Greece* does not correspond with the Swedish legislation on agitation against national and ethnic groups and hence, this conclusion may not be entirely accurate. Even though the European Court of Human Rights found in *Kokkinakis v Greece* that the freedom of religion included not only the right to exercise one's religion but also the freedom to missionise and to influence others through religious preaching, this influence may not be exercised through improper means, such as moral threats.[35] This means that the assumption of the Supreme Court that Sweden would violate Green's right to freedom of religion in accordance with Article 9 if convicted was based on weak arguments. The same objections can also be made in the *Mall Preachers* case.

As we have seen, an emphasis on religious rights can justify a departure from balances of proportionality regarding freedom of expression alone, and direct attention to specific features of the preaching moment which are relevant to

[34] ibid.

[35] *Kokkinakis v Greece* App no 14307/88 (ECtHR, 25 May 1993).

proportionality. It is, however, important in this balancing act to include all relevant rights complexes and to recognise the benefits of expression to the speaker, the cost to the speaker of restricting their expression, and the cost to targets of such expressions of others.[36] Most importantly, before this extensive balance of proportionality, it must be determined whether or not the expressions under investigation are protected as a religious right. Because if they are not, there is no need to assess the proportionality of any other right than the freedom of expression and its limitations. So, the first question that needs to be addressed is whether the mall preachers' statements may generally be regarded as an act protected by religious freedom.

C. Agitation or Religious Manifestation

In the *Mall Preachers* case, the District Court found that defendants X and Y's statements should be seen as a sermon and therefore freedom of religion according to the European Convention was applicable. The Court of Appeal saw no reason to question this conclusion and expressed that the statements made by X and Y should be considered in a religious context due to the fact that the accused themselves regarded their statements as sermons and that these were thus to be held as a manifestation of their faith. The Court of Appeal added that thoughts and ideas that have their roots in a religious view and are manifested in a preaching situation are to be regarded as a distinctive right to expression. This statement is accurate, but the question is whether the act that took place in the *Mall Preachers* case should be regarded as a sermon and thus a religious practice.

In the *Green* case, there is no doubt that the Pentecostal Pastor Åke Green was preaching a sermon because he expressed his religious views in a church in front of his parish. In the *Mall Preachers* case, defendants X and Y expressed similar views to Green, and even harsher, but in public areas preaching to anyone who happened to walk by. The statements of defendants X and Y were also to a certain extent specifically targeted towards passers-by, which may indicate offensive intentions. According to the Court of Appeal, the assessment should not be affected by whether the statements are made in a public area, in a church or in another special place for sermon. Both the District Court's and the Court of Appeal's arguments indicate that it was sufficient that the defendants *regarded* their expressions as preaching for the freedom of religion to be applicable according to the European Convention. The European Court of Human Rights on the other hand held in the *Eweida* case that all behaviour inspired or motivated by religion is not to be regarded as exercising faith in accordance with

[36] Edge (n 28).

Article 9.[37] This would entail that the expressions made by defendants X and Y should not fall under freedom of religion.

The interpretation of the courts in the *Mall Preachers* case was exceptionally wide, especially if considering the absoluteness of the freedom of religion in the Constitution. According to a statement by the Committee on the Constitution (Konstitutionsutskottet, KU), the act of preaching should not generally exclude responsibility from the offence of agitation against a national or ethnic group, but solely citing religious texts may fall outside the scope of this offence.[38] It has also been emphasised that religion may never be used to exclude from liability otherwise criminal acts.[39] This suggests that the decision not to convict defendants X and Y in the *Mall Preachers* case for any of the statements that could be referred to the Bible on the basis that the defendants regarded their statements as preaching, is not in accordance with the Swedish Constitution, nor the European Convention.

It is problematic that the District Court and the Court of Appeal made such a wide interpretation of a sermon and act of preaching as it goes beyond the intention of the absolute status of religious freedom and expands the scope of a limiting provision of another freedom of opinion, in this case the freedom of expression. This extension of the absolute nature of religious freedom in the Swedish Constitution is contrary to the technical design of religious freedom and its relationship with the other freedoms. The legislative solution that all forms of religious practice that can be seen as an extension of other rights, and that thereby lose their absolute status, is thus abolished. As the Court of Appeal expands the meaning of *a sermon* through the *Mall Preachers* case, in principle all religious expressions, wherever stated, could be protected by the freedom of religion and thereby fall outside the scope of agitation of an ethnic or national group.

D. Legitimate Restrictions of Expression

In the *Mall Preachers* case, the District Court gave a description of the rights complexes and the limitations in both the European Convention and the Constitution. The District Court clarified that freedom of expression, but not religious freedom, may be limited by law in accordance with the Constitution. Moreover, the District Court also held that the absoluteness of freedom of religion is only meant to include the core of this freedom, and to exercise one's religion is to be regarded as an extension of other rights and is not considered as absolute. The District Court also noted that according to the Constitution, Chapter 11

[37] *Eweida and others v the United Kingdom* App nos 48420/10, 59842/10, 51671/10 and 36516/10 (ECtHR, 27 May 2013).

[38] Report (betänkande). 2001/02:KU23 p 36–37.

[39] Government bill 1975/76:209 p 114, Bull and Sterzel (n 7) 67. Enkvist (n 10) 95.

Article 14 of the Instrument of Government, a court, which finds that a provision is contradictory to another provision in a superposition, shall not apply the subordinate provision. Therefore, the second question to address is whether the Swedish provision on agitation against an ethnic or national group is considered a legitimate restriction of the freedom of expression.

Even though the provision on agitation against an ethnic or national group is a limitation of the freedom of expression in the Instrument of Governance Chapter 2 Article 1 paragraph 1, the District Court did not asses the provision in relation to the Constitution. The Court of Appeal did not even mention the fundamental freedoms of opinions in the Constitution. Instead, reference was made to the *Green* case and that courts must be able to dismiss statements in preparatory works and case law about the meaning of a certain provision or conditions for the interpretation of rights and freedoms in the European Convention as expressed in decisions of the European Court of Human Rights.

The provision on agitation against an ethnic or national group gives rise to several possible interpretations because the wording is relatively ambiguous. One of the factors that gives rise to different interpretations is the term 'contempt'. According to the preparatory works of the provision it is enough if the statement is disparaging to the reputation of one of the protected groups in order to be categorised as a crime. Even statements of ridicule are considered punishable if they go beyond the boundaries of a factual discussion. The Court of Appeal states that due to the relatively ambiguous wording of the term 'contempt' in the provision on agitation against an ethnic or national group it must be interpreted using the principle of treaty-conform construction, in this case concerning Articles 9 and 10 of the European Convention.

Concerning Article 10 of the European Convention they refer to *Handyside v United Kingdom* from 1976 where the European Court of Human Rights stated that freedom of expression covers not only 'information' and 'ideas' that are received positively or can be considered harmless but also those which 'offend, shock or disturb' a state or any part of the population.[40] Even though this is a correct statement, the Court of Appeal did not consider the possibility of restricting the freedom of expression in national law in accordance with Article 10(2). Neither did the Court of Appeal take into consideration the possibility for Member States to use their wide margin of appreciation according to the European Convention. A statement that would 'objectively fall under the provision of agitation against an ethnic or national group in the Swedish Penal Code' would most likely be seen as a legitimate restriction of expression in accordance with Article 10(2) of the European Convention.

Unlike the Constitution where freedom of religion is regarded as absolute, the freedom of religion in the European Convention is restricted. The Court of

[40] *Handyside v United Kingdom* App no 5493/72 (ECtHR, 7 December 1976).

Appeal, however, never discussed possible limitations to the freedom of religion in accordance with Article 9(2) of the European Convention. Instead the assessment ended with the conclusion that there was no need to question the religious purpose of the plaintiffs. As already mentioned, the individual's right to practise his or her religion in accordance with Article 9 of the European Convention must be interpreted with caution. The purpose of freedom of religion cannot be stretched further than the protection from interventions with regard to the core of the religious beliefs or religion.[41] The *practice* of religion falls outside the scope of the core of religious freedom in the European Convention and may therefore be limited in accordance with Article 9(2).

When conducting a treaty-conform interpretation the judiciary shall apply national law in accordance with the purpose of the relevant international treaty. The purpose of religious freedom in the European Convention was to establish protection against the persecution of people on religious grounds, and it would therefore be a logical conclusion that expressions criminalised through the provision on agitation against national and ethnic groups would also fall under the limitations of the freedom of religion in the European Convention. The provision on agitation against an ethnic or national group would probably have been considered as a legitimate restriction in accordance with the freedom of religion in Article 9(2). It is paradoxical that the Court of Appeal in its reasoning, like the Supreme Court in the *Green* case, referred to the rights and freedoms of the European Convention as a barrier to a convictive judgment when the European Court of Human Rights would most likely have found that there was no unauthorised restriction of Article 9 in either the *Green* case or the *Mall Preachers* case.

The reasoning of the District Court and the Court of Appeal in the *Mall Preachers* case as well as the Supreme Court in the *Green* case, that the conditions for agitation against an ethnic or national group are objectively fulfilled, but that the provision is not applicable due the rights and freedoms of the European Convention, undermines the existence of the restriction rule of the freedom of expression and questions its legitimacy. If such a question is raised, it is important to include and assess the rights pleaded including possible limitations as well as all rights complexes in order to determine a correct ruling. The issue of constitutional rights is highly relevant in this context. If the scope of the constitutional freedom of religion had been assessed in this case, the form of manifestation would most likely have been seen as stemming from the freedom of expression and, consequently, the restriction criteria for freedom of expression would have been applicable. The provision for agitation against an ethnic or national group would therefore be considered legitimate and religious freedom could not have been used as a ground for exemption from criminal responsibility.

[41] Danelius (n 11) 446.

IV. THE FREEDOM OF ASSEMBLY AND THE RIGHT TO DEMONSTRATE

The freedom of assembly and the right to demonstrate are regulated in both the Swedish Constitution and the European Convention. According to Article 11 of the European Convention, everyone has the right to participate in peaceful gatherings in order to protect their interests. The freedom of assembly can be viewed as a special manifestation of the general freedom of expression. The European Court of Human Rights has held that some parts of Article 11 might be seen as a *lex specialis* in relation to freedom of expression in Article 10. It has also been emphasised that cases concerning the freedom of assembly in accordance with Article 11 should be seen in the light of Article 10.[42]

The right to demonstrate is regulated in a similar way in the Swedish Constitution. Chapter 2 Article 1 paragraph 4 in the Instrument of Government stipulates that everyone shall be guaranteed, in his or her relations with public institutions, the freedom to demonstrate: that is, freedom to organise and take part in demonstrations in a public place. Without it being specified in the legal text, the right to demonstrate also includes the manifestation of an opinion, which might also be the most distinguishing feature of this provision. The requirement of a manifestation of an opinion should not to be interpreted too strictly, even symbolic actions and more physical actions can be expressions of an opinion.[43] From this perspective, the right to demonstrate has more in common with the freedom of expression than with the freedom of assembly. At the same time, the preparatory works clearly state that since the legal definition does not include the requirement of a manifestation, there is an intended differentiation from the freedom of expression. Meaning that what is actually protected by the right to demonstrate is the gathering of people.[44]

The right to demonstrate is, as previously stated, relative. Limitation criteria are included in both the Constitution and the European Convention, but the conditions for limiting differ slightly. The general provisions for limiting rights in the Constitution are found in Chapter 2 Articles 20 and 21 of the Instrument of Government and are applicable to the right to demonstrate. In terms of the freedom to demonstrate, however, there is also a special provision for restrictions beyond the general conditions. Chapter 2 Article 24 of the Instrument of Government states that the freedom to demonstrate may only be limited with reference to order, safety, traffic, the security of the nation and epidemics. The part of the right to demonstrate that concerns the gathering of people, the *form* of the demonstration, is the essence of this right and should be assessed in accordance with the limitation rules set out in Chapter 2 Article 24 of the Instrument of Government. The part of the right to demonstrate that concerns

[42] Cameron (n 5) 127.
[43] Bull and Sterzel (n 7) 64–65.
[44] Government bill 1975/76:209 p112.

the manifestation of an opinion on the other hand, the *substance* of the demonstration, should be assessed in accordance with the general limitation rules and with regard to the freedom of expression.[45]

The meaning of the terms order and safety are similar to those of ordinary law. *Safety* here refers to the protection of life and health, but also the protection of the property of others and environmental protection. The meaning of *order* differs from the limitation criterion *public order* in the sense that it is broader in its scope, and also includes disturbances targeted at a certain, even a rather small, group of people and does not necessarily include the general public as a whole. In that sense, not only direct violence and crime, even though they are most common, are encompassed but also disturbances in the form of noise and aesthetic nuisance are included.[46] In order for these limitations not to enjoy too broad a scope, the preparatory works have emphasised that order and safety must always be interpreted in the light of the purpose and the interest of the freedom that is protected. On a practical note, a fear and the risk of a possible disturbance is not sufficient to invoke order and safety, concrete circumstances are required.[47]

It is also important to note that the wording *at* the demonstration also includes disturbances in close proximity to the demonstration and not only those *in* the demonstration.[48] In previous case law, the interpretation was made that limitations were only to be used if the disturbances affected those who were demonstrating and not those in the surrounding of the demonstration. A more recent way of interpret the wording *at* the demonstration suggests that limitations can be made due to disturbances affecting those in close proximity to the demonstration. This, however, does not include other disturbances than those made by the demonstrators themselves.[49]

In accordance with Article 11(2) of the European Convention, peaceful gatherings may be limited by restrictions laid down by law and which are necessary in a democratic society for reasons of state security or public security, for the prevention of disorder or crime, for the protection of health or morals or for the protection of other people's rights and freedoms. The requirement of necessity shall not, as with the other provisions of the Convention, be interpreted too strictly.[50] The fact that the right to demonstrate only protects *peaceful* assembly means that restrictions concerning violent assemblies do not have to be justified by reference to Article 11(2).[51] Furthermore, a state may make the right to demonstrate subject to prior permission as long as permits are refused only on

[45] T Bull, *Mötes- och demonstrationsfriheten* (Uppsala, Iustus förlag, 1997) 460, 496.
[46] ibid 498.
[47] Bull and Sterzel (n 7) 96–99.
[48] ibid.
[49] Bull (n 45) 508–13.
[50] Danelius (n 11) 516.
[51] Cameron (n 5) 127.

the basis of the likelihood of violence on the part of the demonstrators, not with regard to the substance of the demonstration.[52]

A. The Public Order Act as a Limitation to the Right to Demonstrate

An existing limitation to the freedom to demonstrate is found in the Swedish Public Order Act (1993: 1617). When the Public Order Act was drafted, one of the main issues was to ensure that the legislation was compatible with the general and special limitation criteria set out in the Constitution.[53] Accordingly, the Public Order Act is regarded to be in accordance with the freedom and rights as well as the restriction criteria in the Constitution. There is, however, no governmental assessment of the compatibility between the Public Order Act and the European Convention.

According to the Public Order Act, a permission from the Police Authority is required for holding meetings in public places. According to Chapter 2 Section 10 of the Public Order Act, public gatherings may only be refused in respect of order or security at the meeting or, as a direct consequence thereof, in its immediate vicinity or in respect of traffic or in order to counteract an epidemic. Permission may only be refused in exceptional cases and decided solely on the basis of perceived disturbances in the vicinity around the demonstration.[54]

The Police Authority may also issue conditions needed to maintain order and safety when organising general gatherings. These conditions are stipulated in Chapter 2 Section 16 in the Public Order Act and include the possibility to decide time, place, lighting, enclosures or other security equipment needed to secure order and safety. However, the conditions may not lead to unnecessary costs or may not unnecessarily complicate gatherings in any other way.[55] In the case law described below, the question of the freedom of religion of others may constitute grounds for refusing permission or laying down conditions concerning the right to demonstrate under Swedish or international law will be discussed.

In a case called 'the *NMR* case', the Nordic Resistance Movement (NMR) applied for permission to demonstrate in Gothenburg on 30 September 2017.[56] The application contained a suggested route and time, which coincided with the Gothenburg Book Fair as well as with the Jewish holiday Yom Kippur. These were two events that were going to attract a lot of people to the area. The Police

[52] *Stankov and the United Macedonian Organisation Ilinden v* Bulgaria App nos 29221/95, 29225/95 (ECtHR, 21 October 2001).

[53] Government bill 1992/93:210.

[54] K Åberg, *Ordningslagen: kommentarer och rättspraxis* 4th edn (Stockholm, Wolters Kluwer, 2017) 79.

[55] Bull (n 45) 536.

[56] Case no 5083-17, 5084-17, the Administrative Court of Appeal in Gothenburg, of 2017-09-29.

Authority in Region West decided to grant permission for the NMR to organise a general gathering. The Police Authority, however, changed the route and time with reference to the rules of the Public Order Act. They described the situation, with the route and the time proposed by the NMR, as a risk of extensive and systematic security interference.

Due to the Police Authority's decision to grant permission, a number of appeals from, among others, the Jewish Assembly in Gothenburg and the Swedish Mässan Foundation (the book fair) were submitted to the Administrative Court in Gothenburg. They had concerns regarding the date and the location where the NMR had been instructed to organise its demonstration. The Jewish Assembly primarily requested that the Administrative Court change the decision and assign the demonstration to another day so that it would not coincide with the Jewish holiday Yom Kippur. They claimed that due to the religious holiday, the majority of Jews were going to be in or near the synagogue that lay close to the path of the demonstration. Second, the Jewish Assembly requested that the demonstration should be assigned a different route. In both requests issued by the Jewish Assembly in Gothenburg, reference was made to the safety and health of their members.

Concerning the first request, changing the date of the demonstration, the Administrative Court found no reason to make an assessment of the demonstration that differed in any way to the one made by the Police Authority. The Court found it impossible to change the date of the demonstration since that would be regarded as the same as refusing to grant permission. Refusing permission is only to be considered in particular circumstances so as not to violate the freedom of assembly and the right to demonstrate stipulated in the Constitution, and this was not considered to be a particular circumstance.

As regards the second request, laying down the condition that the demonstration take a different route, the Court held that in the case of a decision granting permission to demonstrate, it was possible to take other circumstances other than just the demonstration itself into consideration, such as other major events in connection with the demonstration. However, the Court concluded that the protection of the freedom of assembly and the right to demonstrate should not be dependent on what others do, apart from in exceptional cases. In such exceptional cases, consideration should also be taken of aspects other than public order and security during the actual demonstration, and such a decision should be based on previous experience of the police of similar demonstrations indicating a probable and significant risk of physical attacks. The freedom of religion was not considered to be such a circumstance that could constitute grounds for limiting the freedom to demonstrate in the *NMR* case.[57]

In this case, the Administrative Court ruled that it would take into account the fact that there would be a lot of people moving about the area concerned

[57] Case no 5083-17, 5084-17, the Administrative Court of Appeal in Gothenburg, of 29-09-2017.

because of the Gothenburg Book Fair and the celebration of Yom Kippur, and therefore decided to shorten the length of time of the permission granted as well as change the route of the demonstration. The criteria (order, safety or traffic) upon which this assessment was made, remains, however, unclear. Despite agreeing with the judgment, I found the reasoning behind it rather unsatisfactory.

As a basis for their claims, the Jewish Assembly emphasised that the demonstration would create a major discomfort, which would in turn mean that members of the Jewish Assembly could not participate in Yom Kippur, thereby violating their fundamental religious freedom as stipulated in the Constitution. Similarly, it would entail an unauthorised restriction of religious freedom under Article 9 of the European Convention. Their arguments highlight some fundamentally important legal issues such as: what are the legal boundaries for the interpretation of the freedom of religion according to the Constitution and the European Convention? Should they be considered when determining someone else's right to demonstrate? It is also important to investigate how religious freedom and the right to demonstrate may be set against each other in the event of a conflict?

B. Consideration of the Freedom of Religion of Others

The Jewish Assembly argued that the Administrative Court should take into account their right to freedom of religion. An interesting and very crucial question is whether, and if so how, the freedom of religion can be taken into account in the assessment of permission to demonstrate by a public authority? In this case, the Administrative Court also began to ask whether the rights of the Jewish Assembly should be taken into account in the context of the Police Authority's assessment of the NMR's application for permission to demonstrate. To answer that question it is important to first establish which legal complexes to base the assessment on.

In the possible grounds for limitations laid down in Article 11(2) of the European Convention, the protection of other people's rights and freedoms are clearly stated. The Jewish Assembly specifically urged the Administrative Court to include international instruments signed and ratified by Sweden, including the European Convention, in its assessment. The Court, however, chose not to take into account the international conventions referred to by the Jewish association, inter alia on the grounds that 'the status of the European Convention as a source of law in Sweden is somewhat unclear'.[58] Instead, there was a discussion on whether religious freedom should be taken into account in state decisions concerning the freedom of assembly and the right to demonstrate and the limitations as regulated in the Public Order Act. Sweden has not included

[58] Case no 10510, 10517-17, the Administrative Court in Gothenburg, of 25-09-2017, p 10.

other people's rights and freedoms per se in the legal provisions limiting the right to demonstrate.

The freedom of expression and the right to demonstrate are regulated as two separate rights in the Swedish Constitution. However, as has been discussed above, these two intertwine in many aspects concerning the manifestation of opinion. This also means that it is difficult to determine which limitation rules are applicable and in the end this leads to difficulties when assessing whether to grant permission to demonstrate. The part of the right to demonstrate that concerns the gathering of people, the form, should be assessed in accordance with the limitation rules set out in Chapter 2 Article 24 of the Instrument of Government, and those that concern the manifestation of an opinion, the substance, should be assessed in accordance with the limitation rules concerning the freedom of expression. In theory, this distinction between form and substance is possible, but in practice it is complicated.[59] In the *NMR* case, the Jewish Assembly's fears concerning the demonstration were due to both the form and the substance, but in the assessment of the application, only the form was taken into account.

The fact that other people's rights and freedoms are not per se included in the limitation rules set out in Swedish law does not automatically mean that the Police Authority in its assessment should not take into account the fundamental rights and freedoms of others that are stipulated in both the Constitution and the European Convention. These rights are to be claimed on the basis of their own status as international human rights and constitutional freedoms.

According to the European Court of Human Rights, the freedom of religion is equal to the freedom of expression and assembly. In the case of *Karaahmed v Bulgaria*, the European Court held that it was a violation of the Convention when a governmental body did not take reasonable action to facilitate the equal protection of both the freedom of religion and the freedom of assembly. The European Court decided not, however, to take a stand regarding whether a permission should have been denied or not. That assessment was left to the Member State to decide, as long as both rights were protected accordingly.[60] Consequently, if the freedom of religion had been included in the in the assessment of the *NMR* case, there would have been two conflicting but equally important rights. However, the Administrative Court was, as already mentioned, of another opinion. The Court considered that the limitation rules of the Public Order Act were in such close proximity to the restriction rules in the Constitution, and also clearly designed, that it was not possible to interpret other circumstances than order, safety and traffic when assessing the permission to demonstrate.[61]

[59] Bull (n 45) 460.

[60] Case of *Karaahmed v Bulgaria* App no 30587/13 (ECtHR, 24 February 2015). See also Danelius (n 11) 447.

[61] Case no 10510, 10517-17, the Administrative Court in Gothenburg, of 25-09-2017, p 10.

The Administrative Court also concluded that the limitation rules on the right to demonstrate in the Constitution were better suited as a legal source than the other rights in the same complex. The Court held that Chapter 2 Article 24 of the Instrument of Government 'specifically refers to the issue of freedom of assembly and freedom to demonstrate, and also constitutes a so-called *Lex specialis* in relation to, for example, the Constitutional freedom of religion'.[62] Therefore, religious freedom in the Constitution cannot be taken into account.

It is important to emphasise that the provision in Chapter 2 Article 24 of the Instrument of Government is a limitation rule in relation to the right to demonstrate, it does not constitute a *lex specialis* in relation to any other right, in this case religious freedom. The provision is merely a rule that specifies under what special circumstances restrictions on the freedom of assembly and freedom to demonstrate may be implemented. This rule must also be read and applied in accordance with the more general restricting rule contained in Chapter 2 Article 21 of the Instrument of Government. Therefore, you could instead argue that the freedom of religion would enjoy a higher legal value, *lex superior*, in relation to the provisions in the Public Order Act and thereby be applied.

In light of the above, the reasoning of the Administrative Court can be understood as that the freedoms of opinion in Chapter 2 Article 1 of the Instrument of Government are to be regarded as limitation criteria that cannot be attributed to Chapter 2 Article 24 or to the Public Order Act. With the Court's reasoning, it is not possible to include the constitutional freedoms and rights of others, in this case the religious freedom of the Jewish Assembly, in the assessment of whether permission to demonstrate should be granted. A more reasonable point of departure would be to regard the freedoms of opinion in the Constitution as equivalent conflicting rights. In such a situation, it is important to make a balanced assessment of the various rights, and the Police Authority should have taken reasonable steps to ensure that both the freedom of religion and freedom to demonstrate set out in the Constitution and the European Convention could be exercised.

The European Convention is a legal complex that enjoys a special standing in the Swedish legal system. It could have been included in the assessment regarding whether to grant permission to demonstrate as it is a Swedish law, with the same legal ranking as the Public Order Act, or as part of the international legal framework that Sweden has signed and ratified and is thus obliged to adhere to. Having said that, it is astonishing that the Administrative Court declared that the status of the European Convention was unclear when it is a source of law with dual, or even triple, protection. If the Administrative Court had taken the European Convention into account, it would in all likelihood have come to the conclusion that it had to add the freedom of religion of others to

[62] ibid.

the assessment. It is clear from the practice of the European Court of Human Rights that it is considered to be a violation of the European Convention when an authority does not take reasonable action to ensure that the rights for all are exercised.[63] In view of this practice, the Police Authority must take into account the rights in the Convention and include them in its decision-making, when, for example, assessing whether it will grant the permission to demonstrate.

V. CONCLUDING REMARKS

The starting point for this chapter is the relationship between the freedom of religion and two other freedoms of opinion, namely the freedom of assembly, including the right to demonstrate, and the freedom of expression. Through the two judgments in the *Mall Preachers* case and the *NMR* case, which both relate to the freedoms of opinion and their relationship with the freedom of religion, you can see that the interpretation, reasoning and consequences differ significantly. In the *NMR* case, the freedom of religion of others is not considered relevant in the decision of a permission to demonstrate. Moreover, the freedom of religion is considered subordinate to a limiting provision of another right. In the *Mall Preachers* case, however, religious freedom is considered to be of paramount importance when assessing the boundaries of a limitation clause for freedom of expression and, instead of limiting, increases its scope.

When comparing the two cases, it is obvious that the courts emphasise completely different rights complexes. In the *NMR* case, the Administrative Court declared that the status of the European Convention was unclear and was therefore not considered. The Administrative Court concluded that since the wording of the provision on permission to demonstrate in the Public Order Act was in close proximity to the limitation rules in the Constitution, and since the possible scope of interpretation of the limitation rules in the Constitution is restricted, other rights, such as the freedom of religion based on international conventions, could not be given a superordinate significance when deciding whether to grant permission to demonstrate. This reasoning gives the provisions in the Public Order Act a higher legal value than the freedom of religion in both the Constitution as well as the European Convention. This assumption goes against the established hierarchy of norms in the Swedish legal system as well as the case law of the European Court of Human Rights. The practice of the European Court of Human Rights shows that the freedom of assembly and the freedom of expression are to be considered as equally important as religious freedom and that these rights must therefore be balanced against each other.

The Administrative Court further noted in the *NMR* case that the Constitution only applies vis-à-vis legislative and governmental bodies and not between

[63] Case of *Karaahmed v Bulgaria* (n 60).

individuals. According to the Court, that meant that the freedom of religion for members of the Jewish Assembly did not apply directly to the NMR. As already mentioned, this reasoning did not take the international obligation to safeguard the rights of all into account, nor did it consider the fact that permission was granted by the Police Authority and thus the relationship was not solely between individuals. Moreover, the positive commitments in relation to the European Convention were not mentioned at all. When the Administrative Court in the *NMR* case did not consider the European Convention, the loss of protection for an individual's rights was tremendous.

In the *Mall Preachers* case on the other hand, the importance of the European Convention was highlighted and considered to be of paramount importance, whilst the Constitution was left out of the assessment. This conclusion renders the European Convention as a higher ranking law than the Swedish Constitution. If the scope of the constitutional freedom of religion had been assessed in this case, the form of manifestation would probably have been regarded as an extension of the freedom of expression and, consequently, the restriction criteria for the freedom of expression would have been applicable. If the courts had based their judgments on both of the two rights complexes, and not chosen just one or the other, the outcome in both cases would most likely have been different.

There is also a question of how to apply the limiting rules of the rights in relation to the different rights complexes. In the *Mall Preachers* case the national provision on agitation against national and ethnic groups introduced to limit the constitutional right of freedom of expression were considered to be a violation of the European Convention concerning the freedom of religion. Although certain statements are not protected by the freedom of religion in the Constitution, it is possible that they are protected by Article 9 of the European Convention. However, there are many question marks concerning the arguments put forward, and the assessments made, by the courts in the *Mall Preachers* case.

Even though the European Convention was of paramount importance, the Court of Appeal never discussed possible limitations to the freedom of religion in accordance with Article 9. Instead, their assessment ended with the conclusion that there was no need to question the religious purpose of the defendants, which is also a conclusion that can be called into question as already discussed above. Since religious freedom in the European Convention is not absolute, the scope of the right will be interpreted extensively if the limitations in Article 9(2) are not assessed. The individual's right to practise his or her religion in accordance with Article 9 of the European Convention must be interpreted with caution. The purpose of the freedom of religion cannot be stretched further than the protection from interventions regarding the core of religious beliefs or religion. It would therefore be a logical conclusion that the expressions made in the *Mall Preachers* case would fall under the limitations of the freedom of religion in the European Convention.

It is worth mentioning that the reasoning in the *Mall Preachers* case was based on the *Green* case which in turn was based on an *assumption* regarding what the European Court of Human Rights would have ruled in the same case. The so-called margin of appreciation would, however, be of practical significance for the outcome of the *Mall Preachers* case if it had been tried by the European Court of Human Rights. As Article 9 allows a wide interpretation, there is reason to assume that the European Court of Human Rights would have taken into account the prevailing circumstances and existing legislation in Sweden. This was never discussed in the *Mall Preachers* case.

Finally, it is obvious that the outcome in the *NMR* case as well as the *Mall Preachers* case depended on the legal sources that the arguments and assessments were based on. It is after all up to the courts to decide which rights complexes to be considered, which rights or rights complexes have the greatest legal value as well as which precedent judgments are most relevant. Depending on the basis of those decisions, the outcome may be very different. These two cases show that the application of the same rights and the same rights complexes can be understood and interpreted in different ways. This is problematic, not least for legitimacy purposes, where legal certainty and predictability must be worth more.

7

'... And in Community with Others ...'

EMMA AHLM

I. INTRODUCTION

THIS CHAPTER WILL address the communal aspects of religious freedom, from a European perspective. In so doing, it will take as its starting point Article 9 of the European Convention on Human Rights (ECHR) and present the evolving jurisprudence of the European Court of Human Rights (ECtHR). Moreover, the chapter will address certain issues under EU law – in particular when religious organisations act as employers. EU non-discrimination law, and in particular Directive 2000/78/EC, will be analysed and how it allegedly establishes a 'special legal system' for churches and organisations with a religious ethos, but only so far as the Member States allow for it in the national legal order.

The communal aspects of religious freedom have been accentuated by the ECtHR to safeguard religious organisations from arbitrary State interference. Communal religious freedom includes a basic right for an organisation to exist as a legal person, but also to elect the leader of the organisation. However, when acting in its capacity as a religious organisation, and in particular as an employer, the rights of a religious organisation may potentially clash with the rights of others, such as the right of the employee not to be discriminated on the basis of his or her religion – or lack thereof.

Questions that have arisen in the case law are, among others, whether a hospital run by the Catholic Church may require a greater sense of loyalty from its Catholic employees than from other employees. Likewise, to what extent may a Protestant organisation, while recruiting a communications manager, require that the prospective employee is in fact a Protestant Christian?

The chapter will present case law from both the ECtHR and the Court of Justice of the EU (CJEU) and analyse how a potential conflict at the workplace between the rights of religious organisations and the rights of individuals has been solved by the two Courts.

II. RIGHT TO AN AUTONOMOUS EXISTENCE UNDER ARTICLE 9 ECHR

The European Convention on Human Rights, which was established in the 1950s, has gradually developed a body of case law concerning religious freedom in general and the communal aspects of religious freedom in particular.[1] Article 9 ECHR is the main provision regulating the religious freedom of religious organisations and will thus be the focus of this chapter. Moreover, Article 11 ECHR is also relevant, since it stipulates the general right of freedom of assembly and association, as is also Article 14 ECHR, which prohibits discrimination. However, the latter Article does not stand independently but rather stipulates that the rights enjoyed through the Convention must be protected equally and irrespective of, inter alia, religious affiliation.

Article 9 ECHR reads:

> Freedom of thought, conscience and religion
>
> 1. Everyone has the right to freedom of thought, conscience and religion; this right includes freedom to change his religion or belief and freedom, either alone *or in community with others* [emphasis added] and in public or private, to manifest his religion or belief, in worship, teaching, practice and observance.
> 2. Freedom to manifest one's religion or beliefs shall be subject only to such limitations as are prescribed by law and are necessary in a democratic society in the interests of public safety, for the protection of public order, health or morals, or for the protection of the rights and freedoms of others.

Looking first at the wording, Article 9 ECHR addresses the right of the individual to manifest his or her religion or belief, in worship, teaching, practice and observance – alone, or together with others, in private as well as in public. That is, the starting point is the right of the individual to come together with others. However, the ECtHR has developed a body of case law that strengthens the role of the organisation and grants the organisation a number of rights connected to the organisational freedom of religion.

The ECtHR, and before that the European Commission on Human Rights (EComHR), were earlier reluctant to grant religious organisations any self-standing rights under Article 9 ECHR. Rather, the rights of religious organisations were derived from the right of the individual, and the organisation acted as an agent on behalf of its members. This position started to change

[1] For an account of the development of religious freedom through the ECHR, see, inter alia, C Evans, *Freedom of Religion under the European Convention on Human Rights* (Oxford, Oxford University Press, 2001); P Cane, C Evans and Z Robinson, *Law and Religion in Theoretical and Historical Context* (Cambridge, Cambridge University Press, 2008); MD Evans, *Religious Liberty and International Law in Europe* 1st edn (Cambridge, Cambridge University Press, 2008).

during the 1990s through a body of case law developed by the ECtHR.[2] Rivers argues that:

> Having accepted that religious associations have a separate corporate personality for the purpose of European human rights law, they have become the beneficiaries of a set or relevant right derived both from article 9 and from other provisions such as the right to a fair trial, freedom of expression, non-discrimination, and property.[3]

Nevertheless, it was not until the year 2000, in the case *Hasan and Chaush v Bulgaria* that the Court of Human Rights clearly articulated the rights of religious organisations under Article 9 ECHR, separate from any other (non-religious) organisation.[4] That is, rights held in their capacity as a *religious* organisation, not just as any organisation. *Hasan and Chaush v Bulgaria* concerned the alleged interference of the Bulgarian State, through the Bulgarian Directorate for Religious Denominations, into the internal affairs of the Muslim community. The main criticism against the Bulgarian State was that it had removed the first choice as leader of the Muslim community, the Chief Mufti, and replaced him with a candidate of its own choice.[5] The Court of Human Rights expressed its position in the following way:

> [T]he Court recalls that religious communities traditionally and universally exist in the form of organized structures. They abide by rules which are often seen by followers as being of divine origin. Religious ceremonies have their meaning and sacred value for the believers if they have been conducted by ministers empowered for that purpose in compliance with these rules. The personality of the religious ministers is undoubtedly of importance to every member of the community. Participation in the life of the community is thus a manifestation of one's religion, protected by article 9 of the Convention.
>
> Where the organisation of the religious community is at issue, Article 9 of the Convention must be interpreted in the light of Article 11, which safeguards associative life against unjustified State interference. Seen in this perspective, the believers' right to freedom of religion encompasses the expectation that the community will be allowed to function peacefully, free from arbitrary State intervention. *Indeed, the autonomous existence of religious communities is indispensable for pluralism in a democratic society and is thus an issue at the very heart of the protection which Article 9 affords.* It directly concerns not only the organisation of the community as such but also the effective enjoyment of the right to freedom of religion by all its active members. Were the organisational life of the community not protected by Article 9 of the Convention, all other aspects of the individual's freedom of religion would become vulnerable.[6]

[2] *Serif v Greece* App no 38178/97 (ECtHR, 14 Devember 1999); *Manoussakis and Others v Greece* App no 18748/91 (ECtHR, 26 September 1996); *Canea Catholic Church v Greece* App no 25528/94 (ECtHR, 16 December 1997).

[3] J Rivers, *The Law of Organized Religions: Between Establishment and Secularism* (Oxford, Oxford University Press, 2010) 51.

[4] *Hasan and Chaush v Bulgaria* [GC] App no 30985/96 (ECtHR, 26 October 2000).

[5] ibid paras 10–13.

[6] ibid para 62 (emphasis added). See also Rivers (n 3) 52.

The sentence highlighted in the quote is crucial – it is not only the existence of the organisation but also the *autonomous* existence of the religious organisation which lies at the core of the protection that Article 9 ECHR affords.

Nevertheless, what does the sentence 'the autonomous existence of religious organizations must be protected' mean? One important aspect is, as seen in the *Hasan and Chaush v Bulgaria* case, the right to elect one's own leader. Moreover, the Court of Human Rights held, as quoted above, that the associative life of the community must be safeguarded from any unjustified State interference, meaning that the community must be able to function peacefully, without arbitrary State interference. Rivers argues that:

> The Court [of Human Rights] has repeatedly emphasized the importance of the autonomous existence of religious communities, the existence of associations to enable collective action, and the need for the State to remain neutral and impartial in exercising its regulatory power over them.[7]

III. RELIGIOUS ORGANISATIONS ACTING AS EMPLOYERS UNDER THE ECHR

Religious organisations are not a homogenous group – they come in various sizes and some are more interested in acting as a group or engaging with society at large than others. The vast majority of them are, however, so well organised that they have an organisational structure and have legal personality in order to be able to enter into contracts. A religious organisation must rent or own property, pay for heating and lighting, and more often than not, employ staff.

As stated above, religious organisations indeed enjoy self-standing rights – first of all to exist, but also to be free from arbitrary interference by the State and to have the right to be a legal entity in order to be able to act on behalf of its members.[8] Therefore, it is in fact the religious organisation, in its capacity as an employer, which has proven to be a complicated legal issue. The reason for this is that the workplace is an arena for multiple legal relationships, most predominantly the relationship between employer and employee, which is entrenched with legal rules. In this section, issues addressed by the ECtHR in its case law will be presented, before moving on to the relevant EU law in the following section.

First of all, under Article 9 ECHR, the employee has their own right to religious freedom, which includes the right to be free from religion. The employee

[7] Rivers (n 3) 53.

[8] Rivers divides the right to autonomy of religious organisations into 10 separate rights: a) the right to legal and religious entity status; b) the right of internal structural autonomy; c) the right to select, train, appoint, and dismiss leaders; d) the right to establish places of worship and meeting; e) the right to raise funds; f) the right to uphold religious community life; g) the right of pastoral access to restricted institutions; h) the right to provide educational, charitable and humanitarian institutions; i) the right to public presence; and j) the right to protection; see ibid 55–70.

also has a right to the protection of family and private life under Article 8 ECHR, and the right to organisational freedom under Article 11 ECHR.

A. *Sindicatul 'Pastorul cel bun' v Romania*

In *Sindicatul 'Pastorul cel bun' v Romania*,[9] the ECtHR had before it a case concerning a dissident faction within the Romanian Orthodox Church, with priests who wished to form a trade union. While employed laymen were allowed to form trade unions within the church, priests were not. In *Sindicatul 'Pastorul cel bun' v Romania* the ECtHR held that there is no right to dissent under Article 9 ECHR, but only a right to leave the organisation. Slotte and Årsheim put it in the following way:

> Within a religious community, individuals can reasonably be expected to adjust to the life and ways of the community. If you wish to conduct your religious life in a completely different manner, it would be only reasonable to seek out other like-minded persons instead of destabilizing the group you are already presently in.[10]

However, drawing on the standards of the ILO (the International Labour Organization), the ECtHR held that the relationship between the priests and the Church was de facto an employment relationship, in addition to being a religious and spiritual relationship.[11] As such, the Court of Human Rights found that the actions of the Romanian State constituted an interference with the applicant's rights under Article 11 ECHR. Nevertheless, the interference was justified due to the real risk of a threat to the autonomy of the Church. The margin of appreciation awarded to the contracting states is wide, since there is a lack of consensus in the European setting on State–Church relationships. The Court also held that the duty of the state must be to thoroughly examine whether the risk is substantial and whether the measures taken are proportionate to achieve the aim of protection of the autonomy of the Church:

> It [the religious organization] must also show, in the light of the circumstances of the individual case, that the risk alleged is real and substantial and that the impugned interference with freedom of association does not go beyond what is necessary to eliminate that risk and does not serve any other purpose unrelated to the exercise of the religious community's autonomy. The national courts must ensure that these conditions are satisfied, by conducting an in-depth examination of the circumstances

[9] *Sindicatul 'Pastorul cel bun' v Romania* [GC] App no 2330/09 (ECtHR, 9 July 2013).

[10] P Slotte and H Årsheim, 'The Ministerial Exception – Comparative Perspectives' (2015) *Oxford Journal of Law and Religion* 171, 185; see also I Leigh, 'Balancing Religious Autonomy and Other Human Rights under the European Convention' (2012) 1 *Oxford Journal of Law and Religion* 109.

[11] To characterise the relationship between a priest and the church as an employment relationship is not self-evident, see discussions from a UK context by PW Edge, 'Judicial Crafting of a Ministerial Exception: The UK Experience' (2015) *Oxford Journal of Law and Religion* 244 and Rivers (n 3) 108–22.

of the case and a thorough balancing exercise between the competing interests at stake.[12]

In other words, the right to autonomy does not automatically exclude a right to judicial review. National courts must uphold the rights of the priests, *in casu*, but also the rights of others who might have a conflicting interest vis-à-vis the religious organisation. The scope of judicial review of secular courts was one of the major issues in the case of *Egenberger*,[13] decided by the Court of Justice of the EU (CJEU), which will be examined below.

B. *Fernández Martínez v Spain* (GC)

In another high-profile case decided by the ECtHR, the right to a private life and the freedom of expression of the individual were at stake. The case of *Fernández Martínez v Spain*,[14] decided by the Grand Chamber, concerned Mr Fernández Martínez who was a priest in the Roman Catholic Church, but he was also married and had several children. He worked as a teacher of religion in a Spanish state public school; a position paid for by the Spanish State but approved by the Bishop. When he spoke out in the local newspaper regarding his position on celibacy in connection with his involvement in an organisation of married priests, the Bishop withdrew his approval and Mr Fernández Martínez lost his employment as a teacher of the Roman Catholic faith.[15]

Acting as the employer, it was the Spanish State that had interfered with the rights of Mr Fernández Martínez. The question was whether the interference was justified on the basis of the rights of others – that is the Roman Catholic Church's right to autonomy. The European Court of Human Rights held that there is no right to dissent, but also that the State must be a neutral and impartial organiser of life for religious organisations, in order to achieve public order, religious harmony and tolerance.[16] In emphasising the religious duty of a religious teacher within the Catholic Church, the ECtHR stressed that the State may not assess the legitimacy of religious belief or oblige a religious community to entrust someone with a religious duty:

> The Court further reiterates that, but for very exceptional cases, the right to freedom of religion as guaranteed under the Convention excludes any discretion on the part of the State to determine whether religious beliefs or the means used to express such

[12] *Sindicatul 'Pastorul cel bun' v Romania* (n 9) para 159.

[13] Case C-414/16 *Egenberger* [2018] EU:C:2018:257 [GC].

[14] *Fernández Martínez v Spain* [GC] App no 56030/07 (ECtHR, 12 June 2014).

[15] For a more in-depth analysis of the case, see Slotte and Årsheim (n 10) for an in-depth insight into the Spanish situation regarding State–Church relations, see C Garcimartín, 'The Ministerial Exception: European Balancing in the Spanish Context' (2015) *Oxford Journal of Law and Religion* 260.

[16] *Fernández Martínez v Spain* (n 14) para 127.

> beliefs are legitimate. Moreover, the principle of religious autonomy prevents the State from obliging a religious community to admit or exclude an individual or to entrust someone with a particular religious duty.[17]

In line with this reasoning, the ECtHR also held that individuals, who have positions in a religious organisation, depending on the nature of the post in question, are subjected to a 'heightened duty of loyalty':

> The Court acknowledges that as a consequence of their autonomy religious communities can demand a certain degree of loyalty from those working for them or representing them. In this context the Court has already considered that the nature of the post occupied by those persons is an important element to be taken into account when assessing the proportionality of a restrictive measure taken by the State or the religious organisation concerned. In particular, the specific mission assigned to the person concerned in a religious organisation is a relevant consideration in determining whether that person should be subject to a heightened duty of loyalty.[18]

While the right to autonomy of the religious organisation is allegedly strong, it is not absolute. The ECtHR also stresses that the national courts must ensure a proper judicial review of the circumstances of the case, and perform a thorough balancing act between the interests of the individual and the organisation:

> That being said, a mere allegation by a religious community that there is an actual or potential threat to its autonomy is not sufficient to render any interference with its members' rights to respect for their private or family life compatible with Article 8 of the Convention. In addition, the religious community in question must also show, in the light of the circumstances of the individual case, that the risk alleged is probable and substantial and that the impugned interference with the right to respect for private life does not go beyond what is necessary to eliminate that risk and does not serve any other purpose unrelated to the exercise of the religious community's autonomy. Neither should it affect the substance of the right to private and family life. The national courts must ensure that these conditions are satisfied, by conducting an in-depth examination of the circumstances of the case and a thorough balancing exercise between the competing interests at stake.[19]

IV. EU DISCRIMINATION LAW AND ITS SPECIAL LEGAL SYSTEM FOR RELIGIOUS ORGANISATIONS

A. General Framework

In the Treaty of Amsterdam, which entered into force in 1999, the European Union was granted a legal basis to enact legislation in the field of

[17] ibid 128 (references omitted).
[18] ibid 130.
[19] ibid 131.

non-discrimination law. In order to combat, inter alia, discrimination based on religion and belief, Directive 2000/78/EC ('the Employment Equality Directive') was enacted.[20] The Directive covers the field of employment and occupation, and prohibits both direct and indirect discrimination based on religion or belief, disability, age and sexual orientation. The Directive was implemented in all EU Member States with the aim of enforcing the principle of equal treatment. In addition, the EU has enacted secondary law in order to combat discrimination based on gender, race and ethnicity, which extends beyond the employment sector.[21]

What is more, the European Union has, since 2009, a binding fundamental rights document of its own, which binds the Union institutions and the Member States when they enforce EU law and the Charter of Fundamental Rights of the EU (CFR). Article 10 CFR enshrines the freedom of religion and belief while Article 21 CFR lays down the right to equal treatment. Article 10 CFR is a corresponding right to Article 9 ECHR, and ought therefore to be given the same meaning and scope. Article 6 TEU also states that the European Convention on Human Rights enjoys a special status in the EU legal order and forms parts of the general principles of EU law.

It is possible to imagine several legal issues at the intersection of the right to autonomy of a religious organisation, as established above, and the individual's right not to be discriminated against. There is no doubt that the practice of the Roman Catholic Church to have only male priests is permitted as an aspect of the right to organisational freedom of the Roman Catholic Church, despite otherwise being a directly discriminatory practice on the basis of gender. Likewise, it lies within the prerogative of a Sunni Muslim Community to employ a Sunni Muslim imam, and not a Shia Muslim imam. Nevertheless, when the issue is not about leaders, but other functions – such as a secretary, cleaner, manager, doctor, bookstore keeper and the like – the issue is much less clear. Below, two cases from the CJEU are analysed, one of them dealing with a project manager and the other a doctor in a managerial position at a hospital run by the Roman Catholic Church.

The ECtHR held in the case law presented above that the State may not arbitrarily interfere with the organisational life of a religious organisation; that there exists a right to elect one's leader but not a right to dissent. In particular, the State may not oblige, or prohibit, a certain person to take up a position of a religious nature within an organisation. Moreover, a religious organisation

[20] Council Directive 2000/78/EC of 27 November 2000 establishing a general framework for equal treatment in employment and occupation [2000] OJ L 303, 2.12.2000, p 16–22.

[21] It is not within the scope of this chapter to address the non-discrimination framework of the EU to any great extent, rather, to give a general overview, see S Fredman, *Discrimination Law* 2nd edn (Oxford, Oxford University Press, 2011); and M Bell, *Anti-Discrimination Law and the European Union* (Oxford, Oxford University Press, 2002); for a more specific in-depth analysis of discrimination on the basis of religion and belief, see L Vickers, *Religious Freedom, Religious Discrimination and the Workplace* 2nd edn (Oxford, Hart Publishing, 2016).

may require a certain degree of loyalty from its employees, but the actions of the organisation are not exempt from scrutiny by national courts. This normative framework is, in principle, also valid EU law. The reason is that Article 10 of the Charter of Fundamental Rights shall be interpreted in the same manner, and given the same scope as Article 9 ECHR, according to Article 52(3) of the Charter.

Article 4(2) of Directive 2000/78 contains a few exceptions to the general rules on the prohibition of discrimination. The exceptions, the 'special legal system' to use the words of AG Wathelet,[22] relate to the Member States that had such legislation in place at the time of the adoption of the Directive (a so-called stand still clause).[23] What is more, the ethos of the religious organisation may constitute a general occupational requirement, but may not constitute discrimination on any other ground. Furthermore, if provided for by national law, organisations with a religious ethos may require individuals working for them to act in good faith and to be loyal to the organisation's ethos.[24]

B. *Egenberger*

The Court of Justice has had two occasions[25] on which to adjudicate on the exception provided for churches and religious organisations under Article 4(2) of the Employment Equality Directive. The first case, *Egenberger*,[26] concerns whether or not an organisation with a religious ethos may single-handedly decide the requirements of religious affiliation connected to employment within the organisation. Ms Egenberger sought employment at Diaconie of Germany,

[22] Case C-68/17 *IR v JQ* [2018] Opinion by AG Wathelet, EU:C:2018:363 [2].

[23] While some Member States have transposed Art 4(2) in an extensive manner, others have not done so at all. For an account of the variety of transpositions in the Member States, see, inter alia, Vickers (n 21) 146–48; E Svensson, 'Religious Ethos, Bond of Loyalty, and Proportionality – Translating the "Ministerial Exception" into "European"' (2015) 4 *Oxford Journal of Law and Religion* 224; Garcimartín (n 15); Edge (n 11).

[24] Art 4(2) of Directive 2000/78/EC reads in full: 'Member States may maintain national legislation in force at the date of adoption of this Directive or provide for future legislation incorporating national practices existing at the date of adoption of this Directive pursuant to which, in the case of occupational activities within churches and other public or private organisations the ethos of which is based on religion or belief, a difference of treatment based on a person's religion or belief shall not constitute discrimination where, by reason of the nature of these activities or of the context in which they are carried out, a person's religion or belief constitute a genuine, legitimate and justified occupational requirement, having regard to the organisation's ethos. This difference of treatment shall be implemented taking account of Member States' constitutional provisions and principles, as well as the general principles of Community law, and should not justify discrimination on another ground.

Provided that its provisions are otherwise complied with, this Directive shall thus not prejudice the right of churches and other public or private organisations, the ethos of which is based on religion or belief, acting in conformity with national constitutions and laws, to require individuals working for them to act in good faith and with loyalty to the organisation's ethos'.

[25] Note taken of case law decided before the end of 2018.

[26] Case C-414/16 *Egenberger* (n 13).

a private organisation with a Protestant Christian ethos. The organisation was looking to employ someone to write a report on Germany's compliance with the United Nations Convention on the Elimination of All Forms of Racial Discrimination. In the advertisement, the organisation included the requirement that the applicants were Protestant Christians. While Ms Egenberger in fact belonged to no faith at all, and stated so in her application, she was otherwise clearly qualified for the position since she was a renowned expert in the field.

While *Egenberger* raises several questions relating to the horizontal application of the Charter of Fundamental Rights,[27] the focus of this account is the way the rights of the organisation are balanced with the rights of the individual. The Court of Justice held that The Employment Equality Directive has two aims. One is to protect the fundamental right of workers not to be discriminated on the grounds of inter alia religion and belief. The other aim of the Directive is enshrined in Article 4(2). The Directive takes into account the right of autonomy of churches, as well as the rights of other private and public bodies with a religious ethos. This right is enshrined in Article 17 TFEU and Article 10 CFR, the latter corresponding to Article 9 ECHR. When these two rights clash, the objective of the Employment Equality Directive and Article 4(2) thereof is to ensure a fair balance between these two rights. The requirement is that the balancing act must be performed in such a way that a fair balance between these two fundamental rights can be achieved. Lastly, in the event of a dispute, such a balancing act must be subjected to a review by an independent authority, and ultimately by a national court.[28]

To that end, whether religious affiliation may or may not be a prerequisite for employment with an organisation that is based on a religious ethos, is an aspect that must be reviewed against the requirements put down in Article 4(2) of the Employment Equality Directive. Relying on the *Fernández Martínez* case from the ECtHR, the Court of Justice reiterated that a secular court may not, except under very specific circumstances, review whether or not the religious ethos can be justified or not. However, that said, the national court must ensure that the requirements of Article 4(2) are upheld.

Article 4(2) provides that otherwise discriminatory treatment may be justified by 'reason of the nature of these activities or of the context in which they are carried out, a person's religion or belief constitute a *genuine, legitimate and justified occupational requirement*, having regard to the organisation's ethos'.[29] The Court of Justice stresses that in order to be lawful:

> a difference of treatment on grounds of religion or belief depends on the objectively verifiable existence of a direct link between the occupational requirement imposed

[27] For a take on the horizontal application of the general principle of religious equality in EU law, see L Lourenço, 'Religion, Discrimination and the EU General Principles' Gospel: Egenberger' (2019) *Common Market Law Review* 193.

[28] Case C-414/16 *Egenberger* (n 13) paras 50–53.

[29] Emphasis added.

> by the employer and the activity concerned. Such a link may follow either from the nature of the activity, for example where it involves taking part in the determination of the ethos of the church or organisation in question or contributing to its mission of proclamation, or else from the circumstances in which the activity is to be carried out, such as the need to ensure a credible presentation of the church or organisation to the outside world.[30]

The Court of Justice interprets *genuine* as the professing of a particular belief that must appear necessary in relation to the manifesting ethos of the organisation, or to its autonomy. By *legitimate* the CJEU argues that the requirement of professing a particular belief may not pursue an aim which has no connection to the ethos or autonomy of the organisation. Lastly, by *justified*, the Court means that

> the church or religious organization is also obliged to show, in the light of the factual circumstances, that the supposed risk of causing harm to its ethos or to its right of autonomy is probable and substantial, so that imposing such a requirement is indeed necessary.[31]

At the end of the day, the Court of Justice held that Ms Egenberger was entitled to a full review by the national court as to whether or not the above-mentioned criteria were fulfilled. In the event that the German rules on autonomy of religious organisations, which grant a strong right to self-determination,[32] are not in compliance with EU law, they must be set aside, since: 'The prohibition of all discrimination on grounds of religion or belief is mandatory as a general principle of EU law'.[33]

C. *IR v JQ*

The second case, *IR v JQ*,[34] largely confirms *Egenberger*. Again the case stems from Germany, and again, it concerns the right to autonomy of organisations with a religious ethos. Mr JQ worked as a doctor, in a managerial position, at a hospital run by the Roman Catholic Church. While the hospital employed both Catholic and non-Catholic staff, in both managerial positions as well as ground staff, individuals who were Roman Catholic and held a managerial position were placed under a higher duty of loyalty towards the religious ethos of the hospital. Mr JQ was of the Roman Catholic faith and in his first marriage he had married according to Roman Catholic rites. However, his first wife separated from him

[30] *Egenberger* (n 13) 63.
[31] ibid 65–67, quote at 67.
[32] See G Robbers, *Religion and Law in Germany* 2nd edn (Austin, Kluwer Law International, 2010) 107–72.
[33] Case C-414/16 *Egenberger* (n 13) para 76.
[34] Case C-68/17 *IR v JQ* [2018] EU:C:2018:696 [GC].

and they subsequently divorced. Later Mr JQ married his second partner in a civil ceremony, without the first marriage being annulled. When his employer heard of the second marriage, the hospital dismissed him for breach of loyalty with the Roman Catholic ethos of the hospital. It was in particular with regard to a certain aspect of the Roman Catholic ethos; the 'sacred and indissoluble nature of religious marriage'.[35]

Mr JQ claimed that his dismissal breached the right to equal treatment, since if he had either been a Protestant Christian or had no faith at all, he would not have been bound by the same degree of loyalty, even though he could have held the same managerial position at the hospital. The question that arose before the national court was first of all whether or not the hospital fell within the scope of Article 4(2), and second, whether or not it is the religious organisation which single-handedly may decide the extent of the loyalty requirement.

While the Court of Justice hastily skipped the first question, stating merely that Article 4(2) covers both public and private legal entities, as long as they have a religious ethos, which the hospital did, it spent more effort on the second. The Court of Justice confirmed its standing in *Egenberger*, stating that it is neither the religious organisation which may single-handedly decide on the loyalty requirement, nor is it a matter only for national law, but rather a matter of EU law and must be interpreted accordingly. Thereafter, the CJEU linked the loyalty requirement with the occupational requirements, as described in relation to *Egenberger* above, stating that:

> a church or other public or private organisation the ethos of which is based on religion or belief can treat its employees in managerial positions differently, as regards the requirement to act in good faith and with loyalty to that ethos, depending on their affiliation to a particular religion or adherence to the belief of that church or other organisation only if, bearing in mind the nature of the occupational activities concerned or the context in which they are carried out, the religion or belief is a genuine, legitimate and justified occupational requirement in the light of that ethos.[36]

While it is up to the national court to evaluate the facts and whether or not the requirements of loyalty of Roman Catholic employees in managerial positions are indeed a 'genuine, legitimate and justified occupational requirement' with regard to the Roman Catholic ethos, the Court of Justice provided guidance on the matter. It held that it seemed unlikely that the requirements of loyalty were genuine, since the hospital employed non-Catholics in the same positions, without requiring loyalty. Moreover, it held that it was up to the employer to show that 'there is a probable and substantial risk of undermining its ethos or its right of autonomy'[37] before the national court.

[35] ibid para 57.
[36] ibid 55.
[37] ibid 60.

V. CONCLUDING DISCUSSION

When and how a religious organisation may introduce requirements of faith, moral conduct, marital status and the like on their employees is not a peripheral issue. While the extent of the work performed by these organisations differs from Member State to Member State, they have what AG Tanchev calls a 'quasi-monopolistic position in some regions and fields of work'.[38] Likewise, Vickers reminds us that in the United Kingdom, state-funded faith schools are common.[39] Of course, the French tradition of a strong secularist principle, which extends to work in the public sector, constitutes the complete opposite position.[40] Christoffersen, on the other hand, highlights that the Nordic tradition of a state church system is significantly different, compared to for example, the German one. In the Nordic countries, religious organisations are expected to follow the law of the land, with a limited degree of autonomy.[41] The question is thus to what extent the rulings of the Court of Justice, which emphasises uniformity in the application of EU law, change the legal situation in those Member States that have not implemented Article 4(2) of Directive 2000/78.

What further complicates the issue is when religious organisations either act as part of the State, or on its behalf in carrying out State affairs. Vickers argues that the context of whether or not the religious employer should be seen as a private or public employer is not one of sharp division but rather to be understood as a 'continuum or spectrum'.[42] While arguing that there is currently a trend to hand over public services to private providers, including religiously based charity organisations, the distinction between private and public bodies and workplaces is not an easy one to draw.[43]

The view of the workplace adds a layer of complexity to the discussion on whether or not a court should review the legitimacy of the religious ethos. Vickers distinguishes between a functional and an organic view of the workplace, where according to the former view, the workplace consists of different functions, which in turn may be religious or secular, but again on a spectrum rather than a clear-cut division. The organic workplace, on the other hand, recognises that some workers, and employers, might view all work as worship. As an example, Vickers argues that some Christians might view working in a Christian organisation as part of their mission and faith.[44] Taking an organic,

[38] Case C-414/16 *Egenberger* [2017] Opinion by AG Tanchev EU:C:2017:851 [4] referring to the German situation where a church and religious institution is the second largest employer in the country.

[39] Vickers (n 21) 135.

[40] ibid 136.

[41] L Christoffersen, 'The Argument for a Narrow Conception of "Religious Autonomy"' (2015) *Oxford Journal of Law and Religion* 278.

[42] Vickers (n 21) 79.

[43] ibid 79–80.

[44] ibid 87–88.

rather than a functional, approach to the workplace might enlarge the scope of 'religious' tasks and further complicates the issue of what a secular court may review without overstepping the autonomy of the religious organisation.

The chapter has presented two European legal frameworks: the European Convention on Human Rights and the European Union. The differences between the two systems, and in particular their courts, are manifold.[45] What needs to be highlighted for our purposes, however, are the different ways the two courts treat the historical legacy of the Member States. While the Court of Human Rights uses the margin of appreciation doctrine since there is a lack of European consensus on these issues, the Court of Justice applies a uniform application of EU law.

As a last remark, it is important to note the different scale of judicial review the two courts apply. While the European Court of Human Rights also holds that the State must perform a judicial review which guarantees a proper balancing of the rights of others with the right to autonomy, the Court of Justice arguably extends the scope of that review. The standard of judicial review in EU law is that the occupational requirements are genuine, legitimate and justified depending on the ethos of the organisation. Nevertheless, neither the Court of Justice, nor the national court, may go so far as to review the legitimacy of the ethos itself.

[45] For a specific discussion on religion at the workplace, see ibid 150–58; for a more general discussion, see S Morano-Foadi and L Vickers, *Fundamental Rights in the EU: A Matter for Two Courts* (Oxford, Hart Publishing, 2015).

8

Freedom of Religion: Conscience, Dignity and the Construction of Identity

WILLEM VANCUTSEM*

I. INTRODUCTION

TODAY, HUMAN RIGHTS increasingly appear as a dogma.[1] If they are complied with, it is because the law must be obeyed. If they are challenged, it is because they are seen as unwelcome limitations on sovereignty. The real 'why' of human rights is often neglected, and for defenders as well as contesters, human rights increasingly appear devoid of a 'soul'.

Within this context of a decreasing understanding of human rights, this chapter has two aims. The first is to reconsider the right to freedom of religion – one of the most contentious human rights in the contemporary European political context. Limitations on it are widely debated, and regularly imposed. But often forgotten is the reason for having a right to freedom of religion in the first place. This chapter wants to re-establish that basis, and link it to legal practice, to determine which limitations should, in principle and practice, be allowed.

The second aim, which follows from the first, is to give a new, emancipatory impetus to the debates regarding freedom of religion. Through unconventionally linking securitisation and discourse theory to limitations on freedom of religion, it will be argued that some identity constructions make possible illegitimate limitations on this right. These identity constructs can be analysed, and challenged, offering an alternative perspective on the right to

* An earlier version of this article was published as W Vancutsem, 'Freedom of Religion and the Securitisation of Religious Identity: An Analysis of Proposals Impacting on Freedom of Religion Following Terrorist Attacks in Flanders' (2018) 2 *Global Campus Human Rights Journal* 41–58.

[1] YN Harari, *21 Lessons for the 21st Century* (London, Vintage, 2018).

freedom of religion and its protection. Looking in particular at the example of Flanders post-terrorist attacks of 2016, it will be demonstrated how this works in practice.

This chapter thus links legal, philosophical and political approaches to freedom of religion, and aims to reinvigorate the debate around this right in all aspects. It concludes with two calls to action. The first is for the ECtHR to restrict a State's margin of appreciation in determining the meaning of religious manifestations, as this makes possible illegitimate limitations. And the second is for societies to work towards an inclusive identity, based on human rights and democracy – not on intangible conceptions of what it means to be a nation, as the latter fuels illegitimate proposals to limit the freedom of an incompatible 'Other'.

II. RELIGION, DIGNITY AND CONSCIENCE

Why is there a right to freedom of religion? And what implications does this have? Throughout the decades, several justifications have been raised: from pragmatic and religious to liberal and conscience-based. Yet for a right to freedom of religion to be justified, it needs an inherent and independent value, and be distinguishable from other rights. To determine whether a right to freedom of religion is justified, and which consequences this has for the 'content' of this right, we have to therefore touch the available justifications to these two requirements.

Pragmatic justifications, to start with, argue that, to avoid the suffering that may arise from religious conflict, there should be freedom of religion. Freedom of religion is thus an instrument to protect other rights, like the right to life.[2] But this means that freedom of religion has no independent existence. It has no inherent value and cannot be justified as a right, only as a policy that is useful to the extent that it contributes to another goal.

Religious justifications provide an alternative. Some religions might promote freedom of religion to escape persecution, others for reasons of doctrine.[3] But these justifications are very particularistic. Freedom of religion would only exist for reasons internal to, or for the benefit of, one religion, and thus wouldn't manage to be justified as a universal human right. Again, it would have no independent or inherent value.

More powerful justifications are offered by the liberal tradition. A first one maintains that ideas, religious or otherwise, should never be suppressed, as they may be true.[4] They should circulate freely, so that societies can arrive at

[2] C Evans, *Freedom of Religion Under the European Convention on Human Rights* (Oxford, Oxford University Press, 2001) 23–25.

[3] ibid 25–27.

[4] ibid 28; A Scolnicov, *The Right to Religious Freedom in International Law: Between Group Rights and Individual Rights* (Abingdon, Routledge, 2011) 35.

the best points of view. This justification therefore does attribute an intrinsic value to freedom of religion. But it fails to distinguish it from freedom of opinion and expression. Religion is no different from other ideas, and thus cannot justify a separate right.

The second liberal argument, finally, argues that everyone should be able to live their life in the way they think is 'good'.[5] Since religions describe a 'good' life, one should be allowed to live according to religious precepts. This justification therefore too attributes religion an intrinsic value. But, apart from the impossibility of allowing all ways of life,[6] it runs into problems since religion is just one phenomenon that prescribes a 'good' life. Religion here again is no different from other conceptions of the 'good', and cannot be justified as a separate right.

It thus appears that the most widely-cited justifications fail at justifying a separate right to freedom of religion, and one might therefore conclude that freedom of religion should be abolished. Yet, a final approach – the one from conscience – does succeed at justifying it.

Indeed: despite their differences, one characteristic the justifications above share is that they regard religion – like opinions or ideas – as a choice. The case for specifically protecting religion, beyond ideas, hence disappears. But this changes when one approaches freedom of religion as 'religious liberty for those who regard themselves as claimed by religious commitments they have not chosen'.[7] If religious people do not consider their beliefs a choice, there is a difference with mere ideas. And this leads to a final justification, from conscience and dignity.

As the philosopher Nussbaum argues,[8] dignity – the basis for human rights – is connected with conscience, the 'faculty with which people search for life's ultimate meaning'. Conscience may make people adhere to a religion, and can impose obligations which one feels unable to resist. It compels people to act in certain ways, and when this is prevented, dignity is impacted.

This admittedly resembles the justification from the 'good life'. But there's a difference: conscience is not the same as just any conception of the 'good'. It is concerned with convictions people cannot resist. The dignity that should be protected depends not on choice, but on its opposite: obligation. Religious freedom therefore is 'the freedom to be unfree in a particular kind of way',[9] (the subjection to an alternative authority than that of the state.

[5] Evans (n 2) 29; Scolnicov (n 4) 37.

[6] Cf Evans (n 2) 66.

[7] MJ Sandel, 'Religious Liberty – Freedom of Conscience or Freedom of Choice?' (1989) 3 *Utah Law Review* 597–615, 610.

[8] MC Nussbaum, *The New Religious Intolerance: Overcoming the Politics of Fear in an Anxious Age* (Cambridge, Harvard University Press, 2012) 65.

[9] M Lambek, 'Is Religion Free?' in WF Sullivan, ES Hurd, S Mahmood and PG Danchin (eds), *Politics of Freedom of Religion* (Chicago, University of Chicago Press, 2015) 289–300, 298.

What this amounts to, is the recognition of religion as experienced by believers. This might appear particularistic: it might seem that religion is protected because believers think it should be – which would bring us back to the religious justification. Yet it is not for religious reasons that freedom of religion should be protected – it should be protected to recognise that religion can play a considerable role in human life. It is a recognition of the universality of the possibility of religion.

As such, we finally encounter a right to freedom of religion that cannot be subsumed under other rights, since it has an intrinsic value of its own, based on conscience and dignity.

But what does this mean in practice? It mandates that no one should be forced to act against one's conscience, nor be prevented from acting in the way one's conscience demands – for if one cannot obey one's conscience, this conscience is violated as well.[10] Thus:

1. States should not interfere with religious doctrine. Conscience is personal, and States cannot decide whether doctrine is good or bad. Everyone is allowed to believe whatever one wants to. And States should abstain from judging religious doctrines, and acting on the basis of these judgements.
2. States should not interfere with manifestations on the basis of doctrine. Since religious doctrine is a matter of conscience, it does not suffice to refer to doctrine as a basis to restrict manifestations. Manifestations should be judged independently. That is: would the manifestations also be considered problematic if one didn't look at the doctrine behind it?

Does that mean that States can never intervene? No. But they should take care to do so on the basis of calculations independent of doctrine. Other human rights, too, are based on dignity, and when manifestations objectively impact dignity, restricting them may – and must – be considered.

III. FROM PRINCIPLE TO PRACTICE – ASSESSING THE ECtHR

Only conscience can justify freedom of religion. This, we noted, produces several guiding principles – but does practice live up to principle? In Europe, the leading human rights institution is the ECtHR, and its practice is based on Article 9 of the ECHR. This reads as follows:

> 1. Everyone has the right to freedom of thought, conscience and religion; this right includes freedom to change his religion or belief and freedom, either alone or in community with others and in public or private, to manifest his religion or belief, in worship, teaching, practice and observance.

[10] Nussbaum (n 8) 65–66. A conscience-based justification has implications as well for other forms of conscience. But these cannot be discussed in this chapter.

2. Freedom to manifest one's religion or beliefs shall be subject only to such limitations as are prescribed by law and are necessary in a democratic society in the interests of public safety, for the protection of public order, health or morals, or for the protection of the rights and freedoms of others.

Like its neighbouring articles, the right to freedom of religion therefore is qualified: it can be limited in specific circumstances. Yet this only applies to the freedom to *manifest* religion or belief. Hence, the ECtHR has developed the doctrine of *forum externum* and *internum*.[11]

The *forum internum*, firstly, comprises those aspects of religion and belief that are internal to one's conscience or thought, and refers most notably to the freedom to either choose and maintain or change, a belief.[12] The *forum externum*, on the other hand, is concerned with aspects that are external, or manifested.[13] While the *forum internum* has been interpreted as absolute, manifestations can, according to Article 9(2) be restricted, and they constitute the non-absolute limb of the right to freedom of religion.

At first sight, this distinction appears logical. But, writes Evans, 'the idea that beliefs and actions are separate and distinguishable notions, is controversial', as this is 'not necessarily consonant with the way in which many religions would define themselves'.[14] And indeed: a rigid distinction between *internum* and *externum* does appear artificial when held against a conscience-based justification. This justification recognises that conscience may demand action, and blurs the line between internal and external: limiting the *forum externum* may have the same impact on conscience as limiting the *forum internum*.

The Court's basic doctrine appears to lose sight of this – and problems indeed appear when the Court's further interpretation of the *internum/externum* distinction is scrutinised, in particular when it comes to the protection afforded to manifestations.

Generally, in its case law, the Court has aimed to protect a wide range of beliefs,[15] but has offered protection only to a limited range of manifestations, that 'express the belief concerned'[16] or are 'necessary'.[17] Instead of narrowly defining religion or belief, and widely protecting manifestations – as a conscience-based justification demands – the Court has done the opposite. But it is the Court's interpretation of the limitation criteria, more precisely that of 'legitimate aim', that has most problematically hollowed out protection.

[11] MD Evans, *Religious Liberty and International Law in Europe* (Cambridge, Cambridge University Press, 1997) 299.
[12] R Uitz, *Freedom of Religion* (Belgium, Council of Europe Publishing, 2007) 29.
[13] Evans (n 2) 73.
[14] ibid 74–75.
[15] *Campbell and Cosans v UK* App no 7511/76; 7743/76 (ECtHR, 25 February 1982) para 36.
[16] *Arrowsmith v UK* App no 7050/75 (Commission decision, 16 May 1977) para 71.
[17] Evans (n 11) 307; PM Taylor, *Freedom of Religion: UN and European Human Rights Law and Practice* (Cambridge, Cambridge University Press, 2005) 211.

Indeed: when a State wants to limit freedom of religion, it has to fulfil three conditions. Limitations must be *prescribed by law*, *necessary in a democratic society* and serve a *legitimate aim*, these being 'the interests of public safety', the 'protection of public order', 'health or morals' and 'the protection of the rights and freedoms of others'. The first and second condition cause little problems and don't differ much from the applications with regards to other rights. But when it comes to legitimate aims, the Court shies away from its supervising role almost entirely.

Indeed, when a State Party invokes a legitimate aim, Taylor notes,[18] the Court easily accepts this. There is a reason: not accepting the aim would be politically difficult, and amount to 'accusing the State of bad faith and mendacity'.[19] But as a result, the Court has restricted its role to judging whether the reasons for citing an aim are 'relevant and sufficient'.[20]

Combined with the doctrine that 'where questions concerning the relationship between State and religions are at stake, on which opinion in a democratic society may reasonably differ widely, the role of the national decision-making body must be given special importance',[21] this has made the test of legitimacy an extremely weak one. States may define the 'meaning … of the public expression of a religious belief',[22] and the detrimental effects this has, are made clear especially by the cases of *Dahlab* and *Leyla Şahin* – and in a different way, the case of *Lautsi*.

A. *Dahlab v Switzerland*[23]

This first case concerned Ms Dahlab, who after years without problems, was prohibited from wearing the headscarf in her job as a primary school teacher. While the case, under Article 9, was declared inadmissible, the Court's reasoning in it has been influential – it was referred to in *Şahin*[24] as well as *Lautsi*.[25]

In *Dahlab*, the Swiss government argued that a ban on the headscarf was justified as it pursued the legitimate aims of 'public safety, public order, and the protection of the rights and freedoms of others'.[26] In conformity with its practice of not disputing legitimate aims, the Court accepted that banning the headscarf pursued these.

[18] Taylor (n 17) 302.
[19] Evans (n 2) 148.
[20] *Sunday Times v UK* App no 6538/74 (ECtHR, 26 April 1979) para 62.
[21] *Leyla Şahin v Turkey* [GC] App no 4474/98 (ECtHR, 10 November 2005) paras 109–10.
[22] ibid paras 109–10.
[23] *Dahlab v Switzerland* App no 42393/98 (ECtHR, 15 February 2001).
[24] *Leyla Şahin v Turkey* [GC] (n 21) para 111.
[25] *Lautsi v Italy* [GC] App no 30814/06 (ECtHR, 18 March 2011) para 73.
[26] *Dahlab v Switzerland* (n 23) paras 4–5; 12.

The reasons given by the Swiss government for citing these aims, however, still had to be judged 'relevant and sufficient'.[27] And here too, the Court easily accepted the Swiss argumentation. This was based on the allegation that the headscarf was a 'powerful religious symbol' that could interfere with the beliefs of others and their right to be taught in a neutral environment, and secondly, evoke religious conflict. The Swiss government also argued that the headscarf was 'opposed to gender equality'.[28]

Following its doctrine of subsidiarity regarding religion, the ECtHR had no reason to scrutinise this. If the Swiss government determined the headscarf was a 'powerful religious symbol', the Court's doctrine mandated that it accept this. It therefore did not scrutinise *why* the headscarf – and not, as the Swiss government stated, 'discreet religious symbols ... such as small pieces of jewellery'[29] like a cross – was considered 'powerful', possibly proselytising and opposed to gender equality.

However, there is nothing inherent in a headscarf that leads to this conclusion – rather, it seems that the Swiss government interpreted the *religion* behind the headscarf, as proselytising and opposed to gender equality. That is, the ban was based upon an interpretation of, and value-judgement about, Islam – the Court explicitly stated that '[the headscarf] appears to be imposed on women by a precept which is laid town in the Koran and ... is hard to square with the principle of gender equality'.[30] Islamic doctrines were judged to be 'bad', and its manifestations banned – something Court nor State is qualified to do, as this unduly interferes with conscience.

B. *Leyla Şahin v Turkey* (GC)

This case concerned Ms Şahin, a student at the University of Bursa in Turkey. She had worn the headscarf for four years, and in her fifth enrolled at Istanbul University. There, she was denied the right to wear it.[31] At the ECtHR, the Chamber found no violation of Article 9 – a judgment the Grand Chamber confirmed.

In this case, the Grand Chamber accepted that the ban 'primarily pursued the legitimate aims of protecting the rights and freedoms of others and of protecting public order'.[32] Justifying this, it cited *Dahlab*, noting that 'the State was entitled to place restrictions on ... the Islamic headscarf if it was incompatible

[27] ibid para 12.
[28] ibid paras 12–13.
[29] ibid para 7.
[30] ibid para 13.
[31] *Leyla Şahin v Turkey* [GC] (n 21) paras 15–16.
[32] ibid para 99.

with the pursued aim of protecting the rights and freedoms of others, public order and public safety'.[33]

Having accepted this, the only remaining task for the Court was, as the Chamber stated, 'confined to determining whether the reasons given for the interference were relevant and sufficient'.[34] The Grand Chamber then ruled that the headscarf could be banned to protect gender equality, and that attention had to be paid to 'the impact which wearing such a symbol, which is presented or perceived as a compulsory religious duty, may have on those who choose not to wear it'.[35]

Elaborating on this, it noted:

> the issues at stake include the protection of the 'rights and freedoms of others' and the 'maintenance of public order' ... Imposing limitations ... may, therefore, be regarded as meeting a pressing social need by seeking to achieve those two legitimate aims, especially since, as the Turkish courts stated ..., this religious symbol has taken on political significance ... The Court does not lose sight of the fact that there are extremist political movements in Turkey which seek to impose on society as a whole their religious symbols and conception of a society founded on religious precepts.[36]

Referring to the Turkish Courts, the ECtHR fully adopted the Turkish position. It even invoked a 1984 Supreme Administrative Court decision noting that 'wearing the headscarf is ... becoming the symbol of a vision that is contrary to the freedoms of women'.[37] The Turkish government moreover argued that the headscarf 'was regularly appropriated by religious fundamentalist movements for political ends and constituted a threat to the rights of women'.[38]

These statements led to the Grand Chamber finding of no violation. It accepted that the headscarf was opposed to gender equality, and a symbol for 'extremist political movements'. But this is deeply problematic. As Judge Tulkens noted in her dissenting opinion: 'European supervision seems quite simply to be absent'. The majority, in her opinion, relied 'exclusively on the reasons cited by the national authorities and the courts'. And, she noted, that the majority 'take up position on ... the signification of the headscarf' and that 'it is not the Court's role ... to determine in a general and abstract way the signification of wearing the headscarf'.

This reveals two essential deficits in the Court's doctrine: an excessive margin of appreciation, and the resulting (endorsement of a State's) interpretation of religion. It is readily apparent that the Turkish ban on the headscarf was primarily based not on opposition to the piece of clothing that is the headscarf, but on the interpretation it gave to it. The headscarf was banned because it was thought

[33] ibid para 111.
[34] *Leyla Şahin v Turkey* App no 4474/98 (ECtHR, 29 June 2004) para 103.
[35] *Leyla Şahin v Turkey* [GC] (n 21) para 115.
[36] ibid para 115.
[37] ibid para 37.
[38] *Leyla Şahin v Turkey* (n 34) paras 93–94.

to express 'bad' values – the values of Islam. What the Court's judgment thus amounts to, is a formal endorsement of a State's interpretation of, and value-judgement about, religion.

C. *Lautsi v Italy*

This case, finally, concerned the compulsory display of crucifixes in Italian public schools. Ms. Lautsi complained that this infringed her and her two minor children's rights, more specifically Article 2 of protocol 1, together with Article 9.[39] The Chamber found a violation of both – yet the Grand Chamber reversed this. Because this does not concern a limitation, but a defence, legitimate aims are of less importance. Yet the problems connected to interpretations of religion transpire from this case as well.

Indeed, in *Lautsi*, the Grand Chamber ruled that, in Italy, the crucifix was a religious symbol – but of a 'passive' nature. There was in this case 'no evidence ... that ... a religious symbol on classroom walls may have an influence on pupils ... [T]he applicant's subjective perception is not in itself sufficient'.[40] A far cry from *Dahlab* and *Şahin*, in which influence on others was a predominant consideration.

Moreover, the Grand Chamber concluded that 'whether crucifixes should be present ... is, in principle, a matter falling within the margin of appreciation'[41] and noted that the 'preponderant visibility' did not 'denote a process of indoctrination'.[42] The crucifix, it stated, 'is an essentially passive symbol',[43] explicitly reversing the Chamber's judgment, which ruled that crucifixes should 'be considered "powerful external symbols" within the meaning ... of *Dahlab*'.[44]

According to the Grand Chamber, *Dahlab* could not serve as a basis for this case since the facts were 'entirely different'. But as far as the factors weighing in on the judgment are concerned, the main difference between both cases arguably is that in *Dahlab*, the State aimed to limit a manifestation, while in *Lautsi* the State aimed to protect it. However, the cases are essentially very similar, as the Court, in both cases, accepted the State's argumentation: the Swiss government argued that the headscarf was 'powerful' and negative, the Italian government argued the crucifix was 'passive', and an expression of positive values like democracy and openness[45] and the inclusive nature of Christianity.[46]

[39] *Lautsi v Italy* [GC] (n 25) paras 4; 10–11.
[40] ibid para 66.
[41] ibid para 70.
[42] ibid para 71.
[43] ibid para 72.
[44] ibid para 73.
[45] ibid para 67.
[46] ibid para 15.

Since the determination of the meaning of religious manifestations falls within a State's margin of appreciation, the Court ruled in favour. Again, therefore, this margin resulted therein that a state was free to define the meaning of a manifestation, without supervision, opening the way to an interpretation of, and value-judgement about, religion.

What these three cases therefore make clear, is that the ECtHR fails to adequately protect the right to manifest a religion or belief. This is the case foremost since it is too lenient in accepting limitations, as a result of two factors: the easy acceptance of an invoked legitimate aim, and the margin of appreciation given to States in defining the meaning of a manifestation of religion. This opens the door to limiting manifestations on the basis of interpretations of, and value-judgements about, religion. States interpret, and the Court confirms. And this makes the right to manifest a religion instead of universal, dangerously culturally relativist. By subordinating religion to the margin of appreciation, the right to manifest a religion is emptied of all meaning.

The Court should therefore reconsider its doctrine. It should restrict the margin of appreciation, and investigate *why* a manifestation is targeted: this should not be on the basis of a judgement of religious doctrine. Only in that way can manifestations be adequately protected.

IV. RELIGION, SECURITY AND IDENTITY

We have now demonstrated two points:

1. Only conscience can legitimate a right to freedom of religion.
2. The ECtHR fails to live up to this.

This is problematic inasmuch there is a difference between freedom of opinion and expression, and freedom of religion. If the ECtHR thinks there is no difference with other forms of thought, the doctrine should be the same. But if it thinks there is a difference – which appears to be the case – it should reconsider its practice, and stop allowing states to determine the meaning of a manifestation of religion.

We will now add a third dimension to the analysis: that of security and identity. At the basis of this argumentation lies securitisation theory. Its premise is that security, instead of objective, is socially constructed. Security is about the construction of *existential threats* to justify *extraordinary measures*, a process that takes place when a *securitising actor* describes a threat to a *referent object* in a *speech act*, and the *audience* accepts this as such.[47]

The central concept thus is the 'threat': when someone *securitises* an issue, one constructs this as a *threat* to a *referent object*. And this is directly relevant

[47] B Buzan, O Wæver and J de Wilde, *Security: a New Framework for Analysis* (Boulder, Lynne Rienner Publishers, 1998) 36.

to the legitimate aims that are required to limit manifestations of religion. As noted, these are 'the interests of public safety', the 'protection of public order', 'health or morals' and 'the protection of the rights and freedoms of others'. In securitisation theory, it becomes clear that to invoke these aims, a manifestation has to be considered a threat: a threat to 'public safety', 'public order', 'health or morals' or 'the rights and freedoms of others'.

A manifestation of religion or belief, in other words, must be *securitised* to be limited: it is constructed as a *threat* to a *referent object*, those *referent objects* being the legitimate aims, and the explanation given by States. States cannot limit a manifestation of religion, without securitising it.

The examples used earlier make this clear. In *Dahlab*, the Swiss government considered the headscarf a *threat* to the *referent objects* of public safety, public order and the rights and freedoms of others. The headscarf was a *threat* to these legitimate aims, because it was a 'powerful religious symbol' that could interfere with the beliefs of others and their right to be taught in a neutral environment, and evoke religious conflict. Because the headscarf was a *threat*, it could be limited.

The same is true for *Leyla Şahin*. The Turkish government argued that the headscarf had to be banned because it was a *threat* to the rights and freedoms of others, and public order. The headscarf, it argued, impacted those choosing not to wear it, was opposed to gender equality, and a sign of extremism. It was a *threat* to 'the freedoms of women and the fundamental principles of the republic'.

Securitisation theory thus makes clear that manifestations, like the headscarf, to be limited and comply with a legitimate aim, have to be discursively constructed as a *threat*. If this happens, the ECtHR will most likely – and as demonstrated often problematically – oblige. And discourse theory puts this in an even broader perspective of identity.

Indeed: discourse theory takes securitisation one step further by acknowledging that all of reality – not just security – is discursively constructed. Language, Hansen writes, is 'ontologically significant'.[48] This means that *securitising actors* do not construct threats purely for instrumentalist reasons: they do so because they are embedded in discursive constructions that inform them. *Securitising moves* thus reflect perceived threats in society at large: they reinforce security by institutionalising it.

Second, it has to be realised that threats do not appear out of the blue: they are linked to identity constructions. Discourse theorists have long argued that identity, like all meaning, is discursively, and relationally, constructed: one is defined by what one is not.[49] As Laclau and Mouffe put it: 'to be something

[48] L Hansen, *Security as Practice: Discourse Analysis and the Bosnian War* (Abingdon, Routledge, 2006) 18.

[49] E Laclau and C Mouffe, *Hegemony and Socialist Strategy: Towards a Radical Democratic Politics* (London, Verso, 2001) 106–28; J Torfing, 'Discourse Theory: Achievements, Arguments and

is always not to be something else'.[50] 'We' are defined against an 'Other', and there is 'always the possibility of this relation us/them becoming one of friend/enemy'.[51]

Indeed: when discourses of identity collide, 'social antagonisms' are created.[52] This happens 'when the others, who up to now had been considered as simply different, start to be perceived as putting into question our identity and threatening our existence'.[53] An 'Other' then becomes an enemy, a 'threat'.

Threats are therefore linked to a threatening 'Other'. But this does not mean that we *either* have to agree on everything, *or* are each other's enemy. An 'Other' can be accepted, and become part of an encompassing, higher identity. This happens when a common ground is found that can embrace difference. As Torfing writes, there are 'political attempts to make antagonistic identities coexist ... The political construction of democratic "rules of the game" makes it possible for political actors to agree on institutionalized norms'.[54]

Mouffe further elaborates on this: the aim, she argues, is to construct 'them' in a way 'that it is no longer perceived as an enemy ... but an "adversary", ie somebody whose ideas we combat but whose right to defend those ideas we do not put into question'.[55] This is possible through 'an allegiance to the democratic principles of "liberty and equality for all" while disagreeing about their interpretation'.[56] Hence there can be 'real confrontation ... regulated by a set of democratic procedures accepted by the adversaries'.[57] When this is not allowed, she warns, a 'ground is laid for ... politics articulated around essentialist identities of nationalist, religious or ethnic type and ... confrontations over non-negotiable moral values'.[58]

Identities can thus be constructed in different ways, and correspondingly threats and legitimate differences arise. To be democratic, it is essential that identity is based upon democratic procedures – which must arguably include human rights, and thus freedom of religion. An encompassing 'We' is then

Challenges' in D Howarth and J Torfing (eds), *Discourse Theory in European Politics: Identity, Policy and Governance* (Basingstoke, Palgrave MacMillan, 2005) 1–32, 14–15.

[50] Laclau and Mouffe (n 49) 128.

[51] C Mouffe, 'Democratic Politics And Agonistic Pluralism' (2009) accessible at http://consellodacultura.gal/mediateca/extras/texto_chantal_mouffe_eng.pdf, 7.

[52] M Jørgensen and L Phillips, *Discourse Analysis as Theory and Method* (London, SAGE, 2002) 48.

[53] Mouffe (n 51) 7.

[54] Torfing (n 49) 16.

[55] C Mouffe, 'Deliberative Democracy or Agonistic Pluralism' (2000) 72 *Reihe Politikwissenschaft – Political Science Series* accessible at www.ihs.ac.at/publications/pol/pw_72.pdf, 15.

[56] Mouffe (n 51) 9.

[57] ibid.

[58] ibid.

created, within which legitimate differences can exist. Alternatively, 'We' are defined in 'non-negotiable' ethnic or religious ways, which leads to the construction of an 'incompatible Other'.

This exposé remains quite abstract. But it can be usefully translated to freedom of religion, and limitations on this right, as the following examples make clear. The first example concerns religion 'X'. This religion demands that its followers sit in the middle of a crossroads for one hour daily. They disturb traffic and cause accidents. Reacting to this, a State, say Belgium, forbids this: the manifestation, it claims, is a threat to public order, public safety and the rights and freedoms of others.

This might appear unrelated to identity. But it actually is: it is only because not all of us belong to 'X', that we consider sitting in a crossroads a threat. The act becomes a threat because it has a different meaning to 'Us' and to 'Them', meanings that are incompatible. 'We' think of a crossroads as a means for traffic. 'They' think a crossroads is a religious place. Those meanings, embedded in larger discourses of identity, collide.

In this example, the struggle over the meaning over one particular issue, brings discourses of identity in conflict, not that 'X' is a threat. 'We' do not hold anything against 'X' as such. One can be Belgian and 'X' at the same time. However, because Belgian identity is also constructed upon democratic procedures and human rights, the particular manifestation becomes a threat that qualifies for one of the legitimate aims in Article 9.

Now consider the second example, concerning religion 'Y'. This religion demands that its followers paint a second set of eyes on their faces. Some people take offence at this. They feel that the religion demanding such things is bad and prescribes values they do not agree with, like gender inequality. They think the extra eyes have a proselytising effect, and impacts their rights. This, they feel, does not belong in 'our' society.

In this example too, a manifestation is constructed as a threat because of clashing identity constructions. But the logic is different. Here, the manifestation is threatening not in itself, but because of the meaning attributed to the religion it belongs to. 'Y' is considered incompatible with 'our' values, and its manifestation is therefore not acceptable. It is because the 'Other' is a threat, that manifestations expressing this 'Otherness' become a threat as well.

Here, the 'Other' becomes a threat because it challenges the meaning of 'Us'. Once 'We' are constructed in opposition to an 'Other', a collision develops when this 'Other' wants to become part of 'Us', of 'Our' society – it then challenges the way 'We' had constructed ourselves, since 'We' do not want 'Other' values in 'Our' society. The 'threat' in this example thus involves a value-judgement about a religion and its doctrine. And this not compatible with freedom of religion, as a measure based on a value-judgement about a specific religion violates conscience, and such a 'threat' cannot comply with a legitimate aim.

Apart from a purely legal analysis, identity thus offers an additional lens to analyse freedom of religion. Certain constructs will give rise to 'threats' and corresponding limitations that are not acceptable, since they are based on value-judgements about religion – a dimension the ECtHR neglects in its attitude towards legitimate aims. If a measure relies upon the construction of an incompatible 'Other', it is hard to reconcile with freedom of religion – and the concerned identity should be challenged. While not readily applicable in a purely legal sense, this approach allows to look at freedom of religion in a broader framework of identity, and offers additional ways to protect it.

In practice, this can be done by analysing threats, and the identities behind them, through discourse analysis. This is done mainly by identifying subject positions such as 'we' and 'them',[59] predications that further define these[60] and implicit assumptions.[61] Through such analysis, the identity constructs underlying measures or proposals can be revealed, and addressed or countered if needed. And this analysis can therefore provide an alternative, more emancipatory way to work towards more respect for freedom of religion, as will be demonstrated in the following section.

V. FLANDERS: SECURITISATION OF RELIGION

In the preceding pages, a framework was developed to study the link between identity and limitations on freedom of religion. As a case-study, we will now apply this to three proposals impacting freedom of religion, made in Flanders after the terrorist attacks of 22 March 2016:

- the initiative to change the Constitution;
- the proposal to ban the burkini; and
- the ban on ritual slaughter.

[59] Cf Jørgensen and Phillips (n 52) 15; M Laffey and J Weldes. 'Methodological Reflections on Discourse Analysis' (2004) 2(1) *Newsletter of the American Political Science Association: Organized Section on Qualitative Methods* 28–31; J Weldes, 'Constructing National Interests' in W Carlsnaes and S Guzzini (eds), *Foreign Policy Analysis – Volume II* (London, SAGE, 1996) 315–57, 326; J Milliken, 'The Study of Discourse in International Relations: A Critique of Research and Methods' (1999) 5(2) *European Journal of International Relations* 225–54, 239.

[60] Cf R Doty, *Imperial Encounters: The Politics of Representation in North-South Relations* (Minneapolis, University of Minnesota Press, 1996) 11; D Howarth and Y Stavrakakis, 'Introducing Discourse Theory And Political Analysis' in D Howarth, A Norval and Y Stavrakakis (eds), *Discourse Theory and Political Analysis* (Manchester, Manchester University Press, 2000) 1–23, 10; D Howarth, 'Applying Discourse Theory: the Method of Articulation' in D Howarth and J Torfing (eds), *Discourse Theory in European Politics: Identity, Policy and Governance* (Basingstoke, Palgrave MacMillan, 2005) 316–49, 341; R Wodak, 'The Discourse-Historical Approach' in R Wodak and M Meyer (eds), *Methods of Critical Discourse Analysis* (London, Sage Publications, 2001) 63–94, 73–74.

[61] Cf N Fairclough, *Analysing Discourse: Textual Analysis for Social Research* (London, Routledge, 2003) 56.

A. The Constitution

In the aftermath of the Paris attacks of November 2015, a federal parliamentary initiative was launched to examine whether the Belgian Constitution had to be changed. The initiative was taken by Patrick Dewael of the Flemish liberals, who stated that 2015 had been 'a tipping point'[62] and that 'there is increasing pressure on our fundamental values'. Politics, not courts, had to decide on issues like 'separate swimming hours for men and women'.[63] The starting point for the debate thus was that terrorism was related to the role of religion in society, and that religion was putting increasing pressure on 'our' values. Yet the cited examples revealed that the concern mostly was with one religion, Islam.

Initially, little happened. But the debate suddenly peaked in May 2016, when N-VA-members Vuye and Wauters rejected the other parties' proposals,[64] and brought forward their own. They wanted to make one simple change, adding: 'no one can put himself, on the ground of religious or philosophical motives, above the applicable rules of law, or limit the rights and freedoms of others'.[65]

Rather than 'simple', the purpose of this sentence is not exactly clear. It is, of course, already the case that no one can put himself above the law. Religious exceptions exist, but those are also prescribed by law: slaughter without stunning, for example, was forbidden in Belgium, but an exception existed for religious slaughter.[66]

The impression is therefore evoked that its purpose would be to make impossible such religious exemptions. That would not be a problem for the country's Christian majority, which has historically shaped the law. But a heavy burden would be imposed on relatively new groups, which seek accommodation by a legal system that was set up without taking their needs into account – in this case mostly Muslims, who started to migrate in large numbers to Belgium from the 1960s onwards. This would become impossible, and existing accommodation could be annulled by a simple majority decision.

What this addition would therefore amount to, is giving the majority a means to abolish the right to manifest religion for all non-majority groups. If applied, this would in itself be a violation of the right to freedom of religion – which, contrarily to the proposal, does not only demand a law, but also a legitimate aim and a pressing social need, as set out by Article 9(2) ECHR. And a deeper analysis further problematises it, since this makes clear that the proposal resulted not

[62] 'Lekenstaat – Dewael Vraagt Debat Over Karakter van de Staat en de Fundamentele Grondwaarden', *Belga*, 12 January 2016.

[63] T Peeters, 'Kamer Buigt Zich over Fundamenten van de Staat' *De Morgen*, 18 February 2016.

[64] 'Preambule bij de grondwet – Coalitiepartner MR verslikt zich in fors "njet" van N-VA' *Belga*, 10 May 2016.

[65] T Peeters and J Van Horenbeek, '"God Staat Niet Boven De Wet": N-VA Vraagt Expliciete Toevoeging Aan Grondwet' *De Morgen*, 10 May 2016, accessible at www.demorgen.be/politiek/-god-staat-niet-boven-de-wet-n-va-vraagt-expliciete-toevoeging-aan-grondwet-b13b2b07/.

[66] This has now changed – see s V.C.

from a general concern with religion, but from the construction of Islam as a threatening 'Other'.

Indeed, Vuye and Wauters argued: 'You see that today, there is a problem in Islam. A number of believers think that religious precepts stand above the law. Think, for example, about the burkas. That is not possible, and we have to be clear about that'.[67]

Clearly, they targeted one group in particular. Muslims aiming to live according to religious precepts that are not accommodated, were securitised and constructed as a 'threat'. The only way to be a non-problematic Muslim, was to not ask for accommodation. The message that was conveyed: yes, you can be a Muslim – but you cannot have habits different from what 'We' decide.

This analysis is confirmed by further statements, in which they explicitly stated that the proposed change was a response to the terrorist attacks, and that 'we can only live together in harmony if everyone knows our rules of the game, and accepts them'.[68] Linking the attacks and the need to change the Constitution, they constructed terrorism as an extension of those who want to 'put themselves above the law'. To prevent future terror, they implied, we have to make clear to Muslims that they have to accept 'our' rules of the game, thus creating a continuum from Muslims with incompatible values, to terrorism.

One final statement makes this abundantly clear. Vuye and Wauters wrote:

> This is not a juridical debate. It is political. … Religion belongs in the private sphere. There is a place for religions in our secular society, on the condition that they adapt to our society. … Not the state, but religions have to laicise … What we do not accept, is a society in which fundamental values, such as equality between men and women, are put aside because of religious and belief-related motives. For us no world with burka's in the street. Why not? … this is not how we, in our culture, see the dignity of women.[69]

The debate, they recognise, is political. Religions must 'adapt to our society' – yet the only religion mentioned is Islam. Muslims are welcome, but have to 'laicise', become secular. 'What we do not accept', they write, 'is a society in which fundamental values are put aside because of religious and belief-related motives'. But this does not concern law: it concerns people's convictions, beliefs and religions – those deemed to be of the Islamic kind, exemplified by the burka.

This burka was indeed banned in Belgium – but not primarily because it was deemed contrary to the dignity of women. The law banning the burka also banned all 'clothing that hides the face entirely or to a large extent', and

[67] Peeters and Van Horenbeek (n 65).

[68] H Vuye and V Wauters, 'Grondwetswijziging: Religie Kan Niet Boven de Wet Staan' *Vuyewauters.be*, 11 May 2016, accessible at https://vuyewouters.be/2016/05/11/ grondwetswijziging-religie-kan-niet-boven-de-wet-staan/.

[69] H Vuye and V Wauters, 'God, Allah, Jahweh: Niemand Staat Boven de Wet' *Knack.be*, 17 May 2016, accessible at www.knack.be/nieuws/belgie/god-allah-jahweh-niemand-staat-boven-de-wet/article-opinion-704075.html.

while arguments were made about gender equality, the main reasons were 'living together' and public safety.[70] The authors therefore recognised that this was a façade: the burka had to be banned because it was contrary to 'our culture'. And their proposal was to serve the same aim: banning manifestations that they perceived to be contrary to their values. More specifically: 'Islamic' values.

The concerned proposal, which could impact all religions, thus ensued from the construction of 'Muslims' as a threat, and aimed at the securitisation of manifestations of Islam. Specifically Islamic manifestations were targeted, because of the interpretation of Islam, and not for reasons 'external' to this religion. And such a measure, based on the perception of Islam as a 'threat', is difficult to reconcile with freedom of religion.

B. The Burkini

With the debate about the Constitution subdued, another matter burst into the newspapers. Following a ban on the burkini in several French cities, N-VA proposed to ban the burkini in Flanders too.

This proposal was launched by Nadia Sminate who argued:

> I do not believe that women … want to walk around on the beach in such a monstrosity. If you allow this, you also put women at the margin of society. We live in Flanders, and we make the rules. If we say that we have to draw borders and have our norms and values complied with, we have to also do it.[71]

While almost all parties rejected this,[72] Sminate's proposal was endorsed by Belgian Secretary of State for Asylum and Migration, Theo Francken (N-VA), who stated that the 'burkini is not a new fashion trend but a political struggle symbol for the oppression of women. … Who wears it, mostly has conservative or even Salafist ideas. That is why it does not belong to a modern society like ours'.[73] Even women choosing to wear it, should therefore be prevented from doing so, he argued: 'It might be that they grew up with it, and think a burkini is normal. But we have, as a democracy, the right to say that burkini's are not acceptable'.

Clearly, the proposal targeted only the burkini. It had to be banned because it was allegedly forced upon women, and relegated them to the margins of society. In Sminate's discourse, women wearing the burkini were excluded from 'our'

[70] 'Belgisch Boerkaverbod Goedgekeurd' *Knack.be*, 28 April 2011, accessible at www.knack.be/nieuws/belgie/belgisch-boerkaverbod-goedgekeurd/article-normal-22513.html; Grondwettelijk Hof, 'Arrest nr. 145/2012 van 6 december 2012'.

[71] FEM and DVL, 'N-VA Broedt op Verbod Boerkini's' *Standaard.be*, 17 August 2016, accessible at www.standaard.be/cnt/dmf20160816_02426939.

[72] MJA and WWI, 'N-VA is bijzonder bedreven in het creëren van onbestaande problemen' *Standaard.be*, 18 August 2016, accessible at www.standaard.be/cnt /dmf20160817_02428477.

[73] Bervoet and D'hoore, 'De Publieke Opinie is in Sneltempo aan het Radicaliseren' *De Tijd*, 20 August 2016.

society: their presence had to be 'prevented'. 'We' make the rules, and whoever comes here, has to adapt. Francken moreover made clear that not the burkini, but the ideas behind it were the problem. The burkini was an expression of conservative Islam, which did not belong in 'our' society. 'Our democracy' had the right to decide so.

The proposal thus resulted directly from the construction of Islam as a 'threatening Other'. The façade of a neutrally applicable law was not even made use of: from the earliest moment it was clear that only one piece of clothing was targeted. The burkini had to be banned because of the interpretation of the religion it belongs to. And such a measure, based on a value-judgement about religion, is incompatible with freedom of religion.

C. Ritual Slaughter

The last proposal we will analyse, is the now agreed upon ban on slaughter without stunning. Like the other proposals, it too was discussed in the wake of the Brussels attacks: a ban started to be contemplated in May 2016, and an agreement was reached one year later, in March 2017. However the ban has a longer history, as it was preceded by a ban on slaughter without stunning on temporary slaughter floors.

Contrarily to the analysis of the other episodes, this analysis is therefore not limited to the period *after* 22 March 2016, but includes relevant debates from September 2014 onwards, when ritual slaughter first became a hot topic in Flanders. And because this ban was eventually agreed upon by all parties, their positions are included too.

i. European Regulations and Temporary Slaughter Floors

In September 2014, Flemish Minister for Animal Welfare Ben Weyts (N-VA) announced he would introduce a ban on slaughter without stunning on temporary slaughter floors. At that time, slaughter without stunning was generally prohibited, but an exception existed on religious grounds. Commenting on his decision, Weyts told newspapers that 'there are alternatives: you can donate money. Another possible solution is to work with electro-narcosis … many Muslims accept this as ritual slaughter'.[74]

Clearly, Weyts meant to explicitly target the Islamic Feast of Sacrifice, for which many Muslims slaughter a sheep – which he explicitly confirmed.[75] Muslims would be the only ones affected by his decision, as no other group made use of temporary slaughter floors. The reason for his decision, Weyts argued,

[74] L Casagrande, 'Waar moeten we naartoe met onze 4.000 schapen?' *Het Belang van Limburg*, 15 September 2014.

[75] Vlaams Parlement, 'Vraag om Uitleg over de Slachtcapaciteit tijdens het Offerfeest' *Vlaamsparlement.be*, 13 May 2015, accessible at www.vlaamsparlement.be/ parlementaire-documenten/ vragen-en-interpellaties/969013.

was a 2009 European Regulation,[76] which demanded that slaughter without stunning take place in recognised slaughterhouses.[77]

Interestingly, the reactions of most political parties, N-VA's coalition partners as well as the opposition, were negative – with the exception of Hermes Sanctorum of the Green party and the extreme right Vlaams Belang. Sanctorum, aiming to represent 'vulnerable' voiceless animals,[78] said he did not think a ban violated freedom of religion,[79] since religion could not give people the right to make animals suffer.[80] Vlaams Belang framed it as a question of civilisation[81] and 'Islamization',[82] explicitly stating that 'Islam is a problem'.[83] But other parties were opposed citing human rights.

Indeed, Sonja Claes of the Christian Democrats (CD&V), N-VA's main coalition partner, argued that a ban would violate freedom of religion. 'It is not for us', she said, 'to talk about how they should do religious slaughter', arguing that the measure would make religious slaughter impossible.[84] Similarly, OpenVLD, N-VA's second coalition partner, evoked the ECHR. It noted that 'there is the juridical reality, which makes impossible a total ban on ritual slaughter on the basis of art 9 ECHR'.[85] And SP.A, the socialist opposition, stated that

> freedom of religion is deemed very valuable ... We have to therefore respect it ... Sometimes, it is said that the Muslim community does not care about animal welfare, but ... a Muslim, like any other human being, has respect for animals.[86]

[76] Council Regulation (EC) No 1099/2009 on the protection of animals at the time of killing [2009] OJ L 303/1.

[77] J Truyts, 'Vanaf 2015 verbod op onverdoofd slachten op tijdelijke slachtvloeren' *Deredactie.be*, 12 September 2014, accessible at http://deredactie.be/cm/vrtnieuws/ binnenland/1.2085117.

[78] Vlaams Parlement, 'Verslag Over Het Voorstel Van Decreet Houdende Wijziging Van Diverse Bepalingen Van De Wet Van 14 Augustus 1986 Betreffende De Bescherming En Het Welzijn Der Dieren, Wat Een Pijnloze Manier Van Sterven Van Te Slachten Dieren Betreft' *Vlaamsparlement.be*, 10 November 2016, accessible at www.vlaamsparlement.be/parlementaire-documenten/parlementaire-initiatieven/1094083.

[79] Vlaams Parlement, 'Vraag om Uitleg Over de Erkenning van Tijdelijke Slachtvloeren' *Vlaamsparlement.be*, 22 October 2014, accessible at www.vlaamsparlement.be/ parlementaire-documenten/vragen-en-interpellaties/929225.

[80] Vlaams Parlement, 'Verslag van de Gedachtewisseling over de Stand van Zaken in het Dossier van het Verdoofd en Overdoofd Slachten' *Vlaamsparlement.be*, 10 September 2015, accessible at www.vlaamsparlement.be/parlementaire-documenten/parlementaire-initiatieven/1001559.

[81] Vlaams Parlement, 'Verslag van de Gedachtewisseling over het Onverdoofd Slachten en het Offerfeest' *Vlaamsparlement.be*, 3 July 2015, accessible at www.vlaamsparlement.be/parlementaire-documenten/parlementaire-initiatieven/997110.

[82] Vlaams Parlement, 'Vraag om uitleg over het door de minister aangekondigde label voor onverdoofd geslacht vlees' *Vlaamsparlement.be*, 5 October 2016, accessible at www.vlaamsparlement.be/ parlementaire-documenten/vragen-en-interpellaties/1075365.

[83] Vlaams Parlement, 'Actuele Vraag over het Initiatief van een 'Tijdelijk Erkend Slachthuis' voor het Offerfeest in Antwerpen en het Verbod op Onverdoofd Slachten op Tijdelijke Slachtvloeren' *Vlaamsparlement.be*, 15 June 2016, accessible at www.vlaamsparlement.be/parlementaire-documenten/ vragen-en-interpellaties/1068006.

[84] ibid.

[85] Vlaams Parlement, 'Vraag om Uitleg over de Slachtcapaciteit tijdens het Offerfeest' *Vlaamsparlement.be*, 13 May 2015, accessible at www.vlaamsparlement.be/ parlementaire-documenten/ vragen-en-interpellaties/969013.

[86] ibid.

N-VA however countered that

> in more than half of the Islamic countries, Muslims accept reversible stunning as halal. Sorry, but then Muslims here have to just accept that. … if they do not want to give in, I see that as a problem, but rather their problem. … animal welfare goes above the right to freedom of religion.[87]

In the vision of N-VA, therefore, several things stood out. First, one of the main arguments was that ritual slaughter is not required by Islam. This however, is contrary to freedom of religion: it is not for outsiders to decide what is, or isn't, required. This is a question of conscience, and a state shouldn't interfere. The presumption underlying this, moreover, is that Muslims who practice ritual slaughter, are unreasonable. They have to just 'accept' stunning, and if not, it is 'their problem'.

Second, N-VA was – with the exception of Sanctorum and Vlaams Belang – the only party that saw a rigid opposition between animal welfare and freedom of religion. Supporting ritual slaughter was equalised with being against animal welfare. For the others, this opposition was not necessarily there. N-VA thus was the only major party that thought ritual slaughter was politically significant. And this is essential, because slaughter without stunning was already forbidden for everyone save Muslims and Jews. Muslims were not preventing others from slaughtering with stunning. The debate *only* concerned the exception. But this was deemed unreasonable by N-VA.

Indeed, parties opposing the ban, N-VA said, wanted 'to give only one group, the Muslims, a free letter'.[88] The underlying thought, rather than animal welfare, thus appeared to be that everyone had to act the same. And here the main difference with the opposing parties becomes clearest: while they might have morally opposed the practice, they did not think it had to be tackled politically. Ritual slaughter, for them, did not have to be '*securitised*'. Not because it was preferable, but because their concept of identity embraced freedom of religion for Muslims, who could be 'Flemish' if they continued to do so as well.

Despite this opposition, Weyts decided to go forth with the ban. And N-VA continued defending it, arguing that 'religious prescriptions cannot overrule the law', and that parties opposing the ban, made animal welfare subordinate to electoral gains.[89] 'The norms and rules in Flanders have to be followed', N-VA stated. 'Or do we want to also allow female genital mutilation and child marriages?'[90]

[87] Vlaams Parlement, 'Vraag om Uitleg Over een Mogelijke Erkenning van Tijdelijke Slachtvloeren als Slachthuis' *Vlaamsparlement.be*, 11 February 2015, accessible at www.vlaamsparlement.be/parlementaire-documenten/vragen-en-interpellaties/951476.

[88] Vlaams Parlement, 'Verslag Over het Voorstel van Resolutie Betreffende de Organisatie van het Offerfeest' *Vlaamsparlement.be*, 1 June 2015, accessible at www.vlaamsparlement.be/parlementaire-documenten/parlementaire-initiatieven/973286.

[89] ibid.

[90] ibid.

Stating that 'the norms and rules in Flanders have to be followed', N-VA explicitly focused the discussion on newcomers, bringing 'their', allegedly incompatible, norms and values. Accusing other parties of pursuing 'electoral gains', they moreover delegitimised listening to the Muslim community: defending religious slaughter could not be about freedom of religion, only about appealing to the votes of Muslims. Muslims were thus excluded from the political community, while the radical opposition of ritual slaughter to animal welfare put other parties under pressure. And the reference to female genital mutilation and child marriages further demonised them. By referring to these within the context of Islam, it was implied that if we accept religious slaughter, we open the door to further, threatening manifestations of Islam.

Clearly, therefore, ritual slaughter was constructed as a matter of 'us' against 'them' – of an 'incompatible' Islam against 'our' Flemish identity. At that time, other parties resisted. But things would change.

ii. From Temporary Floors to a Total Ban – And the Turn of Flemish Politics

In March 2016, the debate about slaughter was reinvigorated when Hermes Sanctorum brought forward a legislative proposal.[91] While N-VA in principle supported this, the proposal failed to get government support due to OpenVLD and CD&V's opposition.

Shortly after, Brussels was rocked by the terrorist attacks. But ritual slaughter remained on the agenda, and in a scheduled hearing, N-VA piled up the pressure, stating that even though there might no support for stunning among Muslims, there also is 'no support at all among the Flemish population for slaughter without stunning, 88 percent is against'.[92] Referring to numbers, N-VA again pitted the issue as one of 'us' against 'them'.

The following month, Weyts stated that N-VA would not take part in a future government without a ban on religious slaughter,[93] while Sanctorum tried his luck with his legislative proposal once again, joined by a similar proposal of the extreme right Vlaams Belang.[94] And interestingly, the parties that had initially opposed a ban, changed their positions.

Indeed: SP.A, which had formerly opposed a total ban – first in general, because of freedom of religion, and later because it specifically targeted Muslims – abandoned opposition. While it originally demanded the agreement of Muslim theologians, the party now simply noted that 'when animal suffering

[91] ibid.

[92] Vlaams Parlement, 'Verslag van de Hoorzitting over het Verbod op Onverdoofd Slachten Buiten de Erkende Slachthuizen' *Vlaamsparlement.be*, 14 April 2016, accessible at https://docs.vlaamsparlement.be/docs/stukken/2015-2016/g733-1.pdf.

[93] K Stragier, 'Totaalverbod op Onverdoofd Slachten in Zicht' *Het Laatste Nieuws*, 11 May 2016.

[94] E Vergauwen, 'N-VA wil verbod op onverdoofd slachten, door moslims én joden' *De Standaard*, 11 May 2016.

can be evaded, we have to do so'.[95] A few weeks later, OpenVLD also changed their position,[96] stating that 'we are in favour of a total ban on slaughter without stunning',[97] but asking for 'consultation with the religious communities' first.[98] While both originally invoked freedom of religion to defend ritual slaughter, all traces of this now disappeared.

Only CD&V now still opposed a ban, and on their insistence, an advice was asked from the Council of State, to determine whether a total ban would be compatible with freedom of religion.[99] In this advice, the Council stated:

> The lawmaker can … strive to reduce animal suffering for ritual slaughter as far as possible … without however ignoring the freedom of religion by, as is the case in this case, imposing an unconditional prohibition on slaughter without stunning.[100]

This advice might have led to shelving the issue. But reacting to the advice, Weyts declared that

> this is a societal vision of 20 years ago. It stands so far from the societal reality today in which Flemish people, luckily, attach much more importance to animal welfare. I think it is the damn duty of a civilized society to maximally evade each instance of animal suffering that can be evaded.[101]

N-VA thus designated those opposed to a ban – including judges – as uncivilised, not part of the Flemish people and pro-animal suffering.

Weyts subsequently decided to appoint an 'independent mediator' to mediate between religious groups.[102] But the goal remained the same: a total ban.[103] He thus ignored the Council of State, which stated that an unconditional ban would disregard freedom of religion, and reacted to the objection by announcing that he would do exactly what it had warned against. One month later, moreover, the president of his party, Bart De Wever, published an opinion piece, mentioning religious slaughter. 'Increasing integration', he wrote

> can never mean that you slow down inevitable evolutions to more openness. … No one can systematically rely on a religion to get exceptions from generally

[95] ibid.

[96] L Casagrande, 'CD&V houdt het been stijf' *Het Belang van Limburg*, 25 May 2016.

[97] ibid; Vlaams Parlement, 'Actuele Vraag over het Initiatief van een "Tijdelijk Erkend Slachthuis" voor het Offerfeest in Antwerpen en het Verbod op Onverdoofd Slachten op Tijdelijke Slachtvloeren' *Vlaamsparlement.be*, 15 June 2016, accessible at www.vlaamsparlement.be/parlementaire-documenten/vragen-en-interpellaties/1068006.

[98] Casagrande (n 96).

[99] E Vergauwen, 'CD&V krijgt meer tijd voor onverdoofd slachten' *De Standaard*, 25 May 2016.

[100] Vlaams Parlement, 'Advies van de Raad van State over het Voorstel van Decreet Houdende Wijziging van de Wet van 14 Augustus 1986 … wat Betreft het Invoeren van een Verbod op het Onverdoofd Ritueel Slachten' *Vlaamsparlement.be*, 29 June 2016, accessible at www.vlaamsparlement.be/parlementaire-documenten/parlementaire-initiatieven/1072449.

[101] R Wauters, 'Raad van State tegen verbod op onverdoofd slachten' *De Morgen*, 30 June 2016.

[102] ibid.

[103] B, 'Ex-Boerenbond-topman moet pad effenen naar verdoofd slachten' *Het Belang van Limburg*, 14 July 2016.

> applicable rules. Not to mention blocking democratic decisions, supported by an overwhelming majority of the population.[104]

He thus explicitly shifted the debate from animal welfare to integration and democracy. The issue was one of integration: Muslims do not want to integrate. They sabotage democracy – for if 'we' decide something, 'they' have to listen.

At around the same time, he also referred to CD&V's support for ritual slaughter. 'They accuse me of saying CD&V is a Muslim-party', he said

> [but] I only remark that CD&V is the only party that continues supporting ritual slaughter ... That CD&V branches organize an *iftar* during Ramadan, while lent and Easter pass without attention. May I then conclude that CD&V aims for the votes of Muslims?[105]

Muslims' religious concerns, he implied, should not be listened to.

And a final statement summed it up. De Wever said:

> We promote the '*leitkultur*', inburgering, we are against open borders and we will not say that your own symbols such as Black Pete have to be done away with, and you nevertheless have to tolerate for example slaughter without stunning. The cultural discomfort is stronger with us than the economical, because in the end we all have it relatively well.[106]

He thus clearly constructed the question of ritual slaughter as one, not of animal welfare, but of integration and identity. The issue was with Muslims, bringing 'their' symbols to 'our' society, while 'our' symbols are attacked. It was a 'cultural discomfort', not animal welfare, that drove the ban. People who come here, have to become 'us'. And Islam as it was perceived, did not fit into that.

All political parties eventually agreed on the ban, supposedly with the support of the religious communities. Yet it quickly appeared that there was no compromise at all: the Jewish and Muslim communities rejected the ban.[107] But this did not change anything, N-VA argued. 'We have to make clear to them that laws in this country have primacy over all religious rules', Flemish minister-president Geert Bourgeois said.[108] 'This is how a democracy works'.[109]

One final time therefore, the issue was explicitly focused on 'new' Flemish people. Ritual slaughter was not necessarily about animal welfare: it was about 'new' people adapting to 'our' values – more specifically: Muslims. Their values

[104] B De Wever, 'Onverdoofd slachten is niet meer van deze tijd' *De Tijd*, 2 August 2016.

[105] J Segers, 'CD&V Begrijpt Ons Met Opzet Verkeerd' *Het Laatste Nieuws*, 22 August 2016.

[106] D Dujardin, 'Tussen zes planken willen ze mij buitendragen' *Het Laatste Nieuws*, 26 November 2016.

[107] JC, TT and RW, 'Moslimexecutieve verwerpt akkoord onverdoofd slachten' *De Morgen*, 30 March 2017.

[108] SAN, 'Moslims verdeeld over "historisch akkoord"' *Het Nieuwsblad*, 30 March 3017.

[109] Belga, 'Bourgeois en Weyts: "Wetten hebben voorrang op religieuze gebruiken"' *HLN.be*, 30 March 2017, accessible at www.hln.be/hln/nl/957/Binnenland/article/detail/3117362/ 2017/03/30/ Bourgeois-en-Weyts-Wetten-hebben-voorrang-op-religieuze-gebruiken.dhtml.

were deemed incompatible with being Flemish – and only by shedding theirs, could they truly become Flemish.

It thus clearly appears that NV-A's discourse could not be separated from concerns about 'integration'. To N-VA, a ban on ritual slaughter was about more than animal welfare. It was about 'our' norms, 'our' opinions, 'our' democracy. Ritual slaughter was explicitly framed as a matter of 'cultural discomfort'.

Again therefore, the influence of the Islamic 'Other' on the debate about religious slaughter is clear. Concerns about animal welfare *were* present – but the underlying reason for concern was a 'threatening' Islam. Ritual slaughter – and not eg hunting – became a political concern, because it was deemed an expression of the unwillingness of the 'Other' to 'integrate' in our society, and the threat this posed to 'our' values.

D. Conclusion: Flemish or Muslim, not Both

Throughout the case-studies, it appeared that a construction of Muslims as the incompatible 'Other' fuelled the proposals. This was most explicitly the case for the burkini: it had to be banned because it threatened 'our values'. The same was true, though less directly, for the Constitution and ritual slaughter. The Constitutional change had to prevent 'threatening' manifestations of Islam such as the burka. And ritual slaughter was politicised and banned, primarily because of a 'cultural discomfort'. In a purely legal analysis, the latter two proposals might pass. But from the perspective of identity, it becomes clear that they arose only because 'Islam' was deemed incompatible with 'our' identity. And such a value-judgement about Islam is difficult to square with freedom of religion. Considering a religion a 'threat', cannot comply with a legitimate aim.

Islam, it appeared, was considered incompatible with Flemish values by the largest political party in Flanders, N-VA. 'We' were constructed in opposition to the values of the 'other', 'Islam' – a construction reminiscent of Edward Saïd's *Orientalism*,[110] and its paradigmatic contemporary incarnation, Huntington's 'Clash of Civilizations'. According to Huntington, Western civilisation is fundamentally different from Islam, and they can never be compatible. Islam, he wrote, has 'bloody borders'.[111]

This line of thought appears to lie behind the construction of Flemish identity that made possible these proposals. NV-A's discourse of Flemish identity is one that considers Islam a 'threat'. Being 'Flemish' is identified with adhering to 'Western values', and defined in opposition to 'incompatible' Islamic ones. Not respecting human rights, but intangible values define who is part of 'us', and who is the 'other'. And this construction transforms Muslims into a 'threat'

[110] Edward Saïd, *Orientalism* (New York, Vintage Books, 1979).
[111] Samuel P Huntington 'The Clash of Civilizations?' (1993) 72(3) *Foreign Affairs* 22–49.

when they are not anymore abroad, but living in Flanders, and claim Flemish identity.

As demonstrated, this has a direct impact on the right to freedom of religion for Muslims, as it makes possible the analysed proposals. If this identity construct remains dominant, similar proposals will continue to surface. Indeed – in the meantime, proposals were, for example, launched to prohibit religious symbols for religions that make up more than five per cent of the population – targeting, once again, Muslims.[112] In order to ensure freedom of religion for all citizens, a more inclusive discourse of identity should therefore be worked on.

VI. CONCLUSION

This chapter had two main aims. First, it wanted to reassess the basis for the right to freedom of religion. And second, it wanted to highlight the role of identity in limitations on this right.

To that end, it was, first, demonstrated that only conscience can justify a right to freedom of religion. This justification mandates that manifestations of religion are protected rigorously. But the ECtHR, it was shown, fails at doing so. Rather, it has committed to a doctrine that allows States to interpret, and pass judgement on, religions. When this happens, conscience is violated, and this is incompatible with the essence of this right. In order to consistently protect the right to freedom of religion, we concluded, the ECtHR should therefore review its doctrine, and restrict the margin of appreciation it affords to States in matters of religion. It should not be up to States to define the meaning of religion.

Second, it was demonstrated that clashing identity constructions make possible the 'threats' to legitimate aims that are required to limit manifestations of religion. Different mechanisms of 'threat' exist, and threats that arise because an 'Other' is deemed incompatible with 'Our' values cannot be a legitimate basis to limit freedom of religion, since they do not pursue a legitimate aim and violate conscience. The case-study of Flanders post-terrorist attacks illustrated this mechanism, and made clear that exactly such a construction of identity gave rise to several proposals to limit freedom of religion, including a ban on ritual slaughter. 'Islam' was deemed incompatible with Flemish identity, and this creates a structural problem for freedom of religion for Muslims in Flanders, to which an emancipatory answer is needed.

[112] 'Hendrik Bogaert pleit voor verbod op grote en zichtbare religieuze tekens, maar wordt teruggefloten door eigen partij CD&V: "Dom voorstel"', *Belga*, 18 December 2017, accessible at www.hln.be/nieuws/binnenland/hendrik-bogaert-pleit-voor-verbod-op-grote-en-zichtbare-religieuze-tekens-maar-wordt-teruggefloten-door-eigen-partij-cd-v-dom-voorstel~a25bb50f/.

This chapter thus concludes with a specific demand for the ECtHR to change its doctrine, and a broad call to devote sufficient attention to the identity constructs, and shines a spotlight on the current battle for Flemish identity. It is in all likelihood an illusion to think that any of these will lead to rapid change. But the important matter is that awareness be raised. Freedom of religion *is* contentious, and will remain a very thin line to thread. Religions may indeed have values one does not agree with.

But exactly that is the essence of this human right.

Part III

9

Ban on Faith-based Schools?

LOTTA LERWALL

I. INTRODUCTION

A. Background

IN THIS CHAPTER the possibilities for the Swedish legislator to prohibit – or in other ways limit the actions of – faith-based independent schools, are discussed in the light of the European Convention on Human Rights.[1]

The existence of faith-based independent schools has been a topic of debate for some time in Sweden. Emotions occasionally run high in this debate, although the proportion of faith-based independent schools and the number of pupils who attend them is relatively low. During the 2017/18 academic year, 9,501 pupils attended a primary and lower-secondary school that was faith-based, or what Swedish law describes as a 'confessional focus'. The equivalent figure for upper-secondary school was 827 pupils. In all, this includes 71 schools, five of which are at the upper-secondary level.[2] In all, 60 of the faith-based independent schools have a Christian focus, 10 have a Muslim focus, while one school is Jewish.[3] In March 2018 the Swedish government appointed an inquiry to explore the possibilities of limiting faith-based elements in education.[4] Following a political agreement between the government and the Liberal and the Center Party, the objective for the inquiry was amended in May 2019. The task is

[1] This chapter has previously been published in Swedish, in (2018) 7 *Svensk Juristtidning* 523–41.

[2] The figures were taken from the official statistics of the Swedish National Agency for Education for the 2017/18 academic year. A total of 1,050,000 pupils were enrolled in primary and lower-secondary school during the same academic year, including 156,400 who attended a free school. A total of 347,863 pupils attended upper-secondary school, including 92,191 who attended an independent school.

[3] Since schools are not required to indicate whether or not they have a religious focus, the exact number of schools and pupils involved cannot be determined.

[4] Directive 2018:15 Faith-based elements in the school system (*Konfessionella inslag i skolväsendet*).

now to submit the necessary proposals in order to stop the establishment of new faith-based independent schools.[5]

The arguments for and against banning faith-based independent schools are many and varied. One argument is that a ban would contravene the European Convention. This text addresses the question of whether Article 2 of the First Additional Protocol to the European Convention on Human Rights regarding the right to education prevents a ban on faith-based schools and what other options there are otherwise for the Swedish legislator to change the conditions for running faith-based independent schools.

B. Faith-based or Non-faith-based Education and Teaching

In Sweden, education in publicly administered schools is required to be non-confessional.[6] However, education that is not publicly administered may include a faith-based focus, but *teaching* at such schools may not be faith-based.[7] This means that teaching may not include any faith-based elements in either municipal schools or independent schools. Teaching is a narrower concept than education and refers to 'such goal-oriented processes aimed at development and learning through the acquisition and development of knowledge and values under the leadership of teachers or preschool teachers', while education is a broader concept referring to 'the context in which teaching is conducted based on specific objectives'.[8] Based on this distinction between education and teaching, activities in the schoolyard and dining hall are included in education, but they are not included in teaching. Consequently, devotional practices, morning worship, prayer meetings and other forms of religious practice, along with religious symbols, are permitted as long as they occur outside teaching.[9] In order for these practices to be permitted, participation in confessional elements must be voluntary.[10]

A private entity wanting to operate an independent school must apply for approval as an administrator.[11] Preschools submit their application to the municipality. Most of the remaining school forms submit their application to the Swedish Schools Inspectorate.[12] Approval must be granted if the conditions

[5] Directive 2019:25 Additional directives (*Tilläggsdirektiv till Utredningen om konfessionella inslag i skolväsendet*). The inquiry will submit its report on 19 December 2019.

[6] Ch 1 art 6 of the Swedish Education Act (2010:800).

[7] Ch 1 art 7 of the Education Act.

[8] Ch 1 art 3 of the Education Act.

[9] Government bill 2009/10:165 The new education act – for knowledge, freedom of choice and security (*Den nya skollagen – för kunskap, valfrihet och trygghet*) 225–226 and 636.

[10] Ch 1 art 7 of the Education Act.

[11] Ch 2 art 5 of the Education Act.

[12] Preschool classes, primary and lower-secondary schools, upper-secondary schools, special needs schools at the primary and lower-secondary school level or upper-secondary school level, or after school recreation centres (as specified under ch 2 art 7).

stipulated are met. A private entity who receives permission to operate an independent school is entitled to so-called 'school vouchers'[13] from the municipality. This means that independent schools receive public funding on the same terms as the municipality's own schools.[14]

II. THE RIGHT TO EDUCATION ACCORDING TO THE EUROPEAN CONVENTION

The right to education is recognised in Article 2 of the First Additional Protocol.[15] It states:

> No person shall be denied the right to education. In the exercise of any functions which it assumes in relation to education and to teaching, the State shall respect the right of parents to ensure such education and teaching in conformity with their own religious and philosophical convictions.

The article consists of two sentences; the first stipulates the right to education and the second stipulates that the State must respect the right of the parents to ensure that their children receive an education that is consistent with the religious and philosophical convictions of the parents. The two sentences should be read in light of each other, but also in light of freedom of expression (Article 10), freedom of religion (Article 9) and the right to respect for private and family life (Article 8).[16] There is also a clear link to the democratic society. The European Court of Human Rights has stated that the second sentence in Article 2 'aims first and foremost at safeguarding the possibility of pluralism in education, which possibility is essential for the preservation of "democratic society"'.[17]

The First Additional Protocol was adopted in 1952 and entered into force in 1954 after ratification by 10 States, including Sweden. When the protocol entered into force, Sweden reserved the right regarding Article 2 not to grant exemptions from certain compulsory aspects of public-school education. Moreover, Sweden reserved the right to only grant exemptions from Christianity lessons for children with other religious beliefs. Sweden withdrew this reservation in 1995.[18] Thus from that time forward, Sweden undertook to fully respect the rights of parents to ensure that their children received an education that is consistent with their religious and philosophical convictions.

[13] In Swedish: *skolpeng*.

[14] Ch 8 arts 21–24, ch 9 arts 19–22, ch 10 arts 37–39, ch 11 arts 36–38, ch 14 arts 15–17, ch 16 arts 52–55, ch 17 arts 31–36 and ch 19 arts 45–48.

[15] ETS No 9.

[16] *Hasan and Eylem Zengin v Turkey* App no 1448/04 (ECtHR, 9 January 2008) [cit *Zengin v Turkey*] para 47; *Leyla Şahin v Turkey* App no 44774/98 (ECtHR 10 November 2005) para 155.

[17] *Köse and others v Turkey* App no 26625/02 (ECtHR 24 January 2006) para 26. *Zengin v Turkey* (n 15) para 48.

[18] Council of Europe, Treaty Office.

In 1997 a provision permitting independent schools to have a faith-based focus was implemented for the first time in the 1985 Education Act (1985:1100).[19] The government bill stated that requiring education to be non-faith-based would be inconsistent with Sweden's international commitments (ie the European Convention).[20] The statement gives the impression that the government felt that a regulation banning faith-based elements in teaching would violate the European Convention. The government bill for the 2010 Education Act expresses the opposite view. It states that the purpose of the requirement for teaching to be non-faith-based is precisely to ensure that education is objective, critical and pluralistic, as guaranteed by Article 2 of the First Additional Protocol.[21] Thus not only is non-faith-based teaching considered to be consistent with the Convention, it is also considered to contribute to ensuring compliance with the Convention. However, the question is whether completely banning faith-based schools or requiring *education* to be non-faith-based is consistent with the Convention.

III. 'NO PERSONS SHALL BE DENIED THE RIGHT TO EDUCATION'

A. Access to Existing Education

In spite of its negative formulation, the first sentence of Article 2 entails that basic education is in fact a right. Referring to the preamble to the protocol, the European Court of Human Rights ruled in the 1968 '*Belgian Linguistic case*' that there is no doubt that the Article enshrines a right.[22] The European Court has stated that a narrow interpretation of the first sentence of the Article would be in conflict with the aim and purpose of the article. The Article thus aims to ensure that no one shall be denied access to the education that is available at a certain time. However, this does not require the States to establish certain educational institutions.[23]

The concept that no one may be denied access to the education that is already available also follows from the prohibition of discrimination under Article 14 of the Convention. The *Belgian Linguistic case* also showed that a measure that in

[19] Ch 9 art 2 para 2, Swedish Code of Statutes 1996:1044.

[20] Government bill 1995/96:200 Independent schools, etc (*Fristående skolor m.m.*) 32.

[21] Government bill 2009/10:165 p 226. See also Certain school issues (*Vissa skollagsfrågor*) Part 2, (2 Sept 2014) reg no U2014/5176/S, p 17.

[22] Case 'Relating to certain aspects of the laws on the use of languages in education in Belgium' App no 1474/62 and others (ECtHR 23 July 1968) [cit *Belgian Linguistic case*] s B para 3.

[23] *Belgian Linguistic case* (n 21) paras 3–4, *Leyla Şahin v Turkey* (n 15) paras 135, 137 and 141, *Tarantino et al v Italy* App no 25851/09 and others (ECtHR 2 April 2013) para 43; *Çam v Turkey* App no 51500/08 (ECtHR, 23 February 2016) para 52; *Velyo Velev v Bulgaria* App no 16032/07 (ECtHR, 27 August 2014) paras 31 and 34; *Catan et al v Moldova and Russia* App no 43370/04 and others (ECtHR, 19 October 2012) para 137; *Ponomaryovi v Bulgaria* App no 5335/05 (ECtHR, 28 November 2011) para 49.

itself complies with the requirements of Article 2 of the first Additional Protocol may be in violation of the Article when read in conjunction with Article 14.[24]

It should also be noted that the European Court of Human Rights has ruled on several occasions that Article 2 does not distinguish between education in public and private schools with respect to both the first and second sentences of the article.[25]

B. The Right to Education May be Restricted

Although Article 2 of the First Additional Protocol entails a right to education, formulated without exception, it is not entirely absolute. It may be limited. The State may regulate the right to education, but such restrictions must not curtail the right in question to such an extent as to impair its very essence and deprive it of its effectiveness.[26] According to the Court, any restrictions must be foreseeable for those concerned and must fulfil a legitimate aim, in order to be acceptable restrictions on the right to education. It may be noted that unlike other articles in the Convention, Article 2 of the First Additional Protocol is not bound by an exhaustive list of legitimate aims.[27] Also, as in the case of restrictions on Convention rights in general, the restriction in question must be proportional to the objective pursued. The State must strike a balance between the need for education of the affected individuals and the ability of the State to meet the needs.[28] The Court has expressed that education is a special form of community service to which the individual is entitled, and which also contributes to a democratic society in a broader perspective. Moreover, the right to education is said to be special because it enjoys direct protection under the Convention.[29] The Court has also emphasised that the right to education is indispensable for the promotion of human rights and, therefore, so important that it may not be restrictively interpreted. A restrictive interpretation would not be consistent with the aim or purpose of the Article.[30]

[24] *Belgian Linguistic case* (n 21) para 9.

[25] *Kjeldsen, Busk Madsen and Pedersen v Denmark* App no 5095/71 et al (ECtHR, 7 December 1976) para 50; *Costello-Roberts v United Kingdom* App no 13134/87 (ECtHR, 25 March 1993) para 27; *Leyla Şahin v Turkey* (n 15) para 153, *Tarantino et al v Italy* (n 22) para 52; *Zengin v Turkey* (n 15) para 48; *Folgerø et al v Norway* App no 15472/02 (ECtHR, 29 November 2007) para 84 (b).

[26] *Velyo Velev v Bulgaria* (n 22) paras 32–33; *Tarantino et al v Italy* (n 22) para 44. See also *Konrad v Germany* App no 35504/03 (ECtHR, 11 September 2006) p 7; *BN and SN v Sweden* App no 17678/91 (ECtHR, 30 June 1993); *Ponomaryovi v Bulgaria* (n 22) para 53.

[27] See eg *Catan et al v Moldova and Russia* (n 22) para 140.

[28] *Tarantino et al v Italy* (n 22) para 45; *Leyla Şahin v Turkey* (n 15) para 154; *Ponomaryovi v Bulgaria* (n 22) para 55.

[29] *Velyo Velev v Bulgaria* (n 22) paras 32–33; *Ponomaryovi v Bulgaria* (n 22) para 55; *Çam v Turkey* (n 22) para 52.

[30] *Kjeldsen, Busk Madsen and Pedersen v Denmark* (n 24) para 52 and *Timishev v Russia* App no 55762/00 and others (ECtHR, 13 March 2006) para 64.

In Sweden, the municipalities have the primary responsibility for providing education in the school system.[31] According to Chapter 1, section 8 of the Education Act, everyone shall have equal access to education in the school system regardless of geographical residence, etc. In addition, Chapter 1, section 9 requires education to be equivalent regardless of where it is provided in Sweden. Unlike independent schools, municipal schools are required to provide education within the school system (one of the mandatory tasks of the municipality). However, a (faith-based) independent school has the option to discontinue its operations at any time. The above has two implications: everyone covered by the provisions of the Education Act has equal access to education without discrimination and this access to education is guaranteed without the presence of independent schools. It can therefore not be said that a person 'is denied the right to education' if faith-based schools were not permitted. The existing education system is available on equal terms for everyone. Consequently, the first sentence of Article 2 poses no obstacle to restricting the ability to run a faith-based independent school. No one would be excluded from access to education if such a restriction were to be imposed.

IV. RESPECT FOR THE CONVICTIONS OF THE PARENTS

A. Rights of the Parents versus Rights of the Child

The second sentence in Article 1 of the First Additional Protocol stipulates an obligation for the States to respect the right of the parents to ensure such education and teaching in conformity with their own religious and philosophical conventions. According to the European Court of Human Rights, this obligation is based on the fact that the parents are primarily responsible for the education and teaching of their children, but surrender their natural duty towards their children to the State through the school.[32]

As previously mentioned, the second sentence should be read together with the first sentence regarding everyone's right to education, as well as in light of Articles 8, 9 and 10.[33] Since the second sentence should be read together with the first – about everyone's right to education – the obligation to respect the right of the parents extends only so far that the child's right to education is not restricted. In other words, the child's right to education takes priority over the parents' right to have their religious and philosophical convictions respected.[34] Article 2

[31] The *school system* includes the types of schools specified in ch 1 art 1 of the Education Act.

[32] *Zengin v Turkey* (n 15) para 50.

[33] *Kjeldsen, Busk Madsen and Pedersen v Denmark* (n 24) paras 50 and 52, *Costello-Roberts v United Kingdom* (n 24), *Folgerø et al v Norway* (n 24) para 84 (a) para 27.

[34] *Konrad v Germany* (n 25) p 6 and *BN and SN v Sweden* (n 25).

of the First Additional Protocol overlaps with Article 9 on freedom of thought, conscience and religion, concerning the content of the teaching and the requirement that the parents' right to ensure that the education their children receive is consistent with their convictions. The European Court of Human Rights has ruled that in this regard Article 2 of the first Additional Protocol is *lex specialis* in relation to Article 9, but should be read in the light of the article.[35]

B. Teaching and Education

According to the wording of Article 2, the obligation to respect the convictions of the parents applies to both education and teaching. Thus, the obligation does not concern only the content of the teaching and the way in which it is provided, but refers to what is included in 'education' in Sweden and therefore also includes lunch breaks, work environment etc.[36] Moreover, it can be concluded that the obligation to respect the convictions of the parents applies to *all* teaching and not just when teaching religion.[37] As mentioned above, however, this does not prevent the State from determining the setting and content of the teaching. On the contrary, the Article is formulated in such a way that it 'by its very nature' calls for the State to regulate the structure of education and its curriculum content (etc) and this may vary by time and place.[38]

The requirement in the second sentence of Article 2 of the First Additional Protocol does not mean that education and teaching are required to be completely free of religious or philosophical elements that could be in conflict with the convictions of the parents. On the contrary, the European Court of Human Rights has concluded that teaching could not be carried out with absolutely no religious or philosophical elements. A recurring comment found in the European Court of Human Rights' case law is that 'states are not prevented from imparting through teaching or education information or knowledge of a directly or indirectly religious or philosophical kind'.[39] Such elements are actually a natural aspect of teaching and there is a risk that education would be impossible if it did not include such elements.[40] In other words, parents cannot require the State to provide a certain type of education, nor does the Article give the parents the right to object to the inclusion of religious or philosophical

[35] *Lautsi et al v Italy* App no 30814/06 (ECtHR, 18 March 2011) para 59 and *Osmanoğlu and Kocabaş* v *Switzerland* App no 296086/12 (ECtHR, 10 January 2017) para 35.

[36] See *Lautsi et al v Italy* (n 34) para 63.

[37] *Kjeldsen, Busk Madsen and Pedersen v Denmark* (n 24) para 51, *Zengin v Turkey* (n 15) para 49.

[38] *Konrad v Germany* (n 25) p 7, *Folgerø et al v Norway* (n 24) para 84 (g), *Zengin v Turkey* (n 15) para 51.

[39] *Kjeldsen, Busk Madsen and Pedersen v Denmark* (n 24) para 53.

[40] ibid para 53, *Lautsi et al v Italy* (n 34) para 62. *Folgerø et al v Norway* (n 24) para 84 (g), *Zengin v Turkey* (n 15) para 51.

elements in education.[41] Hence, they cannot deny the child the right to education because of their convictions.[42]

For such religious or philosophical elements to be considered consistent with the convention, teaching must be conveyed in an objective, critical and pluralistic manner. States are forbidden to pursue an aim of indoctrination (see below at IV.C).

C. Requirement for an Objective, Critical and Pluralistic Approach

The purpose of the second sentence of Article 2 of the First Additional Protocol is to guarantee pluralism in teaching, which is considered necessary to ensure a democratic society in accordance with the Convention.[43] Teaching may not be indoctrinating, but must be carried out objectively, critically and pluralistically to enable pupils to develop a critical approach to religion. Inherent to the pluralism requirement is the obligation of the State to take a neutral approach to the different religions and refrain from expressing a position regarding the legitimacy of different religious beliefs and how they are expressed.[44]

In the case *Kjeldsen, Busk Madsen and Pedersen v Denmark* (1976), the parents objected to the requirement that their children participate in compulsory sex education, which the parents considered to be contrary to their convictions. The Danish State argued that the purpose of sex education was to provide the children with information based on science. The European Court of Human Rights found that such information naturally includes considerations relating to a religious or philosophical sphere and that to some extent the purpose of the teaching involved morality. However, no indoctrination aimed at advocating specific sexual behaviour was involved; the purpose was general in nature and the Court ruled that it did not overstep the boundaries of what could be considered to be of public interest in a democratic State.[45]

In the case *Folgerø et al v Norway* (2007), however, the Court found that the national legislation did not comply with the requirements for objectivity and pluralism since there was a both quantitative and qualitative imbalance in favour of the subject Christianity. The conclusion was that the Norwegian State

[41] *Kjeldsen, Busk Madsen and Pedersen v Denmark* (n 24) para 53, *Lautsi et al v Italy* (n 34) para 61, *Folgerø et al v Norway* (n 24) para 84 (g).

[42] *Konrad v Germany* (n 25) p 6 and *BN and SN v Sweden* (n 25).

[43] *Kjeldsen, Busk Madsen and Pedersen v Denmark* (n 24) para 50. *Konrad v Germany* (n 25) p 6, *Folgerø et al v Norway* (n 24) para 84 (b), *Zengin v Turkey* (n 15) para 55, para 48 and 55, *Catan et al v Moldova and Russia* (n 22) para 138.

[44] *Kjeldsen, Busk Madsen and Pedersen v Denmark* (n 24) para 53, *Folgerø et al v Norway* (n 24) para 84 (h) and 85, *Catan et al v Moldova and Russia* (n 22) para 138, *Zengin v Turkey* (n 15) paras 52 and 54.

[45] *Kjeldsen, Busk Madsen and Pedersen v Denmark* (n 24) paras 52–54.

violated Article 2 by not granting an exemption from Christian and religious instruction.[46]

In *Lautsi v* Italy (2011) the question involved whether the presence of crucifixes in classrooms was consistent with Article 2 of the First Additional Protocol and Article 9 of the Convention. The European Court of Human Rights ruled that while a crucifix is a religious symbol, it is in itself insufficient to constitute indoctrination. Moreover, the fact that there is some overemphasis favouring a particular religion does not necessarily mean that the State overstepped its margin of appreciation. An emphasis in teaching about a particular religion can be explained by the country's history and traditions.[47]

The case *Osmanoğlu and Kocabaş v Switzerland* (2017) involved a requirement for participation in compulsory mixed-gender swimming lessons in the context of compulsory schooling. The question was whether denial of exemption from this requirement violated the right to freedom of religion in Article 9.[48] When assessing whether the restriction on the exercise of religious freedom was permitted, the European Court of Human Rights emphasised the Swiss State's argument about the risk of exclusion if pupils do not participate in all teaching and the importance of promotion of social integration in school.

According to the Court, the social factor was particularly important for foreign pupils. The importance attached to ensuring that the applicant's children received the whole of the educational programme on offer at their school so as to further the local authority's vision of social integration outweighed the applicants' wish to have the children exempted from attending swimming lessons. Thus, the child's right to education took precedence over the parents' interest in having their beliefs respected. Moreover, the Court found that the authorities had offered the applicants special arrangements by allowing the daughters to wear a burkini. The conclusion was that the State may require pupils to follow the curriculum and give precedence to successful integration over the parents' interests in obtaining an exemption for their daughters from mixed-gender swimming lessons on religious grounds. As in assessments based on the second sentence of Article 2 of the First Additional Protocol, the Court thereby gave precedence to the child's right to education over the parents' right to respect for their convictions. Switzerland was not found to have exceeded its margin of appreciation.[49]

The European Court of Human Rights has stated in several rulings that the parents are not deprived of the opportunity to educate and advise their children

[46] *Folgerø et al v Norway* (n 24) paras 95–102.

[47] *Lautsi et al v Italy* (n 34) para 71.

[48] The case was tried in relation to Art 9 since the Swiss State had not ratified the First Additional Protocol.

[49] *Osmanoğlu and Kocabaş v Switzerland* (n 34). Warnling-Nerep and Bernitz discuss this decision in (2017) *Förvaltningsrättslig Tidskrift* (a Swedish Administrative Law Journal) 689.

themselves, as the child's natural educators, and to thereby guide them in a direction that is in line with their own beliefs.[50]

Based on the above, the main purpose of the second sentence of Article 2 is to contribute to a democratic society by emphasising pluralism in education.[51] This purpose includes safeguarding the child's right to education and preventing the child from being subjected to indoctrination contrary to the parents' philosophical or religious beliefs. However, when balancing the interests of all parties, the parents' interest in ensuring that their children receive an education that is in line with the beliefs of the parents does not take priority over the child's right to education.

According to the Swedish Education Act, teaching must be non-faith-based, regardless of whether carried out in public or independent schools.[52] As mentioned above, Article 2 of the First Additional Protocol does not prevent the State from determining the setting and content of teaching, as long as it is pluralistic and non-indoctrinating.[53] Swedish curriculums are intended to meet these requirements. The Swedish Supreme Administrative Court has found no 'particular grounds' (which is required by the Education Act) to support home-schooling children in a Jewish orthodox family. The Court declared that the Education Act is formulated in such a way that all pupils can participate, regardless of religious or philosophical beliefs, since the Act requires teaching to be all-incomprehensive and objective.[54] One conclusion is therefore that there are indicators that the Swedish legislation regarding education is in line with the second sentence of Article 2 of the First Additional Protocol.[55]

So far the conclusion can be drawn that Article 2 of the First Additional Protocol does not focus on who has the right to provide education, or the right to specific content in the education. On the contrary, it focuses on safeguarding democratic values regarding freedom of religion by protecting against overly one-sided religious education and promoting the concept that a democratic society is built through a pluralistic education.[56] It is also clear that the right to education applies in both public and private schools, that the education must be provided in an objective, critical and non-indoctrinating manner, and that the child's right to education trumps the parents' interests in having their religious or philosophical convictions respected in the children's education.

[50] *Kjeldsen, Busk Madsen and Pedersen v Denmark* (n 24) para 54, *Köse et al v Turkey* (n 16), *Lautsi et al v Italy* (n 34) para 75.

[51] *Köse et al v Turkey* (n 16), *Zengin v Turkey* (n 15) paras 48 and 54.

[52] Ch 1 arts 6–7 of the Education Act.

[53] *Konrad v Germany* (n 25) p 7, *Folgerø et al v Norway* (n 24) para 84 (g), *Zengin v Turkey* (n 15) para 51.

[54] Swedish Supreme Administrative Court case 2013 No 49, HFD 2013 ref 49.

[55] See also government bill 2009/10:165 p 226 and Certain school issues Part 2 p 17.

[56] *Köse et al v Turkey* (n 16) para 26, *Zengin v Turkey* (n 15) paras 48 and 54.

V. RIGHT TO ESTABLISH A PRIVATE SCHOOL

The wording of Article 2 of the First Additional Protocol does not provide for any right to establish private schools. As noted above, it focuses on the individual's right to education and the State's obligation to ensure the parents' right to receive respect for their convictions when their children participate in education. The above review shows that the Article and the case law of the European Court of Human Rights primarily address the right of individuals to *receive* education, not the right to *provide* education.

Nevertheless, Article 2 of the First Additional Protocol is considered to include a right to establish private schools and universities. In *Kjeldsen, Busk Madsen and Pedersen v Denmark*, the European Court of Human Rights found that there is a freedom of teaching included in the right to education, ie a freedom to establish private schools.[57] The Court referred to the preparatory works (*travaux préparatoires*) to the protocol, which indicate that there were several proposals for how the Article should be formulated. One of these said:

> the right of parents to ensure … and, where schools have been established by the State, to send their children to any other school of their choice, provided that such school conforms with the requirements of the law.[58]

However, this draft text was deleted and the final wording of the Article does not explicitly express the right to establish private schools. Despite the absence of an explicit right, it is considered to exist. The European Court of Human Rights emphasised however, that the preparatory works did not reveal any additional intention to go further than specifically guaranteeing a right to establish private schools.[59] The preparatory works show that the opinions were many and diverse regarding the meaning of Article 2 and the rights of the parents. Lengthy discussions were held before the Member States finally agreed on the wording, and only after some States lodged reservations.[60] According to the European Court of Human Rights, all comments submitted by the different delegates show that the main point was to ensure that *State teaching* in public schools must be carried out with respect for the parents' religious and philosophical convictions. The Court concluded: 'The second sentence of Article 2 (P1-2) aims in short at safeguarding the possibility of pluralism in education which possibility is essential for the preservation of the "democratic society"'.[61]

The standpoint, that the Article mainly focuses on education as a way to achieve a democratic society and the role of freedom of religion contributing to

[57] *Kjeldsen, Busk Madsen and Pedersen v Denmark* (n 24) para 50.

[58] Council of Europe, Preparatory work on Article 2 of the Protocol to the Convention, pp 149, 160 and 201.

[59] *Kjeldsen, Busk Madsen and Pedersen v Denmark* (n 24) para 50.

[60] Council of Europe, Preparatory work on Article 2 of the Protocol to the Convention, p 206–08.

[61] *Kjeldsen, Busk Madsen and Pedersen v Denmark* (n 24) para 50.

a democratic society, is also evident in the subsequent case law of the European Court of Human Rights. As noted in the previous section, the obligation of the States is primarily to protect against limitations to freedom of religion, not to provide – or finance (see below at section VI.D) – an education that is consistent with the convictions of the parents.

VI. POSSIBILITY OF REQUIRING NON-FAITH-BASED EDUCATION?

A. Conditions for Running Independent Schools

Considering the proportionally low number of schools and pupils in Sweden that would be affected by a ban, it can be questioned whether it is actually necessary to ban faith-based schools. The debate refers to more or less horrendous examples of schools and incidents that reflect flagrant inadequacies in compliance with the Education Act, which of course can evoke strong emotions. However, it should be clarified that the problem with these schools is lack of compliance, not the actual existence of faith-based schools. If these schools were to comply with the Education Act and its regulations, as well as associated regulatory requirements, such as the question of the core values (regarding human rights and fundamental democratic values) in Chapter 1, sections 4–5 of the Education Act, the problems described above would cease to exist. *One* way to address the problems described in the discussion of this issue could be to improve and strengthen the supervision and quality review of these schools and to impose sanctions when deficiencies are found – and by extension, revoking their permits.[62]

However, *if* the objective is to limit opportunities to provide education with a faith-based focus, it should be discussed whether and how this could be done without violating the obligations under the First Additional Protocol of the European Convention. In *Kjeldsen, Busk Madsen and Pedersen v Denmark*, the Court only said that there is a right to establish and run private schools, that this right arises through the preparatory works to the protocol and that it is closely linked to the interest in the existing formulation of the second sentence in Article 2 of the First Additional Protocol – to ensure objectivity, pluralism and non-indoctrination in education to guarantee that the parents' convictions are respected.[63]

What options for action are available to the Swedish legislator if the intention is to ban or limit the possibilities to operate independent schools with a faith-based focus? As I see it, there are at least three options that can be discussed:

1) Impose a ban on establishing faith-based independent schools;

[62] Ch 26 art 13 of the Education Act.

[63] *Kjeldsen, Busk Madsen and Pedersen v Denmark* (n 24) para 50. This is the case referred to in subsequent rulings on the right to establish private schools.

2) Allow the existence of faith-based independent schools, but require both teaching and education to be free of faith-based elements;
3) Allow faith-based independent schools, but both teaching and education must be non-faith-based to qualify for public funding.

B. Option 1: *Ban* on Faith-based Schools

This option entails denying permits for 'faith-based administrators' to run a school. In *Kjeldsen, Busk Madsen and Pedersen v Denmark*, the Court ruled in favour of the right to establish private schools, but nothing in the decision says that the right to establish private schools includes the right to establish private schools with a particular focus. On the contrary, the ruling states that an additional intention to go further than specifically guaranteeing a right to establish private schools is not evident from the preparatory works.[64] What this means is unclear.

However, it is clear that Article 2 includes a right to establish private schools and that this right is not unlimited. It can be noted that already in the draft to Article 2, which explicitly included the right of establishment, it was stated that one requirement for opening private schools is that they must comply with the requirements of the law.[65] The legislator can thus set requirements for the education provided in independent schools. This is further addressed under option two below.

As Article 2 includes a right to establish private schools, a ban on establishing independent schools would be in conflict with the European Convention. If this ban only applies to faith-based schools, it would amount to discrimination in violation with Article 14.

Article 14 of the European Convention states that 'the enjoyment of the rights and freedoms set forth in this Convention shall be secured without discrimination on any ground such as … religion … or other status'. Thus, the Article does not define discrimination, but it follows from the Court's case law that discrimination refers to a difference in the way individuals in a similar situation are treated, which cannot be justified by legitimate reasons. '[D]iscrimination means treating differently, without an objective and reasonable justification, persons in similar situations'.[66] To justify such differences in treatment, there must be

[64] ibid para 50.

[65] Council of Europe, Preparatory work on Article 2 of the Protocol to the Convention, pp 149, 160 and 201.

[66] *DH et al v Czech Republic* App no 57325/00 (ECtHR, 13 November 2007) para 175, *Çam v Turkey* (n 22) para 54 and *Enver Şahin v Turkey* App no 23065/12 (ECtHR, 30 January 2018) para 61.

reasonable justification and the measure must be proportionate in relation to these objectives.[67]

By prohibiting only faith-based organisations from establishing independent schools, they are being treated differently than other presumptive administrators and the reason for this differential treatment is associated with religion. Such differential treatment must pursue a legitimate aim and be proportionate; ie the State must be able to justify the discrimination. The fact that the right to establish private schools derives from the discussions held regarding the second sentence of Article 2 at the time that the protocol was drafted suggests that it was religious private schools in particular that were considered to be an alternative to the state school. This, in turn, suggests that it is likely that very weighty reasons would be required to exclude religious organisations from the opportunity to establish independent schools. The presence of problems at a few schools is most likely not sufficient grounds to motivate such a far-reaching measure. The argument that faith-based schools are an obstacle to integration is probably also not sufficient to justify a total ban on faith-based schools. About 10,000 pupils attend faith-based schools at the primary, lower-secondary and upper-secondary levels.[68] The question is whether the impact of a ban on integration could be considered to be more than marginal and it is, in my opinion, uncertain whether such a measure would suffice as 'weighty reasons' to justify exclusion of religious organisations when the total number of students in primary and secondary schools is closer to one and half a million students. My conclusion is that it is most unlikely that the European Court of Human Rights would consider a *ban* on faith-based independent schools to be consistent with the prohibition of discrimination in the Convention.

C. Option 2: Allow Faith-based Independent Schools to Exist, but with the Requirement that Both Teaching and Education are Free of Faith-based Elements

The second option would allow administrators representing a certain religious orientation to operate independent schools (while receiving public funding), but to extend the prohibition on faith-based elements to cover both teaching and education. This would mean that all faith-based elements are prohibited in education, but the right to establish independent schools remains intact.

According to the second sentence of Article 2, the responsibility of the State extends to the 'functions which the state assumes' (in relation to education and to teaching). By financing operations at independent schools, it can be said

[67] *Çam v Turkey* (n 22) para 54, *Enver Şahin v Turkey* (n 65) para 61.

[68] Statistics from the Swedish National Agency for Education, www.skolverket.se/statistik-och-utvardering (obtained 19 April 2018).

that their functions fall within the framework of what the State has 'assumed' and that equal treatment of public and private schools regarding the content of education must be considered to fall within the State's sphere of action. However, the State's right to regulate the content of the education extends even farther.

As was already noted, the State has the right to regulate the setting of the education and its content, and that this may vary over time and space (see section IV.B).[69] The right to establish a private school is not unlimited but may be subject to legal requirements.[70] A regulation specifying requirements for staff qualifications, content of education, minimum number of pupils, etc, to be eligible to run a private school is consistent with the Convention. This is also the conclusion reached in the government bill for the 2010 Education Act.[71] The government bill states that Article 2 'essentially implies a right to establish private schools, but the state can set requirements for the standard and content of the education and the teachers' qualifications'.[72] The preparatory work referred to by the European Court of Human Rights states that private schools should also be subject to national regulations.[73] In other words, the State can set requirements for content even for education that does not receive public funding.

Already now, the education provided in independent schools must meet certain requirements for the independent school to receive a permit under Chapter 2 section 5 of the Education Act. A basic requirement is that the private administrator must have the ability to comply with the regulations that apply for education. As was mentioned above, the school must live up to the core values set out in Chapter 1, sections 4–5 of the Education Act. Moreover, both teaching and education 'must rest on scientific grounds and proven experience' (Chapter 1, section 5, paragraph 3). As an aside, the question may be asked how this requirement can be consistent with allowing faith-based elements in education at independent schools. This question is not addressed in the government bill. As was previously mentioned, the Swedish legislator considered it to be necessary to require that teaching at Swedish schools must be non-faith based in order to live up to the requirements of the Convention.[74] If the content of teaching falls within the State's sphere to decide, an extension to include the content of the education as a whole in the prohibition against faith-based elements, would not violate the convention.

[69] *Belgian Linguistic case* (n 21) paras 31–32, *BN and SN v Sweden* (n 25), *Folgerø et al v Norway* (n 24) para 84 (g), *Zengin v Turkey* (n 15) para 51.

[70] See also *Ingrid Jordebo foundation of Christian Schools and Ingrid Jordebo v Sweden* App no 11533/85 (ECtHR, 6 March 1987).

[71] This is also discussed in Council of Europe, Preparatory work on Article 2 of the Protocol to the Convention, p 167 f.

[72] Government bill 2009/10:165 p 226, Certain school issues Part 2 p 17.

[73] Council of Europe, Preparatory work on Article 2 of the Protocol to the Convention, pp 149, 160 and 201.

[74] Ch 1 arts 6 and 7 of the Education Act, Government bill 2009/10:165 p 226.

The conclusion is that the State is entitled to regulate the content of education and may therefore require education to exclude faith-based elements, regardless of the administrator and regardless of whether or not the State contributes funding. One fact that supports this conclusion is that the European Court of Human Rights has ruled on several occasions that Article 2 does not distinguish between education in public and private schools with respect to either the first or the second sentences of the Article.[75] A change according to this option would thus likely be consistent with the European Convention.

D. Option 3: Require Both Teaching and Education to be Non-faith-based to Receive Public Funding

The third option would require both teaching and education to be free of faith-based elements to receive public funding, but faith-based elements would be allowed in independent schools without public funding. It should be noted here that the current Swedish system prohibits admission fees and other fees.[76] In other words, faith-based independent schools cannot be financed by fees. Consequently, the conditions for running faith-based independent schools would radically change. Thus, this option would require radical changes in the Swedish Education Act in order to allow for admission fees, tuition fees etc. Otherwise, the opportunity to establish independent schools without public funding would in most cases just be an illusion.

From the perspective of the European Convention, it should first be clarified that the right to establish private schools does not entail a right to receive state funding for the school. At the time Article 2 was formulated, there was consensus on omitting the issue of state funding for private schools from the Convention.[77] Wording to this effect was therefore intentionally deleted from the proposal.[78] This was confirmed in the *Belgian Linguistic case*, where the European Court of Human Rights found that the Convention does not affect the freedom of the State with respect to whether or not it wants to fund private schools.[79] This conclusion was repeated in *W and KL v Sweden* in the mid-1980s when the Commission clarified that the State 'did its part' by allowing private schools. Denying these financial contributions was not considered to be in violation of the Convention.[80]

[75] *Kjeldsen, Busk Madsen and Pedersen v Denmark* (n 24) para 50. *Costello-Roberts v United Kingdom* (n 24) para 27, *Leyla Şahin v Turkey* (n 34) para 153, *Tarantino et al v Italy* (n 22) para 52, *Zengin v Turkey* (n 15) para 48, *Folgerø et al v Norway* (n 24) para 84 (b).

[76] See ch 8 art 20, ch 9 art 8, ch 10 art 10, ch 11 art 13, ch 12 art 10, ch 13 art 10, ch 15 art 17, ch 18 art 17, ch 20 art 7 and ch 21 art 6 of the Education Act.

[77] Council of Europe, Preparatory work on Article 2 of the Protocol to the Convention, p 202.

[78] ibid.

[79] *Belgian Linguistic case* (n 21) para 13.

[80] *W and KL v Sweden* App no 10476/83 (ECtHR, 11 December 1985). See also *Verein Gemeinsam Lernen v Austria* App no 23419/94 (ECtHR, 6 September 1995).

Also when considering this option, the issue of discrimination in violation of Article 14 of the Convention is relevant when determining compatibility with the European Convention. Is it discrimination if a system funds some independent schools, but not all of them?

As stated above, the first criterion for determining whether discrimination is present involves determining whether there has been a differential treatment in similar or analogous situations parties are treated differently in the same situation. One view would be to claim that discrimination has not occurred when all independent schools must meet the same conditions to obtain public funding.

Another approach would be to argue that indirect discrimination against religious administrators is present on the grounds of religion. The European Court of Human Rights has ruled that equal treatment in situations that are different may also constitute discrimination.[81] The argument, with this approach, would be that the effect of the relevant requirement on the religious community would be disproportionately severe. With such an approach, the State would have to justify the conditions for public funding.

I have only found two older cases (from the former Commission) that address the issue of discrimination against private schools regarding public financing. The above-mentioned decision *W and KL v Sweden* involved a parent cooperative that wanted to start a Waldorf independent school. The school's application for 'school social assistance' was rejected.[82] The benefit was a publicly funded subsidy for school books, school meals, etc, which was initially paid to pupils based on means testing, but in this case was paid directly to the school without the prior evaluation of student needs. The question was whether the fact that some independent schools received the relevant subsidy, but not others, constituted discrimination in violation of the Convention. The Commission concluded that the discrimination between different independent schools rested on an *objective and reasonable basis* with reference to a wide measure of self-government and independence in matters falling within the jurisdiction of the local authorities. The differences in treatment therefore did not constitute discrimination.

The Commission concluded that the subsidy was paid by the municipalities, which have a considerable amount of autonomy and independence regarding cases that fall within their jurisdiction in Swedish law and that this order is based on long historic tradition. Since the regulation was based on the idea that local authorities are best qualified to decide on school issues within their area, the decision rested on an objective basis, even though differences could arise between different independent schools. The reasoning is somewhat unclear, but

[81] *Thlimmenos v Greece* App no 34369/97 (ECtHR, 6 April 2000) para 44. See also *Çam v Turkey* (n 22) para 54 and *DH et al v Czech Republic* (n 65) para 175.

[82] See government bill 1982/83:1 p 28, UbU 1982/83:10 p 16 f and the Swedish Education Ordinance (1971:235). Hans Liljeson commented on school social assistance in (1985) *Förvaltningsrättslig Tidskrift* pp 125–36.

the conclusion was hence, that because the municipal council decided within the framework of municipal autonomy, the decision did not constitute discrimination in violation of the Convention.

Can corresponding reasoning be used for the third option? To begin with, it can be concluded that a requirement originating from the legislator (State level) cannot be justified under the principle of municipal autonomy. Would the situation be different if the central government instead allowed the municipalities to decide on the right to school vouchers based on the presence of faith-based elements in education? In my opinion, the reasoning in the above-mentioned case is far too unclear to serve as a basis for departure from protection against discrimination. The prohibition of discrimination requires that differential treatment can be justified with objective reasons, which entails that it must pursue a legitimate aim and be proportionate. A general sweeping reference to municipal autonomy therefore probably does not suffice.

In *Verein Gemeinsam Lernen v Austria*, the applicant argued that it was subject to discrimination because church schools were the only private schools financed by public funds in Austria. The applicant, which was an association that ran a private school in Vienna, was not granted public funds since it was not considered to be a 'need', which was a criterion for funding under Austrian legislation. According to the applicant this difference in treatment violated the European Convention's prohibition of discrimination. The Commission stated that Article 2 of the First Additional Protocol does not impose any obligation on the State to subsidise a particular type of education, but Article 14 imposes an obligation not to discriminate if such subsidies are granted.[83]

The government regulation required that the school corresponded to a need of the community to receive government funding. The Commission argued that the church schools were a widespread phenomenon in Austria and that they – unlike the applicant – catered for a large number of pupils, and had done so for a long time. The Commission concluded that treating church schools differently from the applicant's school was justified since there would be a considerable burden on the State if the educational services provided by the church schools fell, as the State would have to make up the shortfall in schools. Consequently there were objective grounds that justified the difference in treatment.

The decisive factor in the above case was the *need* for the schools. Without them, the Austrian State would have had problems. Such an argument cannot be cited for either faith-based schools or independent schools in Sweden. Since providing school services is mandatory for municipalities, they are obliged to provide education regardless of the existence of independent schools. The municipalities already bear the burden of providing education in the event that independent schools should cease operation.

[83] *Verein Gemeinsam Lernen v Austria* App no 23419/94 (Commission decision, 6 September 1995).

The two decisions described above cannot be said to provide guidance on how presumed discrimination under the third option could be justified. The grounds for justifying differential treatment cannot be used in the present situation. Arguing that some independent schools with a faith-based focus demonstrate serious problems probably would not suffice, either. When considering goals and means, it would seem that the problems are not so great that remedial measures should affect all faith-based schools.

The argument that faith-based schools pose an obstacle to integration has also been raised in the Swedish debate. Although it is difficult to predict how the European Court of Human Rights would make its ruling, it can be concluded that integration as a purpose for the school system would be accepted as a reasonable justification. In cases concerning compulsory schooling and the issue of exemption from certain aspects of teaching, both the former Commission and the European Court of Human Rights have accepted arguments about integration and social training to justify requirements for compulsory class attendance in conflict with the desires of the guardian.[84] However, what the position of the Court would be regarding the proportionality assessment is somewhat more dubious when regulation would affect such a small proportion of pupils in the school system under this option.

VII. SUMMARY

In summary, it can be concluded that the first sentence in Article 2 does not prevent a ban on faith-based schools since this part of the Article aims solely to guarantee the right to education. The second sentence in the Article, however, prevents a ban on establishing independent schools. Moreover, a ban on establishment aimed exclusively at faith-based organisations is also inconsistent with the prohibition of discrimination in Article 14 of the Convention.

The Convention probably does allow law-makers to require education and teaching to exclude faith-based elements, since Member States have the right to set requirements for the content of education and Article 2 does not aim to provide education in accordance with specific religious beliefs.

It is more uncertain how a scheme that would require education to exclude faith-based elements to receive public funding would hold up in light of the Convention. The decisive factor would be whether or not the faith-based independent schools are considered to be subjected to discrimination in relation to other independent schools. Personally, I would argue that the third option does not entail any indirect discrimination against the faith-based independent schools. Given that the Convention does not express an absolute right to

[84] *BN and SN v Sweden* (n 25), *Konrad v Germany* (n 25), *Osmanoğlu and Kocabaş v Switzerland* (n 34) para 96.

provide teaching in accordance with a particular belief, nor does it impose an obligation on the States to provide funding for private schools, the State's margin of interpretation should include the ability to set the terms for providing funding.

The above conclusions are drawn without considering many other aspects that should be considered in practice, which are not discussed above. For example, there is nothing to prevent children in schools with a faith-based administrator from staying in school after the end of the school day to participate in faith-based teaching. Moreover, the question of the individual's right to freedom of religion has not been addressed. For example, how should the phenomenon of pupils joining together during breaks, etc to practise their faith be viewed? Thus, it is not without some suspense that we await the findings of the inquiry on faith-based elements in the school system when it presents its final report.

10

The Swedish Education System and its Challenges in a Multicultural Society

HEDVIG BERNITZ

I. INTRODUCTION

THIS CHAPTER AIMS at discussing and analysing the question of how (and whether) the Swedish school system is equipped to take care of and meet the needs of pupils with other religious beliefs and other traditions than those that are regarded as traditionally 'Swedish'. The basis for the discussion is the principle of the best interests of the child, and the right of society to influence pupils to encompass the values of the Swedish community.

Sweden of today is a multicultural society, where old Swedish traditions have been mixed with new influences from all over the world. This phenomenon is not new, as Sweden has had a high influx of immigrants since the Second World War.[1] The number of immigrants has varied over the years, peaking in the 1960s (labour immigration), in the 1980s (refugees mostly from Iran) and in the 1990s (refugees from Yugoslavia). The latest big wave of immigrants came between 2015 and 2017, when about 400,000 people arrived in Sweden. In 2015, there were about 70,000 asylum-seeking children. The majority of those children came from Syria, Afghanistan and Iraq.[2]

The number of immigrants creates a mixture of cultures that appears everywhere and must be integrated into Swedish society. Schools form one part of the social organisation where this variety of cultures is especially noticeable. Irrespective of their background, children registered in Sweden will meet during their nine years of compulsory school (for children aged from six to about 15).[3]

[1] Åke Nilsson, 'Efterkrigstidens invandring och utvandring' (Statistiska Centralbyrån, 2004). Between 1850 and 1930, Sweden was a country of emigration. During that period, 1.5 million people left the country with most going to North America. Since the Second World War about 2.4 million people have moved to Sweden and 1.4 million have emigrated.

[2] www.scb.se.

[3] Swedish Education Act (Skollag (2010:800) c 7.

As many pupils have other traditions and other religious beliefs than those that are considered to be traditionally 'Swedish', most schools have to deal with a multicultural situation.[4] Taking care of and integrating children from all over the world is a huge challenge for the Swedish school system as such and also, of course, for individual schools as well as for individual teachers. This challenge demands adjustments, patience and competence.

As regards religion, Sweden is a Protestant, albeit highly secularised, country. Religious freedom has, until recently, seldom been discussed in modern society. Religion is considered to belong to the private sphere, and it takes up very little space in the everyday life of most Swedes.[5] The large number of immigrants who have come to Sweden in the last few years has, however, emphasised and put the spotlight on religious issues. Public interest in religious questions has therefore increased. The new discussion on religion in society has, however, focused a great deal on Muslim traditions and how they fit into everyday Swedish life.

In the secularised Swedish society of today, the different ideas behind being religious are not really considered. The fact that being religious is more than just belonging to a religious community (that you are in other words, for example, a Muslim, a Catholic or a Jew); is sometimes abstruse for a secularised Swede. In Swedish public debate, it is rarely mentioned that religion and religious life also include a freedom of religious expression and the right to respect for private religious life. Being religious is above all also a question of identity, including for children when they are at school.

Freedom of religion is regarded as part of freedom of opinion in Swedish national law, and is laid down in the very first paragraph of one of the fundamental laws which make up the Swedish Constitution, namely the Instrument of Government. Chapter 1 article 1 states that 'Swedish democracy is founded on the free formation of opinion and on universal and equal suffrage'. What freedom of opinion entails is expounded in Chapter 2, on the rights and freedoms of the individual, and guaranteed by the freedom of expression, the freedom of information, the freedom of assembly, the freedom to demonstrate, the freedom of association and the freedom of worship.[6]

The freedom of worship, that is the freedom of religion, gives everybody the right to practise their religion alone or in the company of others.[7] This also

[4] Swedish schools are, however, very segregated. Children with well-educated Swedish parents often attend certain independent schools, while the number of pupils with foreign parents with a low level of education is increasing in the municipal schools.

[5] According to a survey from 2011, 34 per cent of the Swedish population claimed that religion was 'not at all important'. 38 per cent claimed that is was 'not very important'. Only 8 per cent claimed that religion was 'very important'. World Values Survey, www.worldvaluessurvey.org/WVSOnline.jsp.

[6] Instrument of Government, c 2 art 1 pt 1–6.

[7] The Instrument of Government, c 2 art 1 pt 6: 'Everyone shall be guaranteed the following rights and freedoms in his or her relations with the public institutions: … freedom of worship: that is, the freedom to practice one's religion alone or in the company of others.'

includes the right for pupils and teachers to manifest their religion at school. Freedom of religion also encompasses a legislative protection against discrimination or persecution.

The right to religious identity is, however, not expressly mentioned in the Swedish Constitution. If identity is defined as the right to believe in whatever religion or faith an individual chooses, it is protected by the freedom of religion. If identity is defined as wearing certain religious clothes or symbols, or manifesting your beliefs in public, it is, however, instead protected under the right of (religious) expression. The reason being that freedom of religion shall be interpreted narrowly in Swedish law.[8] It only encompasses a right to 'believe', which also includes a right to manifest that belief in situations where the person in question does not affect his or her surroundings. This means that, for example, praying in private is protected by the freedom of religion, whereas organising a religious demonstration or wearing religious clothes are not.

Religious actions and manifestations that do not affect the right to 'believe' could instead sometimes be protected by the constitutional rights of expression, assembly, information, to demonstration, or association. For example, organising a religious meeting is protected under the freedom of association, and the right to evangelise is protected under the freedom of expression. In this regard, the freedom of religion in the Swedish Constitution differs from the European Convention on Human Rights. Article 9 of the Convention does not only include a 'belief' but also different kinds of actions and manifestations as long as they have an *intimate link* to the religion.[9] The European Convention on Human Rights was implemented as Swedish law in 1995.[10] The Constitution also prescribes that 'No act of law or other provision may be adopted which contravenes Sweden's undertakings' under the Convention.[11]

Whereas the rights of Article 9 in the Convention may be limited by law after a proportionality test according to Article 9.2, the Swedish constitutional freedom of religion may never be limited. The other Swedish freedoms mentioned above may, however, all be limited in law, but only to satisfy a purpose that is acceptable in a democratic society. The limitation must never go beyond what is necessary with regard to the purpose which occasioned it, nor may it be carried so far as to constitute a threat to the free shaping of opinion as one of the cornerstones of democracy. No limitation may be imposed solely on grounds of a political, religious, cultural or other such opinion.[12] This means that the

[8] T Bull and F Sterzel, *Regeringsformen – en kommentar* 3rd edn (Lund, Studentlitteratur, 2015) 67–68.

[9] *Arrowsmith v United Kingdom* App no 7050/75 (Commission Decision, 12 October 1978).

[10] Law (1994:1219) on the European Convention on Human Rights.

[11] Instrument of Government, c 2 art 19.

[12] Instrument of Government, c 2 art 21. The freedom of opinion and the right to express yourself in printed documents or in more technical media is protected in two other fundamental laws: Freedom of the Press Act and Freedom of Expression Act.

right to believe and practise one's religion may never be limited, but the right to manifest that religion by wearing certain clothes, organising or joining religious communities, or holding public meetings may be restricted in accordance with a proportionality test.

The Swedish Education Act (from 2010) emphasises every pupil's right to keep his or her own identity at school, but it does not expressly mention religious identity. There is no doubt, however, that every pupil, as well as every teacher, has full freedom of religion at school and that schools shall acknowledge everybody's right to have and to manifest their own religion. This also includes a right for pupils to organise their own religious activities at school.

The only mention of religion in the Swedish Education Act is a provision laying down that both teaching and education must be non-confessional in municipal schools. In independent schools the teaching must be non-confessional, but there may be religious elements during the rest of the school day, for example, during shorter breaks or the lunch break.[13] Apart from studying different religions and their impact, Swedish schools thus provide no room at all for religion in teaching. Instead, schools shall provide an all-around education that, in accordance with the case law of the European Court of Human Rights, is objective, critical and pluralistic,[14] and has a scientific basis.

Schools have, of course, a very important role to play in conveying the values of Swedish society. The Swedish education system is therefore based on, and strongly emphasises, a set of democratic values that everybody is assumed to accept and support.[15] Those values represent opinions and ideals that most Swedish people can accept and agree on, and are therefore considered to be fully objective and neutral (see further, part 2).

However, it is important to take into account the fact that values stipulated by the state can never really be neutral or completely objective. They always represent the state's own preferences, and mirror the opinions of the majority. This is not in itself a problem; it is part of the democratic process to lay down values that the majority can agree on. Still, as regards the values chosen to govern the Swedish education system, it would probably be more correct to label them as 'Swedish' or maybe 'European', but not as universal. They only represent the opinions of the Swedish majority, and encompass values and principles that the majority thinks ought to be universal.

You should also take into consideration that when it comes to religion, schools encounter other sets of values than those based on democracy and proclaimed by the state. The religious sets of values are based on religious beliefs and religious traditions. Those values govern many people's lives, and when they meet the 'objective' values of the Swedish education system that meeting

[13] Swedish Education Act, c 1 arts 6–7.

[14] See, for example, *Kjeldsen, Busk Madsen and Pedersen v Denmark* App No 5095/71 (ECtHR 7 December 1976).

[15] Swedish Education Act, c 1 arts 4–5.

might be fraught with conflict. Therefore, the responsibilities and duties of the Swedish state when it comes to the multicultural Swedish school system ought to be discussed in the light of the chosen values and their possible clash with the religious values of an individual pupil and his or her family.

Currently, there are no provisions in Sweden restricting the right to run an independent school with a religious profile. Every now and again, there is, however, an intensive political debate on whether faith schools should be allowed or not.[16] The background is that some schools, mostly Muslim ones, have failed to uphold important Swedish principles, such as the equal treatment of boys and girls, which is one of the cornerstones of the basic values of the school system. The question of the wearing of the full veil at school has also been highlighted. When it comes to religious clothing and religious manifestations, the debate has, however, not at all paid attention to the fact that any prohibition or limitation also affects the identity of an individual. The question must be raised regarding whether limitations violate the fundamental rights of the individuals affected, such as equal treatment, the fight against discrimination of persons on grounds of gender, colour, national or ethnic origin, etc, as well as the person's identity.

For some pupils with a foreign background, as well as for their parents, their meeting with the Swedish school system causes no problems and the child, and his or her parents, adapt easily to the Swedish school system with its democratic values and non-confessional conformation. But for other pupils, their meeting with the Swedish school system might come as a shock, especially if a pupil has a set of values at home that differs largely from customary Swedish traditions or the Swedish secular approach to everyday life. Schools and the set of values inherent in schools might also come as a shock to the child's parents, and consequently, an entire family sometimes alienates itself from the school as well as from society.

II. THE VALUE SYSTEM OF THE SWEDISH EDUCATION SYSTEM

The values that have been chosen to govern the Swedish school system mentioned above represent the aims and structure of the Swedish school system. They are summarised in something called the value system of the Swedish education system (*värdegrund*) and are laid down in the Swedish Education Act.[17] They may best be described as representing a set of common values that shall pervade both teaching and all other activities in schools. According to this value system,

[16] Several political parties would like to restrict the right to start and run faith schools. A Commission of Inquiry, appointed by the Government, is now investigating the matter (Government inquiry U 2018:02).

[17] Swedish Education Act, c 1 arts 4–5.

schools shall, among other things, provide an equivalent education throughout the country irrespective of the financial situation of the families and the geographical location of the schools. This includes the quality of education, as well as the competence of the teachers, grading and the minimum number of hours of teaching, etc. According to these basic values, schools must also respect the equal worth of every child and educate the children in accordance with the basic democratic values of Swedish society and firmly establish the respect for human rights. A starting point for the discussion on how well the Swedish school system is able to include pupils with different cultural and/or religious backgrounds and to convey important Swedish democratic principles to them, is the question of how society imposes the principles and the extent to which society must show consideration for the pupil's own religious and/or cultural background.

The value system comprises several prestigious words that are regarded as fundamental for a society such as democracy, freedom of the individual, equality and solidarity. In addition to this, the teaching shall, as mentioned, be non-confessional, and no religion may permeate the teaching. The value system of the Swedish school system is based on the idea that its principles are fundamental to society and that every child must be taught to understand and support these ideals. As regards democracy, for example, it is not enough for pupils to learn about democracy. They shall also be educated to embrace democracy and learn how to act and think democratically.

Educating pupils and ensuring that they become true democrats is promoted through the so-called democratic mission (*demokratiuppdraget*). According to the Government, one of the most important tasks of the Swedish school system is to educate children to become 'democratic citizens' and to influence the socialisation of children.[18] Schools have been given the task of teaching all pupils how to participate in an open and intellectual discourse in order to counteract silent acceptance, a fear of differences, etc.[19] The aim is to educate competent citizens that are capable of dealing with the knowledge and values of Swedish society in order to promote democracy and counteract undemocratic acts and expressions. Educating pupils to become active citizens in our democratic society is conducted at different levels. Schools shall emphasise democracy both in theory, by teaching about democracy, as well as in practice, by working in a democratic way. The task of teaching democracy is considered to be closely related to the child's right to exert influence at school. By allowing the pupils some influence concerning the teaching and by having 'democratic' discussions between teachers and pupils, every child is trained to act in a democratic manner.

[18] Government bill 2009/10:165 p 310–11.

[19] Swedish Schools Inspectorate (*Skolinspektionen*), Skolornas arbete med demokrati och värdegrund, Skolinspektionens rapport 2012:9.

Since the basic values of the Swedish school system shall pervade everything that happens during the school day, pupils from other cultures are strongly influenced to adopt these values regardless of their cultural, social, religious or ethnic background. It is, of course, very important that schools convey the democratic principles and human rights that form the basis of Swedish society to every child growing up in Sweden. It is a great opportunity for society to mould its citizens and to teach them to respect and embrace the very foundation of society. The value system is, however, vague and some of the crucial concepts can be interpreted in different ways. There is also some uncertainty regarding how they can be integrated into teaching and what the sanctions are if a teacher refuses to comply with these basic values. There are some examples of supply teachers who have been dismissed because of their political opinions, but there are no general rules preventing teachers, who do not agree with the basic principles, from teaching.[20] However, what happens if a pupil refuses to comply with these principles for religious (or cultural) reasons? What if a child does not believe in equality between boys and girls, or does not believe in democracy?

The confrontations and conflicts that might arise between individual pupils with other ethnic or religious traditions, and the basic principles of the Swedish school system are not always easy to handle. There are very few guidelines and there is a lack of any real legal framework on how to navigate between conflicting interests. This leaves it up to individual teachers and headteachers to solve the conflicts as part of their daily work, which of course might be a very delicate and sensitive task. An example of such a difficult decision could be an individual teacher having to make a decision without any detailed guidelines to rely on, concerning when and where a female pupil can be asked to remove her full body veil or full face veil. What gives the teacher the right to make such a decision and when can it be made?

III. RELIGIOUS CLOTHING IN SWEDISH SCHOOLS

As mentioned above, the right to wear religious symbols or religious clothes is protected by the Swedish Constitution, at school as well as in public. When it comes to *general* prohibitions against a certain type of religious clothing in schools or elsewhere in society, it could be argued that such a prohibition would violate the freedom of religion as laid down in the Constitution. This fundamental right shall, as mentioned above, be interpreted narrowly, but it is considered to include a protection against discriminating legislation or persecution. A general prohibition against religious clothes, for example, full

[20] See, for example, Skolvärlden, 'Kan man vara lärare och sverigedemokrat?', 21 March 2014.

veils, in Swedish schools (or elsewhere in society) would probably be regarded as discriminatory against practitioners of Islam, and any such provision would therefore probably violate the Constitution. The issue has, however, not arisen yet.[21]

At the level of the *individual*, the wearing of religious clothes is, however, not protected as part of the freedom of religion. Instead it is regarded as a way of manifesting your religion which means that it is protected by the freedom of expression, as the right to present and state your religious opinions.[22] Freedom of expression is also protected in the Swedish Constitution.[23] In contrast to the freedom of religion, freedom of expression may, however, be limited, for example, in order to protect public order or public security.[24] Limitations in the wearing of religious clothes in a particular situation are thus possible after a proportionality test has been conducted if the aim is to secure public order and public security. Any limitation in the right must be laid down in law. In contrast to the European Convention on Human Rights, the concept 'law' here only encompasses legal acts from the Parliament, and no other legal instruments.

Today, there is no law in Sweden clarifying whether and when the right to wear religious clothes or symbols may be limited in schools. Instead the Swedish National Agency for Education (*Skolverket*), the central administrative authority for the Swedish school system, has issued legal recommendations stating that an individual teacher may restrict the use of full veils in situations where he or she considers that the clothing disturbs the contact between teacher and pupil.[25] The teacher may also restrict the use of full veils if he or she considers the clothing to be dangerous to wear, which could be the case, for example, during PE or chemistry lessons. In the absence of a law that clarifies how far the right to wear religious clothes reaches and when it may legally be limited, an authority has thus regulated the area and bypassed the requirement that restrictions may only be laid down in law, by calling it a recommendation. This is in itself a problem. Another problem is that the recommendation addresses only full veils, no other religious clothes or symbols, which is of course questionable from a discrimination perspective.

In contrast to the Swedish Constitution, wearing religious clothes is considered to be a manifestation of religion according to the European Convention on Human Rights. Clothing is therefore protected by the freedom of religion

[21] H Bernitz, 'Frihet till religion och frihet från religion i skolan – elevers och lärares rättigheter' (2017) 3 *Förvaltningsrättslig tidskrift* 451–73.

[22] V Persson, 'Skolkläder och yttrandefrihet' (2009) 1 *Förvaltningsrättslig Tidskrift* 59–80 and V Enkvist, *Religionsfrihetens rättsliga ramar* (Uppsala, Iustus förlag, 2013) 205–15.

[23] Instrument of Government, c 2 art 1 pt 1.

[24] Instrument of Government, c 2 arts 20–23.

[25] Swedish National Agency for Education (*Skolverket*), 'Juridisk vägledning, Elever med heltäckande slöja i skolan' (July 2012).

under Article 9, as long as there is a close link to the religion. As Article 9 may be limited in order to protect, for example, public security and public order, restrictions concerning the right to wear religious clothes laid down in law may be justified.[26]

Both the Swedish Constitution and the European Convention on Human Rights thus accept justified limitations in the right to wear religious clothes at the level of the individual, but the Swedish government has so far not considered it necessary. The lack of legal provisions and legal guidelines leave those difficult and sensitive decisions to individual teachers, which is troublesome and, for the teachers, a very difficult and awkward decision to make. From a discrimination perspective, as well as from a democratic and a legal certainty perspective, it would be much better if the legislator regulated this area. There are, however, for the moment no signs that the legislator will clarify when or where a pupil may be asked to remove his or her religious clothes at school. The Swedish National Agency for Education is now revising its recommendations after severe criticism from academics,[27] and hopefully there will be more general recommendations and more guidelines for teachers in the future.

IV. THE BEST INTERESTS OF THE CHILD

The question of the integration and inclusion of pupils with other traditions and other religions also raises questions with respect to the best interests of the child in the school environment. This principle, as laid down in the UN Convention on the Rights of the Child, has been reiterated in the Swedish Education Act,[28] which states that the best interests of the child shall be the basis of both teaching and all other activities that take place in Swedish schools during the school day. As from 1 January 2020, the Convention will also be incorporated into Swedish law.[29]

According to the government, the spirit of the UN Convention shall permeate the Swedish education system.[30] Both teaching and education shall be organised to promote every child's personal development and guarantee the personal rights of the child. It shall protect the child against insulting or abusive treatment, and guarantee, for example, the child's right to exert influence at school, right to participation, respect for the child's personal integrity and protection against discrimination. The provision in the Swedish Education Act also

[26] In the case *SAS v France*, App no 43835/11 (ECtHR, 1 July 2014) the European Court of Human Rights accepted the French ban on full veils in public. It was considered to fall within the margin of appreciation of France.

[27] See, for example, Enkvist (n 22) 224–26, and Bernitz (n 21) 451–73.

[28] Swedish Education Act, c 1 art 10.

[29] Government bill, 2017/18:186.

[30] Government bill, 2009/10:165 p 231–32.

expressly mentions every child's right to express his or her own opinions freely in all matters that concern the child.

The principle of the best interests of the child in the Swedish Education Act could be interpreted in different ways. A narrow interpretation of the concept limits it to encompassing the child's fundamental rights, such as the right to life and the protection against ill-treatment.[31] A wider, and probably the most likely, interpretation of the concept is, however, to interpret it as an open and dynamic concept in harmony with the cultural and moral values of the society in which the child actually lives. In a school situation in Sweden, this would mean that the principle shall be interpreted in accordance with Swedish values and Swedish law, and related to the basic values that prevail in schools.

At a more overarching level, the Swedish school system is thus responsible for guaranteeing and protecting the best interests of the child as an important part of its 'basic value system'. Teachers and every other person involved in school education shall always take this principle into consideration and it shall permeate everything that happens during the school day. Thus, the integration of the principle gives teachers in Swedish schools a tool to meet the needs of pupils with other traditions and other religions, and adapt the teaching to the actual situation in the classroom.

The principle of the best interests of the child is thus very much taken into consideration as part of the 'basic value system' of the Swedish education system. But how is the principle interpreted and safeguarded at school level?

V. PROPORTIONALITY TESTS

According to the preparatory works of the Swedish Education Act, the Swedish school system is regarded as being fully comprehensive and fully objective. As mentioned above, the teaching shall, for example, be non-confessional in both municipal and independent schools. It shall also be science-based, and use tested methods. This also applies to religious schools, where, in order to guarantee the requirements of the European Court of Human Rights, teaching shall be 'objective, critical, and pluralistic'.[32]

In this comprehensive and objective Swedish school system, there is no such thing as an exemption from attending *compulsory* lessons for any religious, cultural or philosophical reasons. All pupils in Sweden shall participate in all lessons, regardless of their individual opinions and beliefs. This means that there is currently no real legal way for a child to be excused from lessons such

[31] J Schiratzki, *Barnets bästa i ett mångkulturellt Sverige* 2nd edn (Uppsala, Iustus, 2005).

[32] *Kjeldsen, Busk Madsen and Pedersen v Denmark* para 53. See also Government bill 2009/10:165 p 226.

as, for example, sex education, religious studies, swimming, PE or cooking.[33] If a pupil finds a specific situation offensive, the school shall primarily adapt the teaching, for example, by regrouping the pupil. In exceptional cases, the head-teacher (but not the teachers) may, however, grant an exemption from a specific part of the teaching, but only very rarely.[34]

As exemptions for religious or other reasons are rare according to the Swedish Education Act, pupils might try to invoke the European Convention on Human Rights. The European Court of Human Rights has emphasised that the refusal to grant an exemption for religious reasons might violate the right of the parents to ensure the provision of an education and teaching in conformity with their own religious and philosophical convictions (First Protocol, Article 2).[35] In Sweden, the parent's right according to the First Protocol is considered to be protected by the right to choose a faith school. As for exemptions from specific lessons, the Swedish conclusion is that it is unnecessary in the objective and neutral Swedish school system.

According to both Swedish administrative law[36] and the case law of the European Court of Human Rights,[37] a proportionality assessment must, however, be made in every decision concerning an exemption for religious or other reasons. Despite the strict Swedish view on exemptions, where exemptions from compulsory lessons are hardly ever granted, there are practically no guidelines on how this proportionality test shall be carried out. There is also very little Swedish case law clarifying when and how exemptions from compulsory education may be granted on religious grounds.

There is, however, one interesting case from 2013, which sheds some light on the situation. A girl was granted an exemption from attending PE, when dancing was being taught, for religious reasons after a proportionality test had been conducted.[38] The court argued that the pupil was able to obtain the same knowledge and skills through other activities and that the girl's religious reasons for not dancing were therefore stronger than the school's interests ensuring that every pupil participated in compulsory lessons. The outcome of this case must, however, be seen as exceptional, and does not give any general right to an exemption on religious grounds. The lack of guidelines places individual headmasters in a very difficult position when balancing the interests of the child against the interests of the school.

[33] It should be noted that Sweden has about 70 independent religious schools. As regards the religious features in those schools, the Education Act states that participation shall be voluntary (Swedish Education Act, c 1 art 7).

[34] Government bill 2009/10:165 p 339 ff. and 707. Swedish Education Act, c 7 art 19.

[35] *Folgerø v Norway* App no 15472/02 (ECtHR, 29 June 2007).

[36] Swedish Administrative Procedure Act (2017:900) art 5.

[37] See, for example, *Kjeldsen, Busk Madsen and Pedersen v Denmark*, *Bernard and others v Luxemburg* App no 17187/90 (Commission Decision, 8 September 1993) and *CJ, JJ and EJ v Poland* App no 23380/94 (ECtHR, 16 January 1996).

[38] Administrative Court of Appeal in Sundsvall, 1493-12, 4 July 2013.

Another subject where pupils request an exemption is swimming. In Sweden, as in many other countries, there are children who sometimes refuse to participate in swimming lessons for religious reasons. In those specific situations, a proportionality test must be carried out and it is important to take into consideration that swimming is not just about exercise (as in the case of dancing), it is primarily a lifesaving activity. Swimming is also, as the European Court of Human Rights has put it, an important aspect of integration into the society where the child lives.[39] It could therefore be argued that it is in the best interests of the child to participate in compulsory swimming lessons.[40]

However, for a teacher standing by the pool together with a child that refuses to swim, the principle of the best interests of the child does not solve the problem. Even if it is considered that it is best for the child to learn how to swim, it is sometimes not an easy task to persuade the child to go along with it. It would be considered a criminal act were a teacher to force a child into the water. Any problems concerning a child's participation in swimming lessons should therefore preferably, after a proportionality test, be solved, not with exemptions or force, but with adjustments such as helping the girls to rent 'burkinis',[41] talking to and persuading the parents, etc. Splitting boys and girls into different groups may also help sometimes. You could argue that separating boys and girls might contravene the principle of gender equality – the separation of boys and girls is normally not permitted during PE or during any other lessons in Swedish schools. There are, however, two decisions from the Swedish Equality Ombudsman (DO)[42] concerning adults that indicate that it might be legally acceptable to make such a separation when it comes to swimming lessons. According to the DO, it is acceptable, in exceptional cases, to organise special times for women in public swimming baths. The key principle should always be equal treatment, but if the separation of men and women aims to provide for women, who, for religious or cultural reasons, would otherwise never learn how to swim, the separation might be justified.[43] Sweden is a country with long coastlines, 96,000 lakes and 2,500 km of shoreline. Teaching everyone to swim is a matter of health and safety.

As the Swedish school system is considered to be fully comprehensive and fully objective, *home education* is also practically impossible, even if a child invokes religious or philosophical reasons. The teaching and the education

[39] *Osmanoğlu och Kocabaş v Switzerland* App no 29086/12 (ECtHR, 10 January 2017).

[40] H Bernitz and W Warnling-Nerep, 'Kan det vara "barnets bästa" att lära sig simma eller är det tvärt om?' (2017) 9 *Svensk juristtidning* 689–708.

[41] A burkini is a kind of swimsuit that covers the whole body, except for the face, hands and feet.

[42] The Equality Ombudsman (DO) is a government agency that works on behalf of the Swedish Parliament and government to promote equal rights and opportunities, and to combat discrimination.

[43] Swedish Discrimination Act, c 1 art 4, and c 2 arts 12 and 12a. DO's decisions: 2016-12-14, GRA 2016/9 and 2016-12-14, GRA 2016/8.

provided are considered to be designed to include and suit all children, and therefore, according to the government, there is no need for home education on the grounds of a family's religious or philosophical convictions.[44] In other very specific situations, home education might exceptionally be granted for a short period of time, for example, if a child is participating in the production of a film.

There is very little case law in Sweden regarding home education for religious reasons, but there is one interesting case from 2013 from the Supreme Administrative Court. The case concerned Jewish children who had previously been granted home education under the former Education Act, based on their special needs for prayers, food, safety, protection against bullying, etc.[45] The court denied them home education under the present Education Act, basing its decision on the children's young age and the need for social skills training. This reasoning is similar to that of the European Court of Human Rights in the *Konrad* case, where the social skills training provided by German schools was accepted as a reason for denying home education.[46] The Swedish Supreme Administrative Court did not, however, mention the *Konrad* case, nor did it mention the European Convention on Human Rights. It is likely, however, that the court was influenced by the reasoning of the European Court of Human rights in the *Konrad* case.

It is the individual teacher or headteacher who has the full responsibility for making sure that the pupil participates in all lessons, even if the pupil or his or her parents find it difficult for cultural or religious reasons. Here, the principle of the best interests of the child does not seem very dynamic as it is always considered to be in the best interests of the child to attend compulsory schooling such as sex education, swimming, etc, even if it clashes with the child's religious beliefs.

As concerns *non-compulsory* activities in school, such as speech day ceremonies in church, the pupil may choose not to attend for, among other things, religious reasons. If a pupil chooses not to attend non-compulsory activities, the school must, however, be very careful not to breach the negative freedom of religion, laid down in the Swedish Constitution.[47] According to this freedom, the state, which includes both municipal and independent schools,[48] may not coerce anybody to divulge an opinion in a religious, cultural or other such connection. The school is therefore prevented from asking the pupil whether it is for religious reasons that he or she, for example, does not

[44] Government bill, 2009/10:165 p 523.
[45] Supreme Administrative Court, 2013 ref 49.
[46] *Konrad v Germany* App no 35504/03, (ECtHR 11 September 2006).
[47] Instrument of Government, c 2 art 2.
[48] Swedish government official report 2016:4 p 266. See also J Hirschfeldt and L Lerwall, 'Friskolorna – några konstitutionella synpunkter på deras ställning' in S Blomstrand (ed), *Bertil Bengtsson 90 år* (Stockholm, Jure, 2016) 169–75.

wish to attend an end of term ceremony held in a church. The same article also protects against being coerced into participating in a meeting organised for the shaping of opinion, which probably includes religious meetings. This means, for example, that a study visit to a Mass might cause constitutional problems, depending on how much the pupils are participating in the religious ceremony.

VI. FINAL REMARKS

To relate the concept of the best interests of the child to the value system of the Swedish school system is no easy task. Regardless of a child's, or his or her parent's, opinions, in Sweden, it is considered to be in the best interests of the child to attend normal schooling and to attend all lessons. According to Swedish opinion, it is in the best interests of the child to learn how to swim, to cook all kinds of food, to participate in sex education, and to learn about democracy and human rights, irrespective of the religious beliefs of the children. The reason is that it corresponds to fundamental Swedish values.

There is, however, a fine line between indoctrination and an education that aims at helping the pupils to understand the society in which they live. As discussed above, basic principles, such as those governing the Swedish school system, are clearly connected to the views of the majority, and include rights, positions and attitudes that the majority considers to be right. The basic values of the Swedish school system are clearly worded in accordance with the Swedish Constitution and its fundamental democratic principles. They aim at educating independent citizens, providing them with tools so that they are able to choose their own set of values, but at the same time they also convey values that everybody is assumed to embrace. This is important for society, but to enforce values on pupils, and assume that everybody accepts (or is willing to learn to accept) them might cause problems from a constitutional point of view, as well as from the perspective of the best interests of the child. You should, therefore, consider to what extent the school system has the right to enforce its basic principles on the pupils. You should also consider how schools should deal with pupils who, for example, do not believe in democracy, human rights or gender equality, or pupils who do not believe in a secular society.

There are no simple answers to these questions. A school may, of course, encourage its pupils to become interested in democratic questions, and teach them to understand the importance of human rights, gender equality, etc, by discussing these topics in class and trying to promote the advantages of a society characterised by democracy and human rights.

According to the freedom of opinion, as laid down in the Swedish Constitution, the state, which includes both municipal and independent schools, may not, however, force anyone to embrace a particular opinion, such as, for example, the secular values of the school or other important and basic principles for a democratic society. Nor can anyone be forced to embrace any political opinion, not even democratic values, as everybody has the right to their own opinions. When it comes to influencing pupils to adopt those views, there is reason to be cautious.

The Swedish school system, as mentioned above, is regarded as playing an important role in providing children with a broad education, as part of the Swedish school system's democratic mission. There is, however, no limit concerning the freedom of opinion that could give schools the right to impose their basic principles on pupils. Therefore, every pupil has the freedom to choose whether he or she wants to embrace democratic ideas or a secular approach. A constitutional perspective calls for caution and demands a balance between a school's desire to convey its basic values, and the constitutional rights of an individual pupil to hold whatever opinion of his or her choosing. Even if it is very important for Swedish society to learn about democracy, no one can be forced to believe in democracy.

Does the neutral Swedish school system take multicultural pupils with different religions and values into account? The answer is no, not when it comes to teaching and influencing the pupils to adapt to the basic values of the Swedish school system.

There is, however, a discussion regarding adapting to a situation but this is on a completely different level; in Sweden, every year, there is a public debate about end of term ceremonies in municipal schools being held in churches. This debate is taking place in the light of the non-confessional conformation of the Swedish school system and the multicultural Swedish society. The focus of the issue of multicultural pupils is the question of whether it is acceptable to hold an end-of-term ceremony in a church or not. In my opinion, it is perfectly possible as long as there is no sermon or blessing. Just using a church as an assembly hall can never be regarded as 'confessional' and therefore the prohibition against confessional education is not violated. Most schools have now, however, moved this kind of ceremony from the local church to the school's own assembly hall or to a local sports centre as a way of adapting to the new multicultural society.

As regards the ceremonies, society has thus shown some respect for multicultural pupils. In class, however, no consideration is taken at all to the pupils' cultural or religious traditions. This is considered unnecessary as the Swedish values upon which the school system is based are said to be objective and neutral, so that everybody can adjust to them. However, the values are not universal, they are Swedish or at least very European. A pupil who does not approve cannot object, nor can his or her parents. A pupil can respond to cultural differences in two ways; either by assimilating to the new situation which could mean alienating himself or herself from his or her parents and their values, traditions and religion, or by finding himself or herself in two different worlds that must blend as much as possible. As shown above, there are concerns about the basic values of the Swedish school system that must be taken into consideration. If there is no flexibility in how these values are put into practice, schools could become a way for the majority population to teach the minority 'how to think'. The desire for a society where everybody shares the same ideals could then lead to the creation of a society with structural discrimination. At the same time, it is an important democratic task to convey value-related issues to all pupils and teach them to take an interest in our common system of values.

11

Religious Refusals in Health Care as a Matter of Freedom of Religion

KAVOT ZILLÉN

I. INTRODUCTION

ACCOMMODATING RELIGIOUS BELIEFS and values of health care professionals in an increasingly multicultural and diverse setting is a challenge the Swedish health care system faces today. Health care professionals sometimes experience difficulties in carrying out their duties, particularly when trying to fulfil their job requirements while simultaneously acting in accordance with their religious and moral beliefs.[1] Several studies in the field of medicine and ethics show that health care professionals' ethical, moral and religious beliefs affect how they perform their work.[2] Health care professionals' religious backgrounds may challenge the health care system in a number of different ways. For example, there have been recent controversies regarding midwives refusing to participate in abortion care on religious grounds. Conflicts can arise from such situations, namely between health care professionals' interests in acting in accordance with their beliefs while at work and patients' interests in receiving good care on equal terms. Caregivers have an important role in balancing both sets of interests. There is therefore a need for a better

[1] B Farsides et al, 'Aiming Towards "Moral Equilibrium": Health Care Professionals' Views on Working Within the Morally Contested Field of Antenatal Screening' (2004) 5 *Journal of Medical Ethics* 505, 505 ff; M Moller, 'Human Embryonic Stem Cell Research, Justice, and the Problem of Unequal Biological Access' (2008) 3 *Philosophy, Ethics, and Humanities in Medicine* 3, 22.

[2] See R Lawrence and F Curlin, 'Physicians' Beliefs About Conscience in Medicine: A National Survey' (2009) 9 *Academic Medicine* 1276–82; R Lawrence et al, 'Obstetrician-gynecologist Physicians' Beliefs about Emergency Contraception: A National Survey' (2010) 4 *Contraception* 324–30; L Ramondetta et al, 'Religious and Spiritual Beliefs of Gynecologic Oncologists May Influence Medical Decision Making' (2011) 3 *International Journal of Gynecoligical Cancer* 573–81; C Sprung et al, 'The Importance of Religious Affiliation and Culture on End-of-life Decisions in European Intensive Care Units' (2007) 10 *Intensive Care Medicine* 1732–39.

understanding of when health care professionals' religiously-based objections should be accommodated in health care.

This chapter explores whether Article 9 of the European Convention on Human Rights (ECHR) on freedom of religion offers a certain amount of religious accommodation in health care. The purpose is not to examine all aspects of health care professionals' freedom of religion but to clarify whether freedom of religion includes a right for health care professionals to refuse to provide medical care and services that are contrary to their religious and moral beliefs, defined here as *conscientious objections* or *religious refusals* in health care.[3] Special attention will be given to situations where health care professionals refuse to provide certain sexual and reproductive health care services, such as abortion, when they are incompatible with their convictions.

II. THE REGULATION OF CONSCIENCE CLAUSES AND SWEDEN'S STANDPOINT

In order to respect health care professionals' freedom of religion and conscience, some Council of Europe Member States have developed and adopted regulation that gives health care professionals the right to refuse to perform or participate in medical procedures that are contrary to their religious and moral beliefs, defined here as *conscience clauses* in health care. The scope and regulation of conscience clauses varies in the different Member States and the content and reach of these regulations are therefore limited in different ways, depending on the legal and social considerations in the given national context. Most of the existing conscience clauses adopted by the Council of Europe Member States concern specific medical procedures such as abortion. This is due to the fact that conscientious objection in health care most often arises in cases involving sexual and reproductive health care services, such as abortion and contraception, where health care professionals might be confronted with issues concerning the moral status of the foetus and the woman's right to bodily integrity and self-determination.[4]

[3] The question of conscientious objection in Sweden has been further elaborated in K Zillén, *Hälso- och sjukvårdspersonalens religions- och samvetsfrihet. En rättsvetenskaplig studie om samvetsgrundad vägran och kravet på god vård* (Uppsala, Uppsala University, 2016); K Zillén, 'Conscientious Objections in Clinical Healthcare Education as a Manifestation of Religion' in A Sjöborg and HG Ziebertz (eds), *Religion and Human Rights* (Cham, Springer International Publishing, 2017); K Zillén, 'Conscientious Objection to Abortion in Sweden – A Commentary on the Swedish case of *Ellinor Grimmark*, AD 2017 nr 23' (2017) 3 *Giornale di Diritto del Lavoro e di Relazioni Industriali* 791–801.

[4] A Lamačkova, 'Conscientious Objection in Reproductive Health Care: Analysis of Pichon and Sajous v. France' (2008) 15 *European Journal of Health Law* 7–43, 8; C McCafferty (special rapporteur), *Women's Access to Lawful Medical Care: The Problem of Unregulated Use of Conscientious Objection*, report to The Social, Health and Family Affairs Committee, Council of Europe (adopted 20 July 2010) doc 12347.

Conscience clauses are regulated in 21 out of the 28 EU Member States.[5] In some countries such as Latvia, Malta, Finland, Bulgaria and Sweden, the matter of conscientious objection is still unregulated.[6] In addition, the Council of Europe has addressed the issue of conscientious objection in abortion-related care. In October 2010 the Parliamentary Assembly of the Council of Europe adopted Resolution 1763 on conscientious objections in lawful medical care. This has given rise to some renewed discussion on the issue of conscientious objection. The Resolution, which is not legally binding, invites Member States of the Council of Europe to develop comprehensive and clear regulations that define and regulate conscientious objection regarding health care and medical services such as abortion.[7]

The Swedish Parliament decided not to comply with Resolution 1763 to establish a right to conscientious objection in abortion care, arguing that this risked undermining women's legal right to abortion and compromising their access to safe abortion care.[8] The question of health care professionals' religious refusals in the medical field is highly controversial in Sweden and there is, as pointed out, no right for Swedish health care professionals to object to participate in certain health care on the basis of religion. Health care professionals in Sweden therefore have no statutory right on the basis of religion, conscience or other principles to refuse to participate in certain types of care as the government has not yet identified reasons for introducing such a right into Swedish health care legislation. Nevertheless, lately the question of conscientious objections in health care has emerged in discussions in Sweden. This is mostly because of a recent case brought before the Swedish Labour Court[9] about a midwife, Ellinor Grimmark, who was denied employment in several clinics (specialised in care for women) on the grounds of her religious refusals to participate in abortion care.[10] The case raises a question about what possibilities Swedish employees have for abstaining from certain work requirements that are inconsistent with their beliefs. A description of the *Grimmark* case will be provided in the following section as the case clearly illustrates the challenges pertaining to an employee exercising freedom of religion in the workplace when manifested as a refusal to provide care and medical services in Sweden.

[5] United Kingdom, France, Belgium, Austria, Hungary, Slovakia, Poland, Portugal, Italy, Cyprus, Denmark, Finland, Germany, the Netherlands and Spain all allow health care professionals to object to performing abortions under specific circumstances, see A Heino et al, 'Conscientious Objection and Induced Abortion in Europe' (2013) 4 *European Journal of Contraception and Reproductive Health Care* 231–33.

[6] McCafferty (n 4) 5 referred to in Zillén, 'Conscientious Objections in Clinical Healthcare Education' (n 3) 168.

[7] Council of Europe resolution 1763 *The right to conscientious objection in lawful medical care* (adopted 7 October 2010).

[8] Swedish Parliamentary rapid protocol 2010/11:100 (adopted 11 May 2010), § 18.

[9] The Swedish Labour Court is a special court that hears and rules on labour-related disputes as a final instance court. Its judgments cannot be appealed.

[10] The Swedish Labour Court (Arbetsdomstolen) case AD 2017 nr 23 [12.4.2017].

III. THE *GRIMMARK* CASE IN THE SWEDISH LABOUR COURT

During the last couple of years, the question of religious objections has emerged in discussion in Sweden after several midwives' religiously-based refusals to participate in abortion care. The responsibilities of Swedish midwives in relation to abortion care are typically restricted to contraceptive services, including prescription of the contraceptive pill and insertion of an intrauterine device, as well as pre-abortion counselling and post-abortion care. In certain cases of medical abortions, midwives can administer medical abortion pills to women. This may involve several tasks such as counting, calculating, mixing, labelling, preparing and ultimately giving the medication to the woman. Their responsibilities in cases of surgical abortion are generally limited to assisting the physician and to caring for the patient in the treatment of complications or evacuations of incomplete abortions.[11]

As indicated, midwives are sometimes confronted with issues concerning the moral status of the foetus and the woman's right to abortion, which can give rise to moral conflicts as well as legal claims brought before courts. One example is the Swedish Labour Court case of *Grimmark*.[12] The applicant in the case, a midwife, had been denied employment in several clinics specialised in care for women in County Council hospitals (women's clinics) because of her religious refusal to participate in abortion care services. One of her central claims was that the hospitals' refusal to accommodate her religiously-based request to abstain from providing abortion care services amounted to a violation of her freedom of religion under Article 9 ECHR.[13] The case was initially handled by the Swedish Equality Ombudsman (DO) and thereafter by the District Court, which affirmed the DO's decision, stating that Grimmark had not been subjected to unlawful treatment. The District Court's judgment was then appealed to the Swedish Labour Court.

In the autumn of 2016, the Swedish Labour Court handed down its judgment, stressing that the working conditions for the position of midwife in Sweden – which required all the tasks of a midwife to be performed, including assisting with abortions – did not constitute a violation of a midwife's freedom of religion under Article 9 ECHR. The Court held that the County Council's

[11] The Swedish Association of Midwives (Svenska Barnmorskeförbundet) Description of competence for registered midwifes (kompetensbeskrivning för legitimerad barnmorska) 2018 p 7 and 11.

[12] AD 2017 nr 23 [12.4.2017]. See also the case of *Linda Steen*, similar to the *Grimmark* case, about a midwife with a conscientious objection to abortions. The case was appealed to the Labour Court but the Court decided not to grant a leave of appeal, upholding the decision of the District Court, decision by the Labour Court, case number B 124/16 [8.5.2017]. For an extensive legal analysis of the Swedish Labour Court *Grimmark case* see K Zillén, 'Conscientious Objection to Abortion in Sweden' (n 3).

[13] The Labour Court was also asked to consider two other claims, namely whether the County Council's decision not to hire Grimmark amounted to discrimination on religious grounds and whether the decision also infringed her right to freedom of expression. These two claims will not be elaborated since the chapter's sole focus is on health care professionals' freedom of religion.

decision for not hiring her constituted a legitimate restriction on her freedom of religion with reference to the legitimate aim of protecting the health of others, particularly women seeking abortion. The Labour Court accepted the County Council's reason, stating that the decision was in place to safeguard women's access to safe and effective abortion care.

So far, the Court's decision clearly upholds the Swedish legislators' standpoint that health care professionals should not be allowed to derogate from general work requirements due to religious reasons. The result of the Court's assessment is clear – employers do not need to satisfy health care professionals' desires to be relieved from performing certain tasks that contradict their beliefs. It should also be noted that Grimmark together with her lawyers have brought a complaint before the European Court of Human Rights (ECtHR), arguing that the caregivers' actions violated her freedom of religion and conscience, as well as her freedom of expression under the ECHR. The Court has not yet examined whether the complaint is admissible or not. One central question likely to be addressed if the ECtHR considers the complaint is whether the Labour Court's conclusions regarding religiously-based refusals are in line with the case law under Article 9 of the ECtHR. This question will be further elaborated in the following section.

IV. ARTICLE 9 ECHR AND THE JURISPRUDENCE ON RELIGIOUSLY-BASED REFUSALS

A. Religiously-based Refusals as Manifestation of Religion

There are various provisions concerning freedom of religion and its limitations in national, regional and international human rights law. One of the main legal sources for freedom of religion and conscience in the European system of human rights protection is Article 9 of the ECHR. The provision includes a freedom to *manifest* one's religion or beliefs, which has been given a fairly broad interpretation by the Convention organs.[14] Yet, the manifestation of a religion can be subjected to limitations in accordance with Article 9(2) if the restriction is prescribed by law, has a legitimate aim and is necessary in a democratic society.

Article 9(1) refers to a number of different forms of manifestations that are protected, such as worship, teaching, practice and observance. However, the examples in the list are not exhaustive. Instead, they should be viewed as a sample of protected manifestations. The case law makes clear that other acts, such as conscientious objections to military service, are covered.[15] It is

[14] D Harris et al, *Law of the European Convention on Human Rights* (Oxford, Oxford University Press, 2009) 426.

[15] *Bayatyan v Armenia* [GC] ECHR 2011–IV 1 App no 23459/03, para 110.

noteworthy that manifestation of religion or beliefs does not cover each and every act or form of behaviour that is motivated or influenced by a religion. The ECtHR generally makes a distinction between an activity central to the expression of a religion or beliefs – which falls within the realm of Article 9 – and one which is merely inspired or even encouraged by it – which falls outside the scope of Article 9.[16]

The ECtHR has in its recent case law adopted a rather generous approach to religiously-based refusals as a manifestation of religion and beliefs as set out in Article 9 ECHR. As an example, when dealing with an objection to military service, the ECtHR stated in its Grand Chamber judgment in *Bayatyan v Armenia* that a person's opposition to military service, where it is motivated by a serious and insurmountable conflict between the obligation to serve in the army and a person's conscience or his deeply and genuinely held religious or other beliefs, constitutes a conviction or belief protected under Article 9.[17] In the present case, the applicant, a Jehovah's Witness, refused to perform military service for reasons of conscience and was convicted of draft evasion and sentenced to prison. The Grand Chamber found that the applicant's conviction constituted a violation of Article 9. Even though Article 9 does not explicitly refer to a right to refuse to do military service, the ECtHR is clearly of the opinion that objection to military service falls within the ambit of that provision, given that such an objection is grounded on genuinely held religious convictions.[18]

B. Religious Refusals in Health Care

A religiously-based refusal to participate in an activity that is incompatible with one's beliefs can be expressed in a number of different ways, such as the above-mentioned opposition to mandatory military service or a refusal to provide care and medical services. As previously mentioned, conscientious objections in health care arise when health care professionals refuse to provide some care, service or information due to religious or moral beliefs. The practices of conscientious objection in health care and military service both focus on situations when individuals refuse to perform a task or an obligation due to religious or moral reasons. With regard to religious refusals in health care, the ECtHR has held that a worker's religiously-based refusal to perform certain tasks may be

[16] *Eweida and Others v the United Kingdom* ECHR 2013–I 215 App nos 48420/10 and 3 others para 82.

[17] *Bayatyan v Armenia* (n 15) para 110.

[18] *Bayatyan v Armenia* (n 15) paras 111, 124. The *Bayatyan* case is the first in which the ECtHR examined the applicability of Art 9 in relation to conscientious objection to military service. See also the cases of *Savda v Turkey* App no 42730/05 (ECtHR, 12 June 2012) and *Adyan and Others v Armenia* App nos 75604/11 and 21759/15 (ECtHR12 October 2017).

recognised as a manifestation of religious belief that may also permit an exemption from certain work tasks. In *Eweida and Others v the United Kingdom*, one of the applicants, a therapist who provided therapy and relationship counselling to couples, refused to provide his services to same-sex couples.[19] The applicant stated that he had difficulty reconciling working with same-sex pairs with his Christian belief that homosexual activity is sinful. He was later dismissed for refusal to provide certain services on equal grounds, which he claimed violated his right to freedom of religion by arguing that national law had failed adequately to protect his rights in Article 9. The ECtHR found that the applicant's objection was directly motivated by his orthodox Christian beliefs about marriage and sexual relationships, and held that his refusal to counsel homosexual couples constituted a manifestation of his religion and belief as set out in Article 9.[20] Consequently, the sanctions against him were seen as a restriction on his right to manifest his belief. However, the Court found that the dismissal was motivated by a legitimate aim, namely to protect the rights of others, particularly the right of homosexual couples not to be discriminated against in a health care setting. The Court therefore held that there had been no violation of the therapist's freedom of religion.[21]

As shown, a health care professional's religiously-based refusal may be categorised as a manifestation of religion as set out in Article 9. However, not all action taken in respect to a practitioner's refusal or failure to comply with a legal or administrative obligation on the grounds of personal belief is protected under Article 9. In the case of *Blumberg v Germany*, an insurance doctor refused to conduct the medical examination of an apprentice as he feared a 'possible bias' which could lead to difficulties if he had to work with the apprentice in the future.[22] The applicant did not elaborate his view about the potential bias. He was later dismissed for refusing to conduct the medical examination. The applicant claimed that the dismissal had been in breach of his freedom of conscience as guaranteed in Article 9, stating that a moral dilemma had prevented him from carrying out the requested examination. The ECtHR first noted that Article 9 does not always guarantee the right to behave in the public sphere in a way which is dictated by one's personal beliefs. In particular, the term 'practice', as employed in Article 9(1), does not cover each act which is motivated or influenced by one's belief. The Court also reiterated that conscientious refusals have to be based on views that attain a certain level of cogency, seriousness, cohesion and importance to be protected by Article 9. Consequently, the Court found that the applicant's refusal to examine the apprentice did not constitute a manifestation of his personal beliefs, as protected by Article 9, since the refusal was

[19] *Eweida and Others v the United Kingdom (McFarlane)* ECHR 2013–I 215 App nos 48420/10 and 3 others,

[20] ibid, para 108.

[21] ibid, para 109.

[22] *Blumberg v Germany* (decision on admissibility) App no 14618/03 (ECtHR 8 March 2008).

not based on a coherent view of a fundamental problem that amounted to a specific religion or belief. Instead, he had expressed that an examination of the apprentice for the purpose of employment could have resulted in a conflict of interest but without specifying what that conflict of interest might be. The Court therefore found that his refusal did not fall within the realm of Article 9.

Furthermore, the ECtHR has previously held that Article 9 does not always guarantee a right for health care professionals to behave in a manner governed by their religion. In the case of *Pichon and Sajous v France* the ECtHR found that a pharmacist's religious beliefs did not justify a refusal to sell contraceptive pills in their dispensary since they could manifest those beliefs in many ways outside the professional sphere.[23] The ECtHR held that as long as the sale of contraceptives is legal and occurs on medical prescription in a pharmacy, the applicants cannot give precedence to their religious beliefs and impose them on others as justification for their refusal to sell such products. Similarly, the ECtHR has in following cases stated that the practice of conscientious objection in health care settings should not be allowed to jeopardise patients' access to lawful medical care and services, for example, women's access to reproductive care and abortions.[24]

Although a right to religiously-based refusals is not, as such, guaranteed by Article 9 of the Convention or any other provision of the Convention or any of its Protocols, the ECtHR has accepted that health care professionals' refusal to provide certain types of care can constitute a manifestation of religion or belief. Given the principle laid down in the previously mentioned cases, such a religiously-based refusal must be motivated by a serious and insurmountable conflict between the obligation to perform certain work tasks and a person's conscience or deeply and genuinely held religious or other beliefs. The refusal must in other words be closely linked to a religion or belief in order to constitute a manifestation, and this needs to be determined on the facts of each case.

With regard to the reasoning of the Swedish Labour Court in *Grimmark*, it found that the midwife's refusal to participate in abortion care due to religious constraints constituted a manifestation of her religion in the meaning of Article 9(2). So far, the Labour Court's reasoning about the worker's religiously-based refusal to perform certain tasks as a manifestation of religion seems to be in line with the abovementioned cases from the ECtHR, especially the case of *Eweida and Others*. The Swedish Labour Court expressly referred to the case of *Eweida and Others* and followed the conclusion herein, namely that a health care professional's conscientious objection to perform certain tasks may be recognised as a manifestation of religious belief as set out in Article 9. Furthermore, in determining whether a measure is necessary and proportionate, both the ECtHR and the Swedish Labour Court held that there had been no violation

[23] *Pichon and Sajous v France* (dec) ECHR 2001–X 371 App no 49853/99.

[24] See *Tysiąc v Poland* ECHR 2007–I 219 App no 5410/03; *A, B and C v Ireland* [GC] ECHR 2010–VI 185 App no 25579/05 and *RR v Poland* ECHR 2011–III 209 App no 27617/04.

of freedom of religion since the restriction on the manifestation of religion in both cases was necessary and justified.

Given the above, and as an answer to the question at hand, health care professionals' religious refusals can under certain circumstances constitute a manifestation of a religion or beliefs in accordance with Article 9 ECHR. However, what is important to clarify is that the scope of Article 9 of the Convention does not protect a *right* for health care professionals to refrain from participating in certain types of health care and services that conflict with their convictions. As emphasised in this chapter, such a right is not expressed in Article 9 and the case law of the ECtHR clearly illustrates that not all religiously-based refusals in health care can constitute a manifestation of a religion under Article 9, and even so the manifestation can be restricted if there is a public interest against such a manifestation.

V. CONCLUSION

The goal of health care is to enable patients to receive good quality care that is based on science and proven experience, as well as to ensure that the system provides quality care to patients on the basis of need throughout the populace. It also requires health care professionals to respect patients' self-determination and provide patients with essential health care information before the patients themselves consent to care. As illustrated, health care professionals sometimes decline to provide such care or services on the basis of their religion or conscience. In the wake of recent controversies over midwives refusing to participate in abortion care in Sweden, the Swedish Association of Midwives and the Swedish Medical Association have raised concerns about the consequences of allowing health care professionals to deny women legally and medically permitted interventions such as abortions.[25]

A central argument for allowing professionals in health care to opt-out of participating in certain health related services based on religious grounds is that freedom of religion requires it. However, an established conclusion is that the protection of religious freedom under Article 9 does not entail an absolute right for health care workers to refrain from participating in care and services that contravene their religion or beliefs. The manifestation of religion or beliefs may in certain circumstances be limited, for example, with regard to the protection of public health or the rights and freedoms of others.

[25] See the following article: H Karlsson et al, 'Aborträtten hotas av samvetsfriheten' *Aftonbladet* (12 November 2015) (www.aftonbladet.se/debatt/a/6nVRrO/abortratten-hotas-av-samvetsfrihet). The debate article was signed by representatives of the Association of Midwives, the Medical Association, the Association of Doctors and others). See also C Zätterström (the Association of Midwives), 'Att åberopa samvetsklausul är en oetisk vägran att ge vård' (www.barnmorskeforbundet.se/aktuellt/forbundet/att-aberopa-samvetsklausul-ar-en-oetisk-vagran-att-ge-vard/).

The question of conscientious objection in health care is an ethically and morally sensitive issue upon which the Council of Europe Member States have so far failed to reach a consensus. This accounts for the wide margin of appreciation afforded to States in addressing the issue under the ECHR. In addition, the ECtHR has stressed that questions related to the religion of members of the health care workforce and the impact those issues may have on the safety and quality of care is a matter best resolved by the Member States themselves, thus indicating a wide scope for variation in the matter of conscience clauses among the different Member States.

As stressed, there is no right for health care professionals in Sweden, such as midwives, to refrain from participating in certain types of health care that are contrary to their religious beliefs. The Swedish legislator has not found it reasonable to insert a conscience clause in Swedish health care legislation which would give health care professionals a general right to 'opt out' of certain types of health care and services on religious grounds. There is in other words no broad political consensus in Sweden that favours the legal recognition of health care professionals' right to religiously-based refusals in health care. The standpoint is that a deviation from current work requirements in health care, such as the obligations to participate in care, including to participate in abortion care services, may jeopardise the right of patients to have the highest attainable care, particularly with regard to women's rights to sexual and reproductive health. This approach is illustrated in the abovementioned *Grimmark* case where the Labour Court came to the conclusion that the midwife's refusal to participate in abortion care could cause disruption at work and affect timely access to safe abortions. The Court accepted the limitations on her freedom of religion without considering other alternatives that perhaps could satisfy both the caregivers' and the midwife's needs. It could, for example, be argued that a request to be exempted from activities related to abortion from one single midwife could have been granted without risking women's access to abortion. Perhaps this could be realised by shifting tasks between midwives so that women seeking abortions only have an appointment with clinicians who are willing and able to perform the procedure. The situation at hand raises a number of questions about the balance of rights between the public interest and individual interests, how much weight should be given to health care professionals' freedom of religion, and to what extent it can be legally permissible to refuse to give lawful medical care.

The conclusion reached thus far is that Article 9 ECHR does not put a direct or indirect obligation on Swedish employers to satisfy health professionals' desires to be relieved from performing certain tasks on religious grounds. However, the question of health care professionals' religious refusals in Sweden might become the subject of renewed discussion as the majority of the Council of Europe Member States have deemed it necessary to introduce conscience clauses in health care regulation and the Council of Europe has itself passed two resolutions encouraging Member States to introduce such measures.[26] In the meantime, the approach to conscientious objections in health care should be to accommodate what is legally as well as ethically acceptable to both the patient and the physician with an acknowledgement of the underlying tension between different rights, namely the patient's right to access sexual and reproductive health care, the health care professional's freedom of religion and a woman's right to reproductive self-determination.

[26] Council of Europe resolution 1763 *The right to conscientious objection in lawful medical care* (adopted 7 October 2010) and resolution 1607 *Access to safe and legal abortion in Europe* (adopted 16 April 2008).

12

Understanding Religion: A Portal to the Past or the Key to the Future?

VICTORIA ENKVIST

I. INTRODUCTION

IN MOST EUROPEAN countries, the state has had a long relationship with religion in one way or another. The status of this relationship has not been the same in all European countries, but in most states there has been a long and lasting relationship between the *Church*[1] and the state.[2] This means that different forms of Christianity have enjoyed a strong position in European countries.

The relationship between European states and religions other than Christianity and even Christian minority groups has, throughout history, been strained to say the least. This is partly due to the belief that a strong state presupposed unity in religion.[3] 'The others' were often seen as enemies of the state or at least a problem in society. This view was in some countries, like in Sweden for example, reflected in different forms of legislation during the nineteenth century.[4] This way of thinking is familiar today, although it is not as explicit concerning certain religious groups, and it still has an impact on legislation. It is especially evident in discussions concerning immigrants.

The relationship between religion and European states is, in other words, to a great extent embodied in the relationship between the state and the Christian majority Church that was legitimised by the state and not by religion as a whole.

[1] Different forms of the Christian Church such as, for example, the Roman Catholic and Orthodox Churches.

[2] T Rasmussen and E Thomassen, *En historisk introduktion* (trans P Beskow, Skellefteå, Artos, 2007).

[3] In the eighteenth and nineteenth Century this was the prevailing belief in, for example, Sweden.

[4] I Montgomery, *Enhetskyrkans tid* (Stockholm, Verbum, 2002) 38–40.

Over time, the relationship between the state and the Church, ie religion, has changed, and many European states have adopted a more secular form of governance. The development has not been the same in all European countries. In some European countries, religion still has a great deal of influence in society, while in others a strictly secular view has become the prevailing form of government.[5] However, even in strictly secular states[6] like the Nordic states, you can find traces in contemporary legislation that stem from Lutheran heritage. The research focus of a multidisciplinary project covering the Nordic states and Germany, the ProNoLa project, has been to study the kind of traces that can be found.[7] The impact of religion on society has been studied in the research programme The Impact of Religion – Challenges for Society, Law and Democracy.[8]

The ProNoLa project focuses on the traces of Protestantism in secular law while the Impact of Religion programme studies the impact of religions and non-religions from several perspectives. In both projects, research has been conducted on religious values that are explicitly and implicitly expressed and taken for granted. One important conclusion in both projects is the acknowledgement of religion as a companion to both those in power and to those who are not in power.

As regards the interpretation and application of human rights instruments that regulate freedom of religion, the lack of unity regarding the role of religion in society, has, for example, affected the interpretation and application of Article 9 European Convention on Human Rights (ECHR) and resulted in a wide margin of appreciation.[9] The consequences of the wide margin of appreciation have been thoroughly discussed and heavily debated in jurisprudence by legal scholars.[10] From a human rights perspective, it is important to highlight the fact that the wide margin of appreciation has a negative impact on the protection of minorities. Great consideration is taken concerning the culture and tradition of the majority.[11] From a democratic and majority ruling perspective this is self-evident. In that sense, democracy and human rights clash due to the

[5] Compare, for example, Italy and France.

[6] The definition of secularity is debated and the concept has several different meanings.

[7] Protestant Legacies in Nordic Law: Uses of the past in the construction of secularity of law. ProNoLa aims to provide a nuanced and critical genealogy of the negotiations of law and religion in the Northern parts of Europe from the Reformations and up to the present. This project is funded by Humanities in the European Research Area (HERA).

[8] The research programme The Impact of Religion: Challenges for Society, Law and Democracy (IMPACT) is a multidisciplinary research programme at Uppsala University. IMPACT ran over a 10 year period 2008–18 funded by the Swedish Research Council and Uppsala University.

[9] See case law concerning headscarves and religious symbols. For example *Sahin v Turkey* App no 44774/98 (ECtHR, 10 November 2005) para 108 and *Eweida and others v the United Kingdom* App nos 48420/1, 59842/10, 51671/10 and 36516/10 (ECtHR, 15 January 2013).

[10] Se for example I Cameron, *An Introduction to the European Convention on Human Rights* 5th rev edn (Uppsala, Iustus, 2006).

[11] See for example *Lautsi v Italy* App no 30814/06 (ECtHR, 18 March 2011).

wide margin of appreciation. The majority opinion almost always prevails in Article 9 cases.[12]

Closely linked to the margin of appreciation is the principle of neutrality that is firmly established in many western societies.[13] Religion, secularism and neutrality are all concepts that have a great impact on the understanding and application of freedom of religion.

It has been called into question whether the neutrality of the state is compatible with multicultural societies. Another challenge to neutrality is that some people are always going to be treated more favourably than others, due to culture, language, tradition and history. The alleged neutrality can be called into question on grounds of bias. And the overarching question is, of course: neutrality in relation to what?

Are secular values neutral and is it necessary to be neutral? Conflicts may arise when the dominant religious orientation and the liberal state attempt to attract the same audience because neither of them is founded on rational principles and both of them are expressions of traditions, non-neutral traditions.[14] But what is neutrality? What do we mean when we speak of neutrality – a neutrality of facts or a neutrality of reasoning? In the *Lautsi* case from Grand Chamber of the European Court of Human Rights Judge Bonello states in a concurring opinion that

> seen in the light of the historical roots of the presence of the crucifix in Italian schools, removing it from where it has quietly and passively been for centuries, would hardly have been a manifestation of neutrality by the State. Its removal would have been a positive and aggressive espousal of agnosticism or of secularism – and consequently anything but neutral. Keeping a symbol where it has always been is no act of intolerance by believers or cultural traditionalists. Dislodging it would be an act of intolerance by agnostics and secularists.[15]

Secularism is another concept that is often brought up when religion and freedom of religion are discussed. Are secularity and neutrality the same thing? Countries like France and the Nordic states see themselves as secular countries but in different ways. The relationship between secularism or the secularity of the law and/or neutrality leads to questions concerning the rule of law. Even if a piece of legislation/a law is universal some groups may be targeted by certain legislation. An example of that is the Swedish law prohibiting the slaughter of animals without the animals first being stunned.[16] This prohibition has a huge impact on Jews and Muslims and their possibility to manifest their religion.

[12] *Sahin v Turkey* (n 9) para 108 and *Lautsi v Italy*, ibid.
[13] R Fahlbeck, *Bed och arbeta* (Malmö, Liber, 2011) 54.
[14] V Enkvist, *Religionsfrihetens rättsliga ramar* (Uppsala, Iustus, 2013) 252.
[15] *Lautsi v Italy* (n 11).
[16] See for example the animal welfare legislation in, for example, Sweden.

Moreover, are secular societies more open to pluralism than religious ones? This cannot be taken for granted.

II. OPPORTUNITIES OR CHALLENGES – A WAY OF THINKING

Over the last decade, migration has been one of the greatest challenges for politicians in Europe to solve. When migration is debated in the media and in politics, religion is often set in relation to migration and integration. The religion of the migrants is often portrayed as a problem or at least as a challenge. One reason for this is that most of the immigrants have roots in different parts of the world where Christianity is not necessarily the dominant religion. New manifestations of religions challenge societal and old religious norms. The immigrants and their beliefs are often described as a problem, a challenge for those in power to solve. 'The others' are seen as a threat to the European way of life. But is the question of immigration really connected to religion to the extent that some tend to believe? What is the underlying notion? In all probability, the old view that there is a unity in religion, or unity in conviction, is one explanation. 'The others' challenge the norms and the values that are taken for granted and regarded as the truth.

In the media and political discourse, we often hear opinions linking religion, security and terrorism to each other. This puts another important question on the agenda – how do we use power, how do we use legislation? Do we use them to protect us from harm or to guide us? Are they used as a way of prohibiting or of allowing? And how do we draw up new legislation? Do we introduce legislation that is detailed or legislation that is open to almost unlimited possibilities of interpretation? Are pragmatic solutions a threat to freedom of religion?

There has been a huge influx of Islamic immigrants arriving in Europe and in some cases demands for religious manifestations clash with the values that have prevailed in European societies for hundreds of years. New and perhaps different views concerning what religious manifestations entail challenge the old notions of our western democracies. One of the most important questions many European societies must find an answer to is which path they shall choose. Shall they go down the path of inclusion or the path of exclusion? In addition, why do we choose one way over the other?

During the past 10 years, politicians that advocate an 'us and them' mindset have gained influence, and the gaps between different groups in society are growing. At the same time, we can see grassroots movements fighting for a more inclusive society and the future is wide open for new interpretations and a more inclusive way of thinking. Maybe gaining an understanding of 'the other' is the solution instead of forcing these 'others' into a norm that has been unchallenged for hundreds of years.

III. THE FREEDOM OF RELIGION – A TIGER WITHOUT TEETH

When the ECHR was established in the 1950s, one of the aims was to shape a dynamic human rights convention, a human rights instrument that could evolve at the same pace as society at large. Article 9 on the freedom of religion has proved not to be as dynamic as, for example, Article 10, the freedom of expression. The wide margin of appreciation is interesting in many ways but one major consequence is that the protection of minority groups is not as strong as it might be. Therefore, even though freedom of religion is often promoted as a fundamental right in a democracy, the impact of that right is quite small compared to other rights. Freedom of religion seems to be defined as a right to have a religion, no more, no less.

But is freedom of religion, as well as all human rights, relative, dynamic and open to interpretation? If freedom of religion can be interpreted differently in different contexts – what does the freedom protect? What is the core of the right? Moreover, the current development of the right – is it a positive development or is the relativisation of the right a path to destruction?

Another important question concerning the freedom of religion is the question about representation – who may represent whom? May a religious umbrella organisation, such as in the *Cha'are Shalom Ve Tsedek v France*,[17] decide to speak out on behalf of smaller groups within the same religion? This may sometimes give rise to conflicts between representatives of minority religions and representatives of the majority society, but also between members within smaller religious groups.

The way forward is perhaps testing uncharted waters and maybe it demands that we leave some traditions and notions behind and start a new quest, in order to find new traditions and to create new common denominators. The opposite way is also an alternative – to recognise the fact that maybe Europe is not united in its attitude concerning the role of religion in European states and to acknowledge that the margin of appreciation gives us the opportunity to find different solutions.

> Pluralism, tolerance and broadmindness are hallmarks of a democratic society. Although individual interest must on occasion be subordination to those of a group, democracy does not simply mean that the views of a majority must prevail: a balance must be achieved which ensures the fair and proper treatment of people from minorities and avoids any abuse of a dominant position.[18]

[17] *Cha'are Shalom Ve Tsedek v France* App no 27417/95 (ECtHR, 27 June 2000).
[18] *Sahin v Turkey* (n 9) para 108.

IV. INTERPRETATION IS A HIGHLY IMPORTANT TASK – BUT BY WHOM AND FOR WHOM?

In the early days of the ECHR, the Commission handled the cases about freedom of religion. Since the re-organisation in 1998, the Court has been the sole decision-maker concerning these cases.[19] When the Commission held that responsibility, the definition of religion, belief and faith were considered to be important questions to answer.[20] Were these concepts defined and labelled with different names, or was there an important distinction between the concepts? And more importantly, who decided the definitions? The legislators, the judges, agency officials or the religious individuals that were affected by the legislation?

These questions do not seem to be as important to the Court as they were to the Commission. The case law of the Court shows an acceptance of the opinion of the applicants concerning which manifestations originate from religion and which have their roots in culture or tradition.[21] This is a path that can be chosen when freedom of religion is constructed as a relative right. In the Swedish case, freedom of religion is constructed as an absolute right in the Constitution. One of the most important consequences of this construction is that the definition and interpretation of religion and the word manifestation are very important. Manifestations that fall within the protection of the freedom of religion are absolute and therefore impossible to restrict. In the Swedish preparatory works of different pieces of legislation on religious matters, it is possible to discern a tendency to debate whether a manifestation has its roots in religion, tradition or culture.[22] Is it even possible to define a difference between religion, tradition and culture?

From a judicial perspective it is quite important to understand how religion and manifestation are understood and applied as this might be a decisive reason for protecting a manifestation. These are highly complex questions but a simple answer as stated above is that there are different answers depending on the context. When approaching the matter of religion, it is important to understand that the answer will probably differ depending on the question you raise. The horizon of understanding and the possible outcomes that we expect are actually as important as the questions themselves.

In all forms of judicial work, interpretation is essential. How do those who apply legislation and judicial rules, interpret the words in the regulations and why do we understand the words the way we do? Prejudices cannot be ignored in the process of interpretation. The way we understand religion is affected by the society in which we grow up and live.

[19] Cameron (n 10) 39–43.

[20] See *X v Germany* App no 8741/79 (Commission Decision, 10 March 1981).

[21] Case of *Cha'are Shalom Ve Tsedek v France* (n 17).

[22] Government bill 2000/01:81 p 18 (preparatory works for the law concerning religious motivated circumcision). See also Enkvist (n 14) 244–45.

In a post-Christian society like Sweden, it is more likely that the way we understand religion is based on Christian (Lutheran) values. This presupposes that religions or convictions that are similar to the Christian faith are more likely to be protected than completely different religions and the manifestations of minority religions. Manifestations of other religions are sometimes defined as manifestations of culture and tradition.[23] The way we understand different words and concepts changes over time, and the context and the way we experience daily life have an impact on the way we perceive the reality around us, and also the way we interpret legislation.

V. DEFINING DEMOCRACY – A SERENDIPITY MOMENT

A concept frequently used by politicians both in their speeches but also in legislation is *democratic values*. All citizens are expected to adhere to democratic values and all citizens are expected to know how these values are defined. This is quite interesting; it is a kind of assimilation process that we all indirectly accept without really knowing what we are accepting. The preamble to the legislation concerning the Swedish education system (the Swedish Education Act, SFS 2010:800), for example, states that the aim of the education system is to educate the pupils in democratic values. The question is how far the state is prepared to go in its quest to mould democratic individuals and exactly what democratic values we are talking about. Are they a well-kept secret or are they perhaps obvious to a true democrat? Or is this a guessing game and a serendipity moment when an agreement is made concerning a definition of democratic values? In this context it is important to recognise that democratic values in a state like Sweden are affected by Christian values. This is not a problem, just a mere fact but one consequence of this is that other religions may not be fully respected or treated equally or in the same way as the majority religion. These values are seemingly democratic values but beneath the surface 'the same' values are called Christian values.

Each era of time has its own conditions or fundamental base that are seen as self-evident prerequisites for interpretation. When older values that are taken for granted are replaced there has been a change at a deeper level.[24]

[23] See the discussion about religious slaughter of animals in Sweden. See also the case law from European Court of Human Rights concerning headscarves. The political debate about prohibition of headscarves in several European states is another example.

[24] K Tuori, *Critical legal positivism* (London, Routledge, 2002) and CA Aurelius, *Luther i Sverige – Den svenska Lutherbilden under fyra sekler* 2nd edn (Skellefteå, Artos och Norma, 2015) 11.

Index

Introductory Note

References such as '178–79' indicate (not necessarily continuous) discussion of a topic across a range of pages. Wherever possible in the case of topics with many references, these have either been divided into sub-topics or only the most significant discussions of the topic are listed. Because the entire work is about 'religion' and 'human rights', the use of these terms (and certain others which occur constantly throughout the book) as entry points has been restricted. Information will be found under the corresponding detailed topics.

www.ingramcontent.com/pod-product-compliance
Ingram Content Group UK Ltd.
Pitfield, Milton Keynes, MK11 3LW, UK
UKHW020812290926
15470UKWH00003B/1117

9 781509 935864